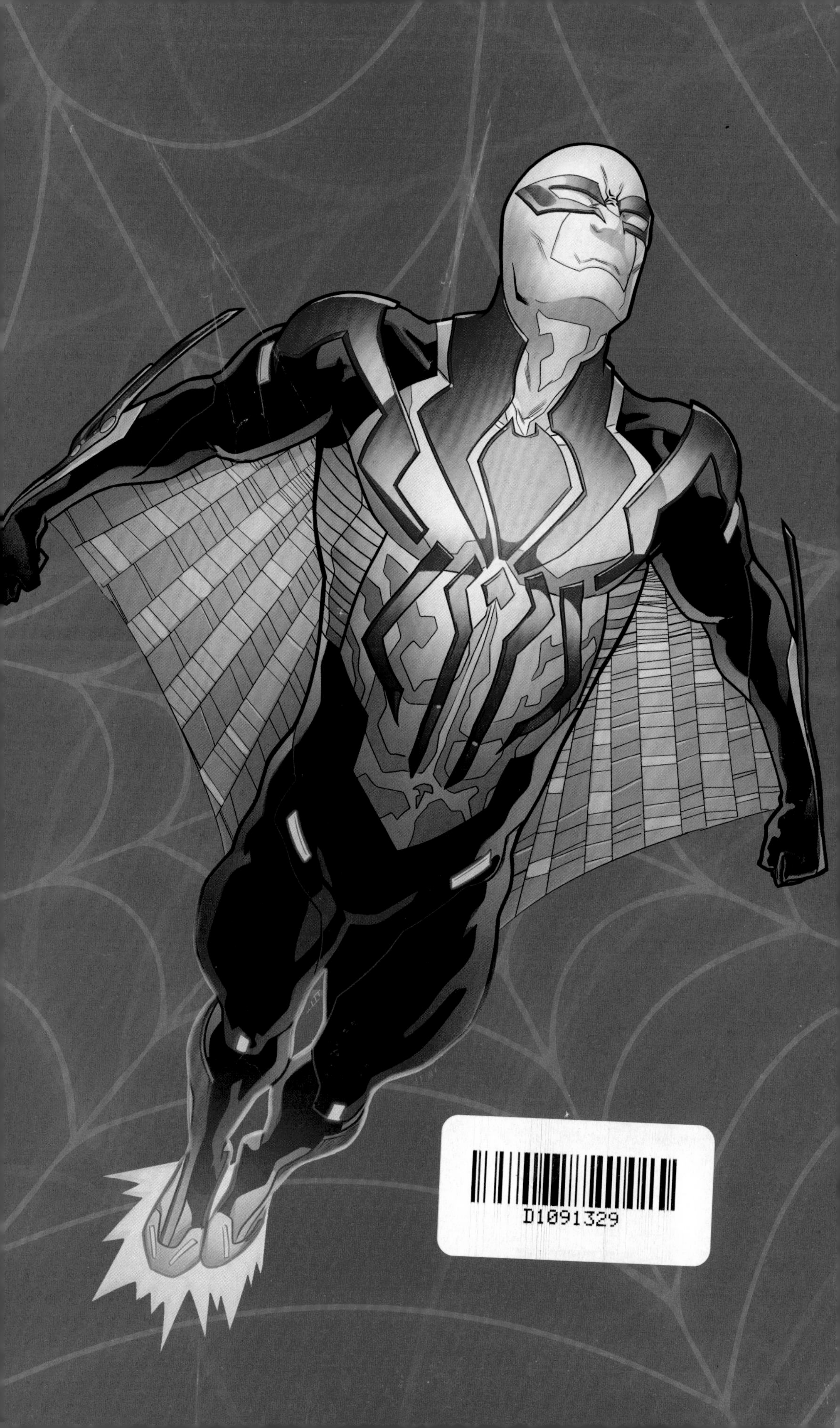

FIGHTING CRIME BEFORE HIS TIME!

SPIDER-MAN 2099

PETER DAVID
writer

WILL SLINEY
artist

FRANK D'ARMATA [#1-2 & Amazing Spider-Man (2015) #1]
with ANDRES MOSSA [#2] & RACHELLE ROSENBERG [#3-5]
colorists

VC's CORY PETIT
letterer

FRANCESCO MATTINA [#1-5] & ALEX ROSS [Amazing Spider-Man (2015) #1]
cover art

DEVIN LEWIS
editor

NICK LOWE
senior editor

SPIDER-MAN created by STAN LEE & STEVE DITKO

---

collection editor SARAH BRUNSTAD
associate managing editor ALEX STARBUCK
editors, special projects JENNIFER GRÜNWALD & MARK D. BEAZLEY
vp, production & special projects JEFF YOUNGQUIST
book design ADAM DEL RE

svp print, sales & marketing DAVID GABRIEL
editor in chief AXEL ALONSO
chief creative officer JOE QUESADA
publisher DAN BUCKLEY
executive producer ALAN FINE

SPIDER-MAN 2099 VOL. 3: SMACK TO THE FUTURE. Contains material originally published in magazine form as SPIDER-MAN 2099 #1-5 and AMAZING SPIDER-MAN #1. First printing 2016. ISBN# 978-0-7851-9963-2. Published by MARVEL WORLDWIDE, INC., a subsidiary of MARVEL ENTERTAINMENT, LLC. OFFICE OF PUBLICATION: 135 West 50th Street, New York, NY 10020. Copyright © 2016 MARVEL. No similarity between any of the names, characters, persons, and/or institutions in this magazine with those of any living or dead person or institution is intended, and any such similarity which may exist is purely coincidental. **Printed in Canada.** ALAN FINE, President, Marvel Entertainment; DAN BUCKLEY, President, TV, Publishing & Brand Management; JOE QUESADA, Chief Creative Officer; TOM BREVOORT, SVP of Publishing; DAVID BOGART, SVP of Business Affairs & Operations, Publishing & Partnership; C.B. CEBULSKI, VP of Brand Management & Development, Asia; DAVID GABRIEL, SVP of Sales & Marketing, Publishing; JEFF YOUNGQUIST, VP of Production & Special Projects; DAN CARR, Executive Director of Publishing Technology; ALEX MORALES, Director of Publishing Operations; SUSAN CRESPI, Production Manager; STAN LEE, Chairman Emeritus. For information regarding advertising in Marvel Comics or on Marvel.com, please contact Vit DeBellis, Integrated Sales Manager, at vdebellis@marvel.com. For Marvel subscription inquiries, please call 888-511-5480. **Manufactured between 3/4/2016 and 4/11/2016 by SOLISCO PRINTERS, SCOTT, QC, CANADA.**
10 9 8 7 6 5 4 3 2 1

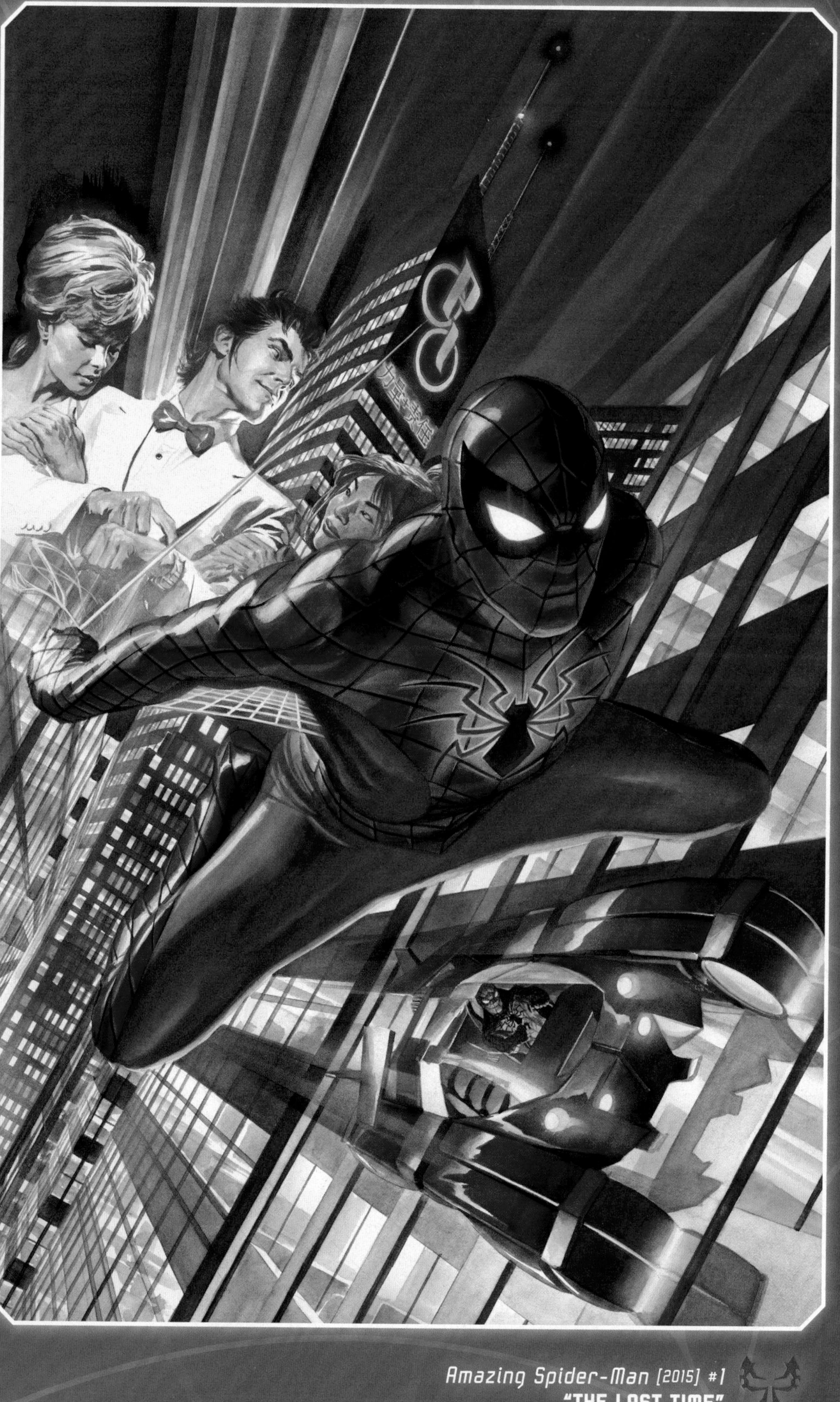

Amazing Spider-Man [2015] #1
"THE LAST TIME"

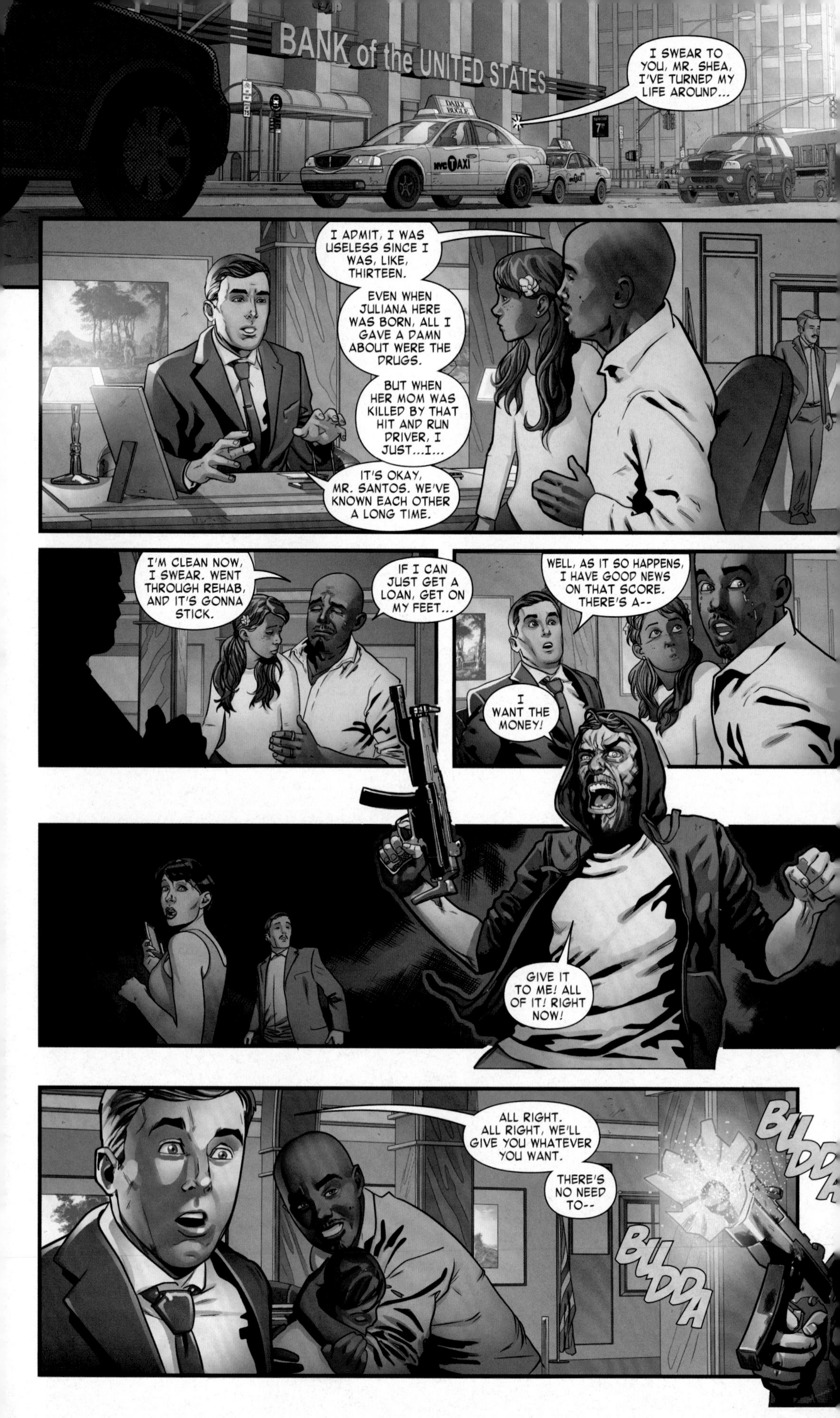
BANK of the UNITED STATES
DAILY BUGLE
NYC TAXI
I SWEAR TO YOU, MR. SHEA, I'VE TURNED MY LIFE AROUND...
I ADMIT, I WAS USELESS SINCE I WAS, LIKE, THIRTEEN.
EVEN WHEN JULIANA HERE WAS BORN, ALL I GAVE A DAMN ABOUT WERE THE DRUGS.
BUT WHEN HER MOM WAS KILLED BY THAT HIT AND RUN DRIVER, I JUST...I...
IT'S OKAY, MR. SANTOS. WE'VE KNOWN EACH OTHER A LONG TIME.
I'M CLEAN NOW, I SWEAR. WENT THROUGH REHAB, AND IT'S GONNA STICK.
IF I CAN JUST GET A LOAN, GET ON MY FEET...
WELL, AS IT SO HAPPENS, I HAVE GOOD NEWS ON THAT SCORE. THERE'S A--
I WANT THE MONEY!
GIVE IT TO ME! ALL OF IT! RIGHT NOW!
ALL RIGHT. ALL RIGHT, WE'LL GIVE YOU WHATEVER YOU WANT.
THERE'S NO NEED TO--
BUDDA
BUDDA

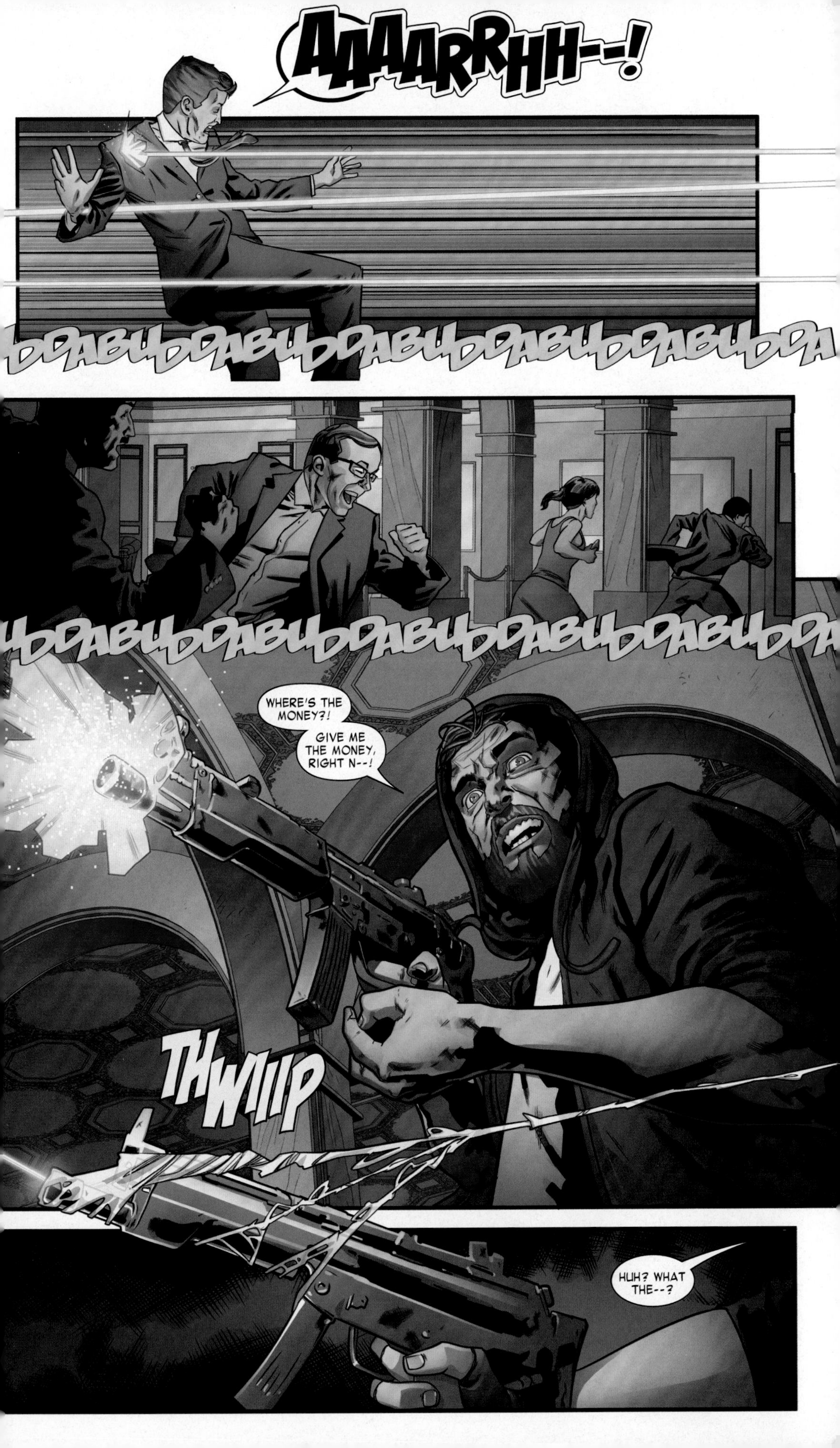
AAAARRHH--!
DDABUDDABUDDABUDDABUDDABUDDA
UDDABUDDABUDDABUDDABUDDABUDDA
WHERE'S THE MONEY?!
GIVE ME THE MONEY, RIGHT N--!
THWIIP
HUH? WHAT THE--?

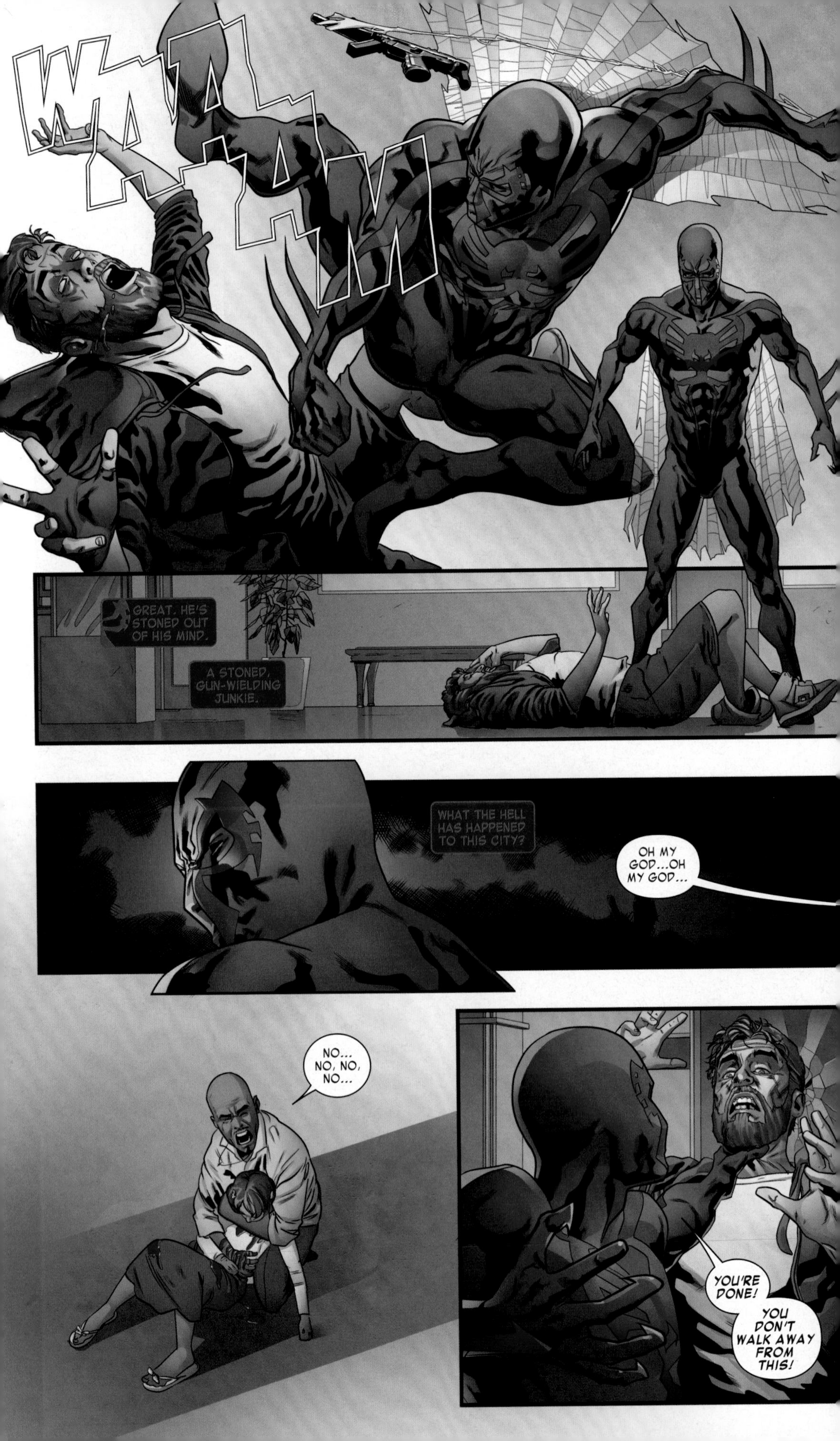
WHAM
GREAT. HE'S STONED OUT OF HIS MIND.
A STONED, GUN-WIELDING JUNKIE.
WHAT THE HELL HAS HAPPENED TO THIS CITY?
OH MY GOD...OH MY GOD...
NO... NO, NO, NO...
YOU'RE DONE!
YOU DON'T WALK AWAY FROM THIS!

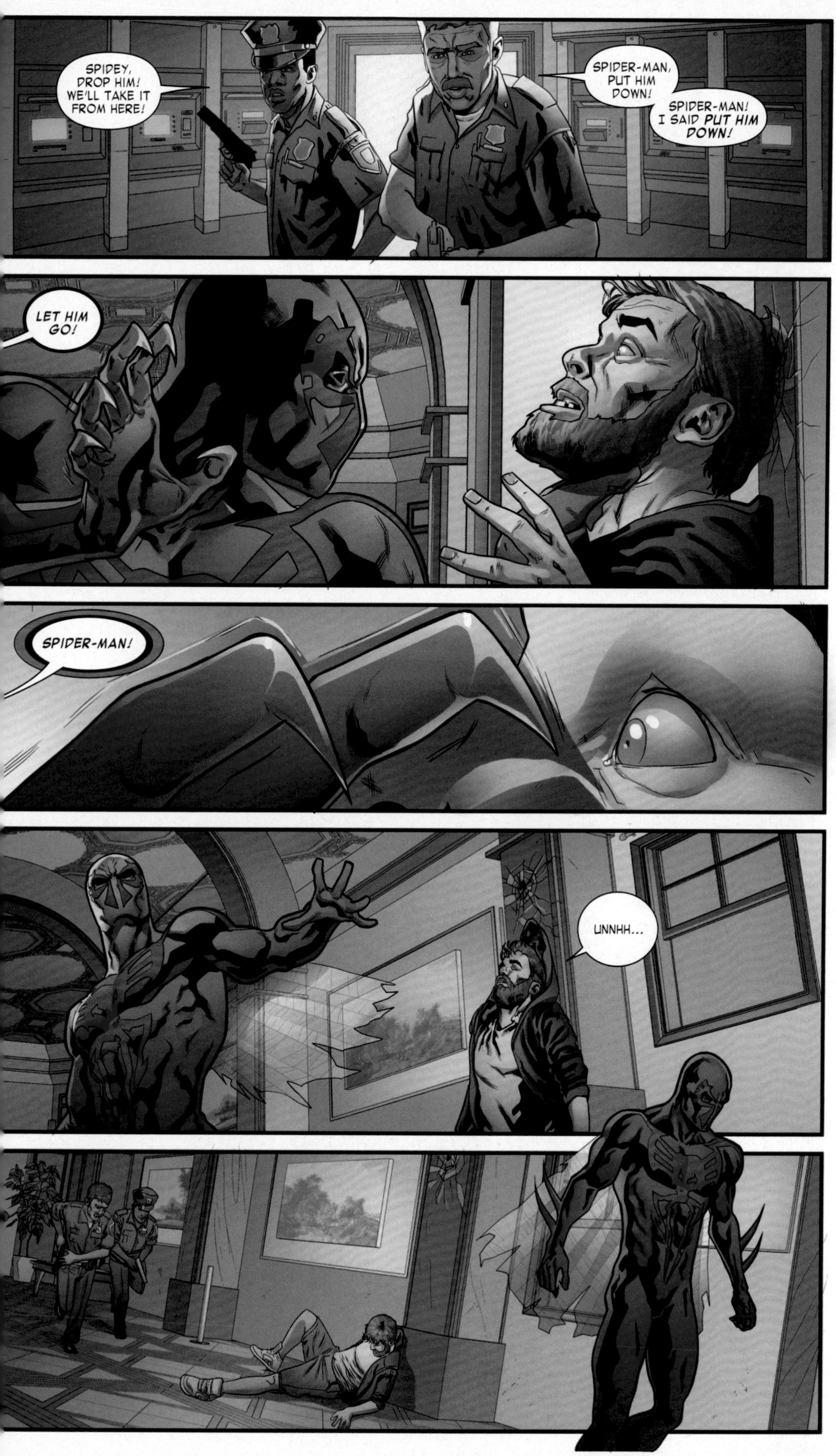

SPIDEY, DROP HIM! WE'LL TAKE IT FROM HERE!
SPIDER-MAN, PUT HIM DOWN!
SPIDER-MAN! I SAID **PUT HIM DOWN!**
LET HIM GO!
SPIDER-MAN!
UNNHH...

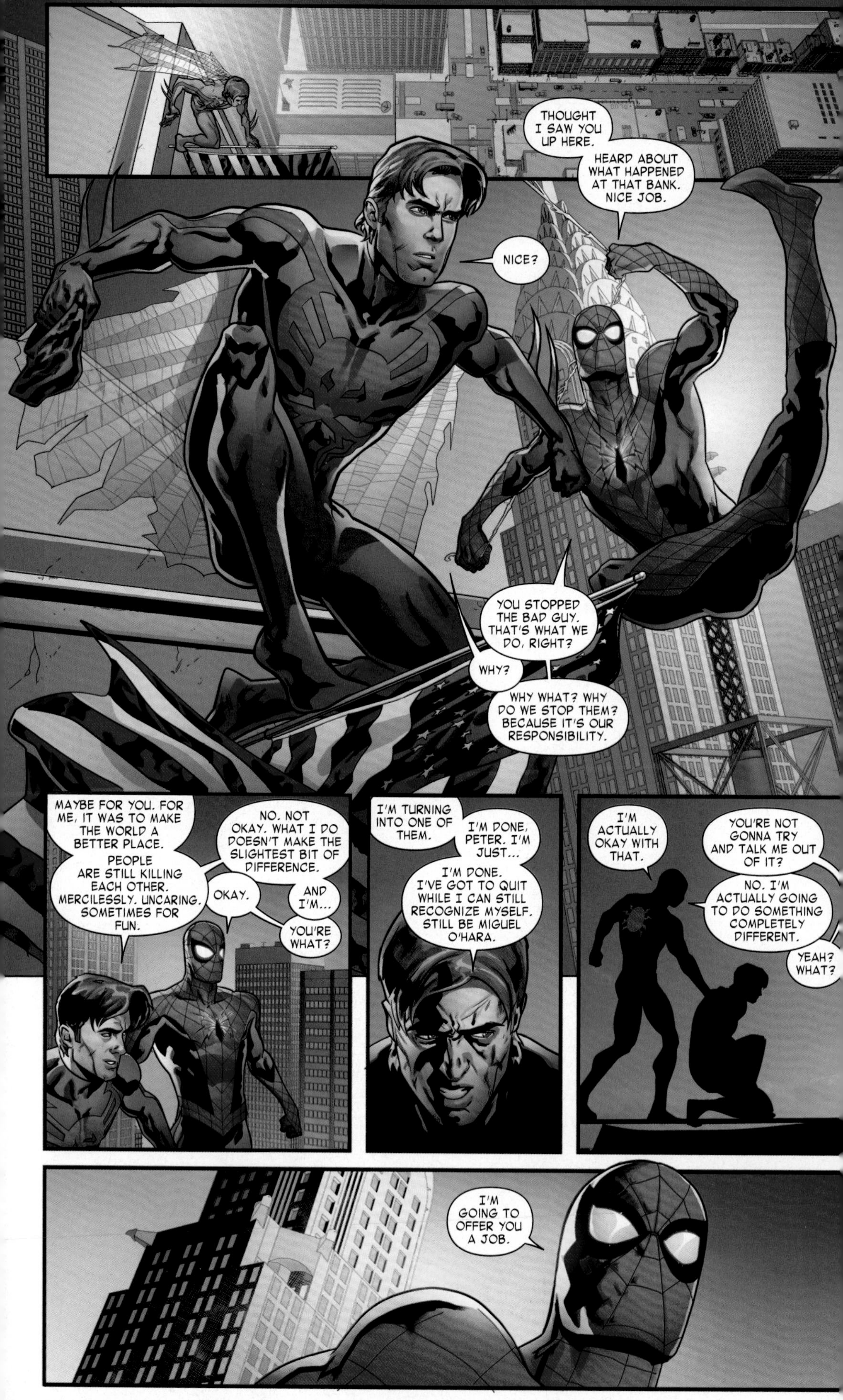

THOUGHT I SAW YOU UP HERE.
HEARD ABOUT WHAT HAPPENED AT THAT BANK. NICE JOB.
NICE?
YOU STOPPED THE BAD GUY. THAT'S WHAT WE DO, RIGHT?
WHY?
WHY WHAT? WHY DO WE STOP THEM? BECAUSE IT'S OUR RESPONSIBILITY.
MAYBE FOR YOU. FOR ME, IT WAS TO MAKE THE WORLD A BETTER PLACE.
PEOPLE ARE STILL KILLING EACH OTHER. MERCILESSLY. UNCARING. SOMETIMES FOR FUN.
OKAY.
NO. NOT OKAY. WHAT I DO DOESN'T MAKE THE SLIGHTEST BIT OF DIFFERENCE.
AND I'M...
YOU'RE WHAT?
I'M TURNING INTO ONE OF THEM.
I'M DONE, PETER. I'M JUST...
I'M DONE. I'VE GOT TO QUIT WHILE I CAN STILL RECOGNIZE MYSELF. STILL BE MIGUEL O'HARA.
I'M ACTUALLY OKAY WITH THAT.
YOU'RE NOT GONNA TRY AND TALK ME OUT OF IT?
NO. I'M ACTUALLY GOING TO DO SOMETHING COMPLETELY DIFFERENT.
YEAH? WHAT?
I'M GOING TO OFFER YOU A JOB.

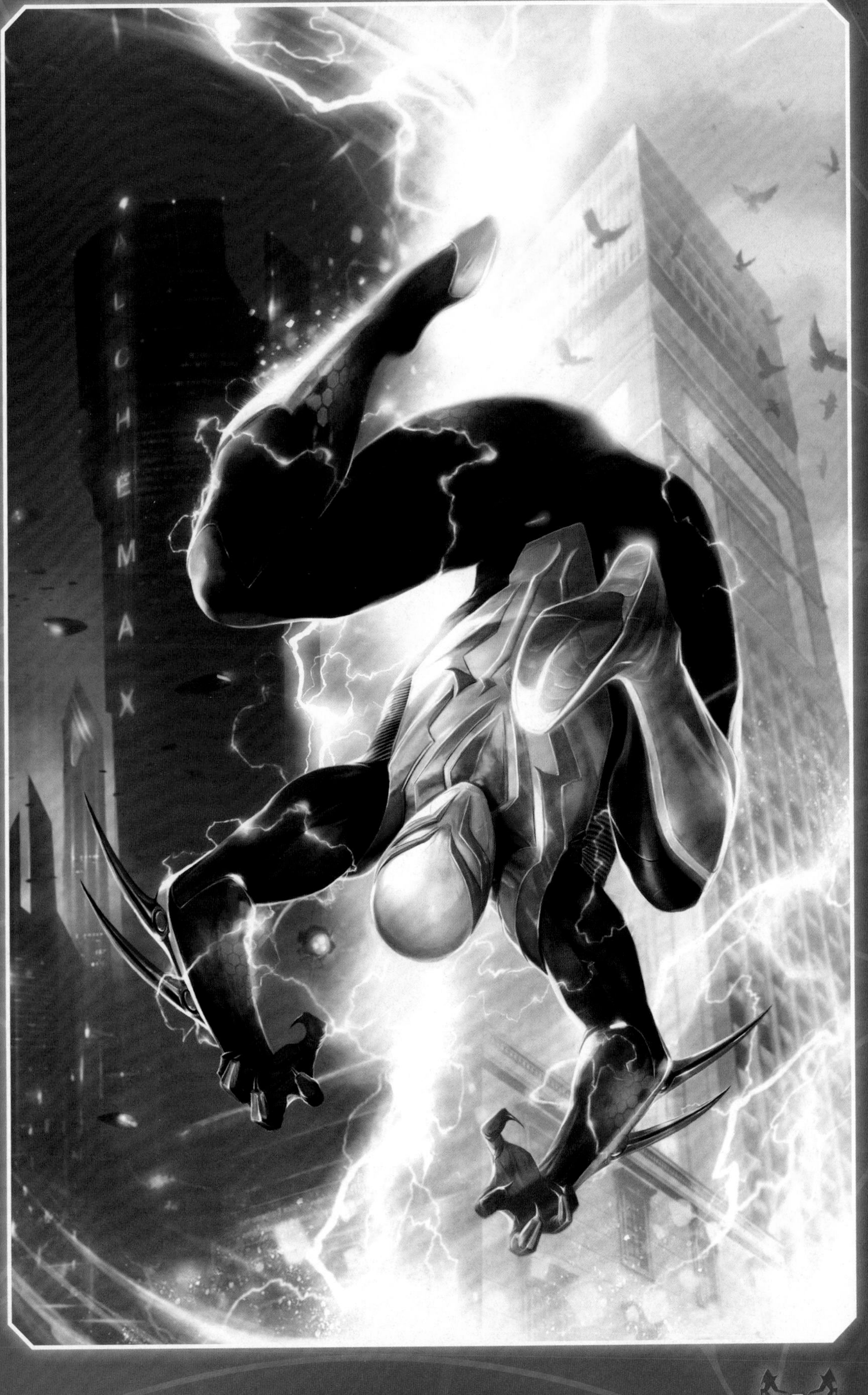
ALCHEMAX

1

MIGUEL O'HARA WAS A YOUNG GENETICS GENIUS EMPLOYED AT THE MEGACORPORATION ALCHEMAX IN THE FUTURE CITY OF NUEVA YORK! O OF HIS EXPERIMENTS--TO REPLICATE THE POWERS OF THE PRESENT-DAY SPIDER-MAN--WAS TURNED AGAINST HIM AND REWROTE HIS DNA MAKE IT 50% SPIDER! AFTER LEARNING HOW TO USE HIS AMAZING NEW ABILITIES, MIGUEL SOON BECAME...

SPIDER-MAN 2099

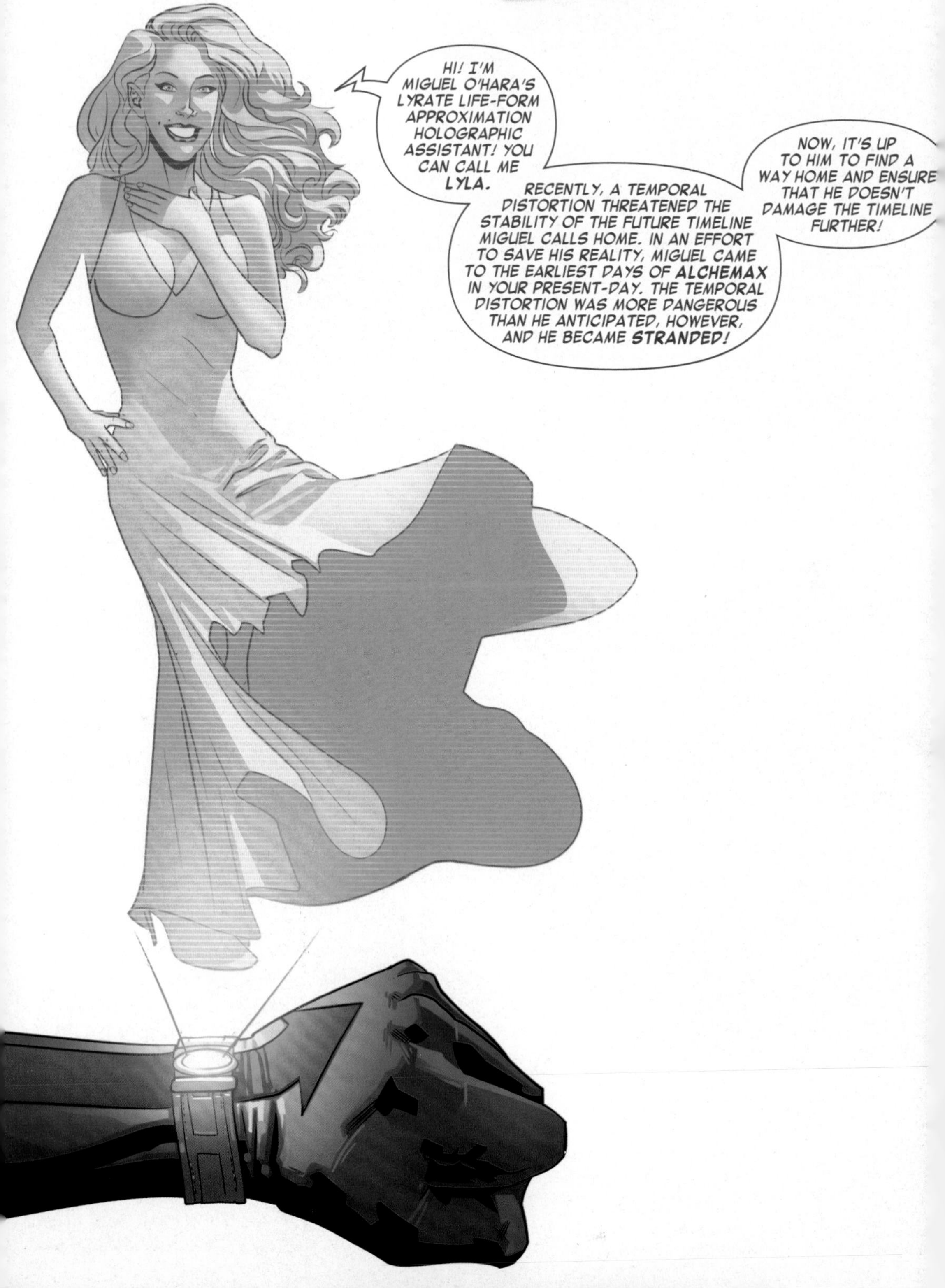
HI! I'M MIGUEL O'HARA'S LYRATE LIFE-FORM APPROXIMATION HOLOGRAPHIC ASSISTANT! YOU CAN CALL ME **LYLA.**
RECENTLY, A TEMPORAL DISTORTION THREATENED THE STABILITY OF THE FUTURE TIMELINE MIGUEL CALLS HOME. IN AN EFFORT TO SAVE HIS REALITY, MIGUEL CAME TO THE EARLIEST DAYS OF **ALCHEMAX** IN YOUR PRESENT-DAY. THE TEMPORAL DISTORTION WAS MORE DANGEROUS THAN HE ANTICIPATED, HOWEVER, AND HE BECAME **STRANDED!**
NOW, IT'S UP TO HIM TO FIND A WAY HOME AND ENSURE THAT HE DOESN'T DAMAGE THE TIMELINE FURTHER!

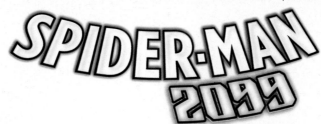

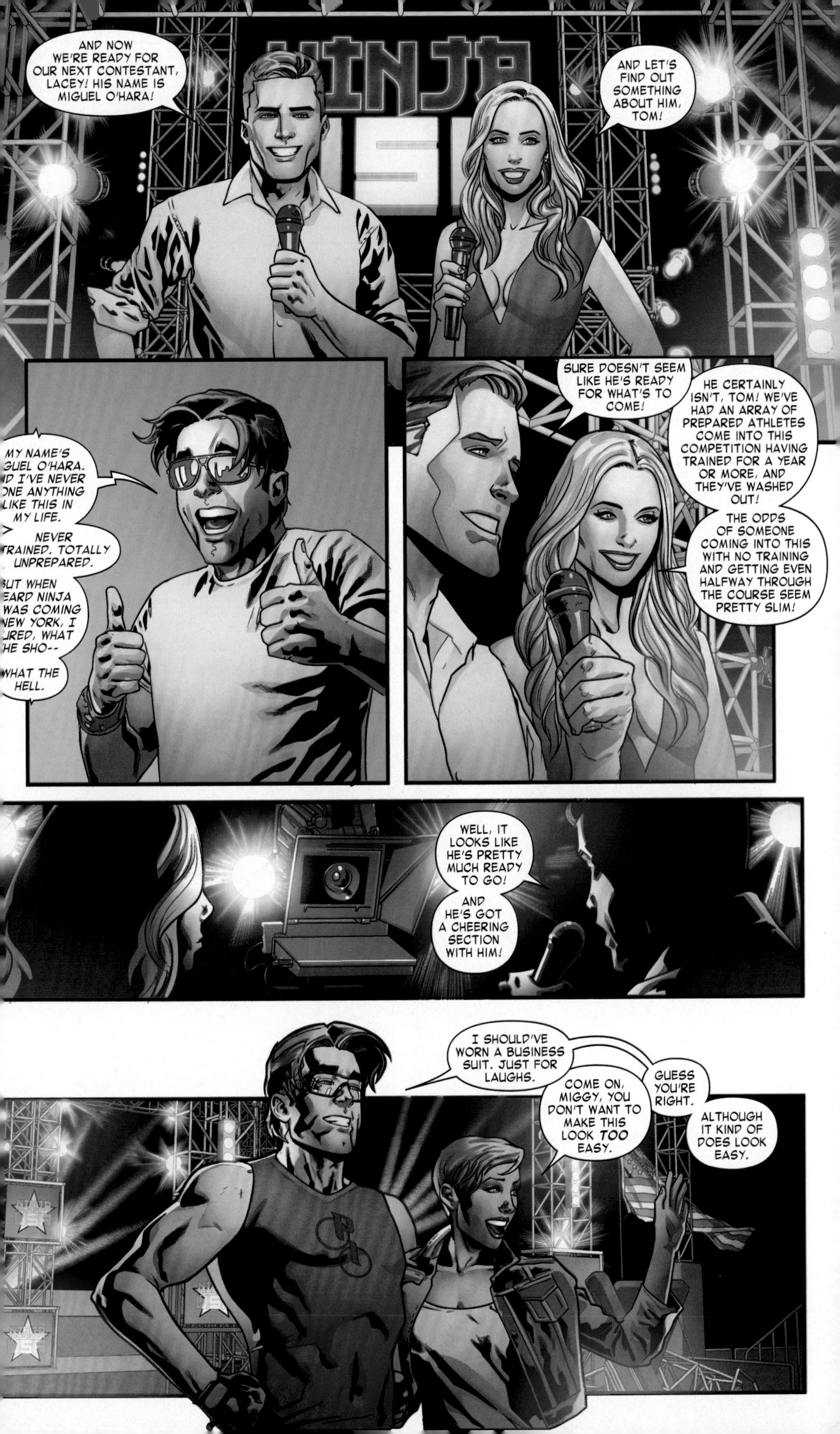

AND NOW WE'RE READY FOR OUR NEXT CONTESTANT, LACEY! HIS NAME IS MIGUEL O'HARA!
AND LET'S FIND OUT SOMETHING ABOUT HIM, TOM!
MY NAME'S GUEL O'HARA. D I'VE NEVER ONE ANYTHING LIKE THIS IN MY LIFE.
NEVER TRAINED. TOTALLY UNPREPARED.
UT WHEN EARD NINJA WAS COMING NEW YORK, I URED, WHAT HE SHO--
WHAT THE HELL.
SURE DOESN'T SEEM LIKE HE'S READY FOR WHAT'S TO COME!
HE CERTAINLY ISN'T, TOM! WE'VE HAD AN ARRAY OF PREPARED ATHLETES COME INTO THIS COMPETITION HAVING TRAINED FOR A YEAR OR MORE, AND THEY'VE WASHED OUT!
THE ODDS OF SOMEONE COMING INTO THIS WITH NO TRAINING AND GETTING EVEN HALFWAY THROUGH THE COURSE SEEM PRETTY SLIM!
WELL, IT LOOKS LIKE HE'S PRETTY MUCH READY TO GO!
AND HE'S GOT A CHEERING SECTION WITH HIM!
I SHOULD'VE WORN A BUSINESS SUIT. JUST FOR LAUGHS.
COME ON, MIGGY, YOU DON'T WANT TO MAKE THIS LOOK TOO EASY.
GUESS YOU'RE RIGHT.
ALTHOUGH IT KIND OF DOES LOOK EASY.

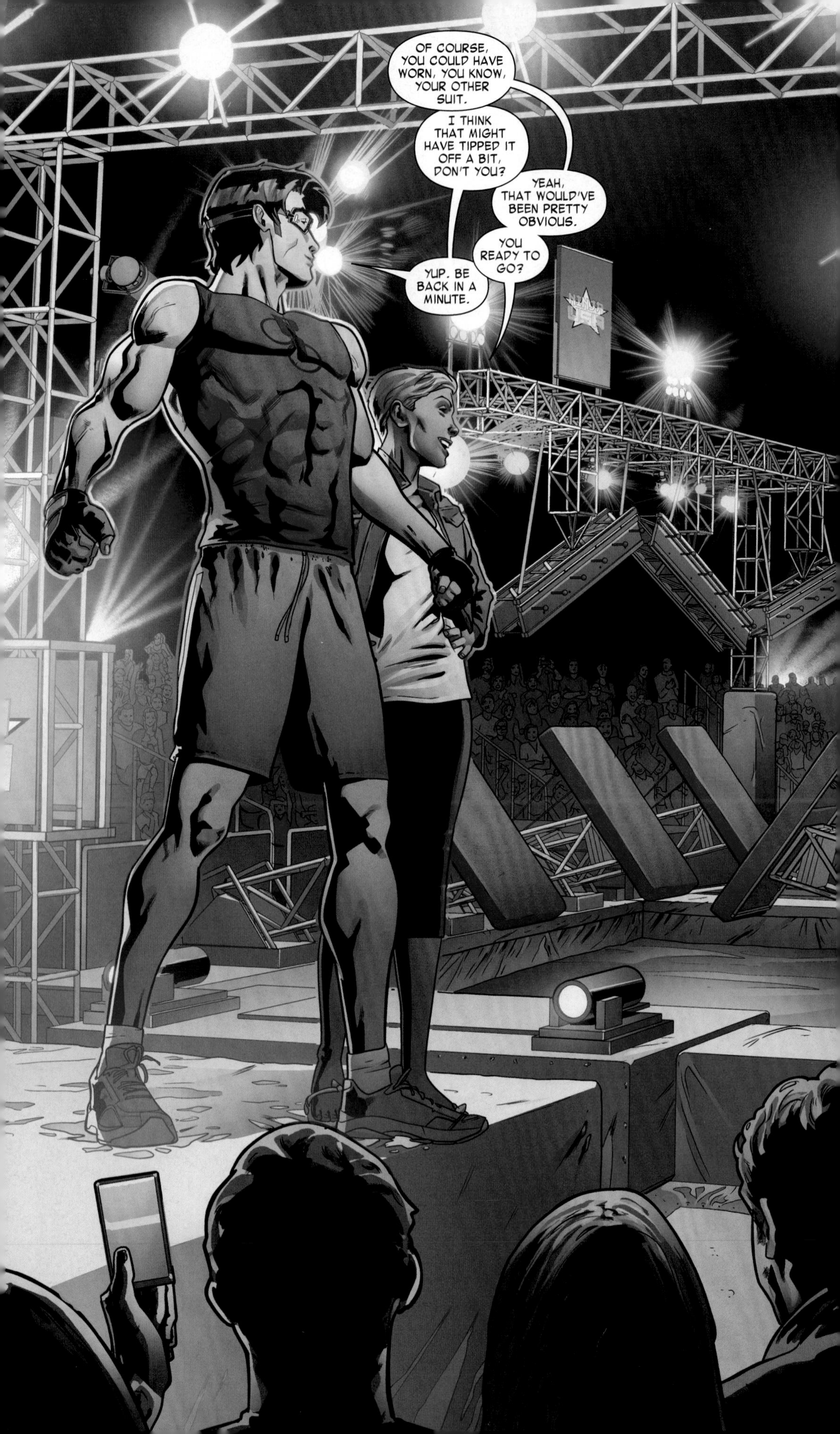
OF COURSE, YOU COULD HAVE WORN, YOU KNOW, YOUR OTHER SUIT.
I THINK THAT MIGHT HAVE TIPPED IT OFF A BIT, DON'T YOU?
YEAH, THAT WOULD'VE BEEN PRETTY OBVIOUS.
YOU READY TO GO?
YUP. BE BACK IN A MINUTE.

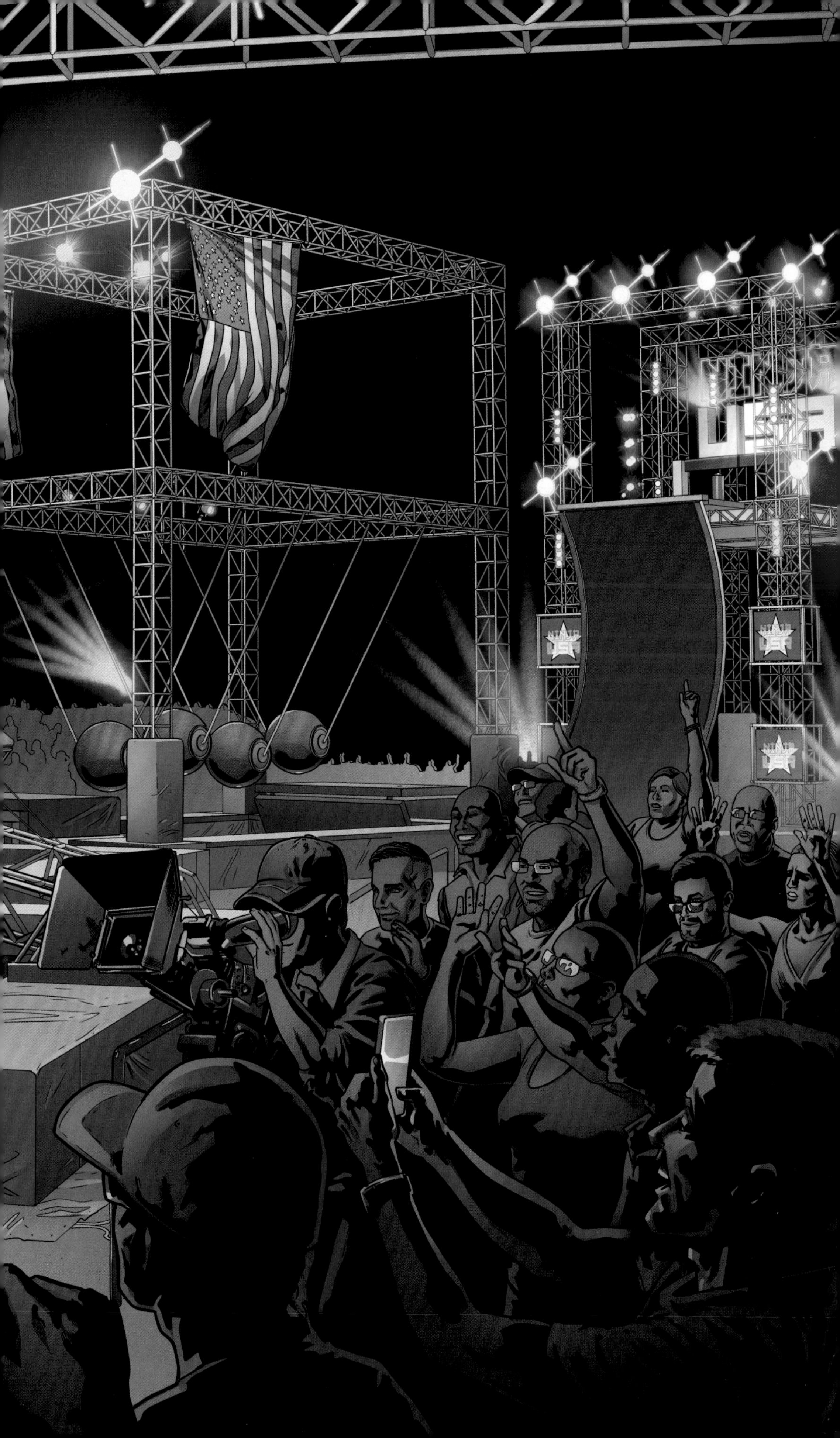

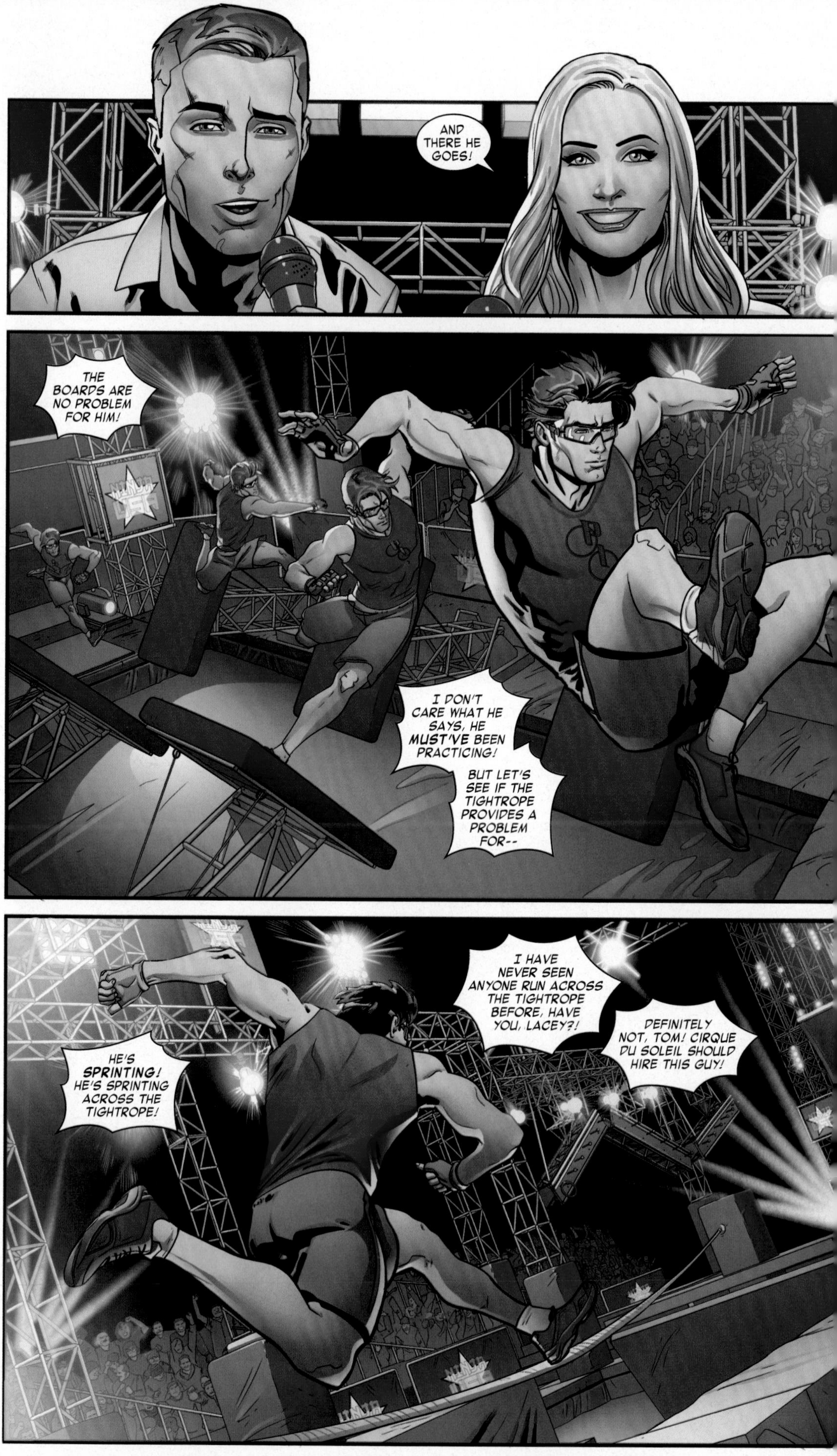
AND THERE HE GOES!
THE BOARDS ARE NO PROBLEM FOR HIM!
I DON'T CARE WHAT HE SAYS, HE **MUST'VE** BEEN PRACTICING!
BUT LET'S SEE IF THE TIGHTROPE PROVIDES A PROBLEM FOR--
HE'S **SPRINTING**! HE'S SPRINTING ACROSS THE TIGHTROPE!
I HAVE NEVER SEEN ANYONE RUN ACROSS THE TIGHTROPE BEFORE, HAVE YOU, LACEY?!
DEFINITELY NOT, TOM! CIRQUE DU SOLEIL SHOULD HIRE THIS GUY!

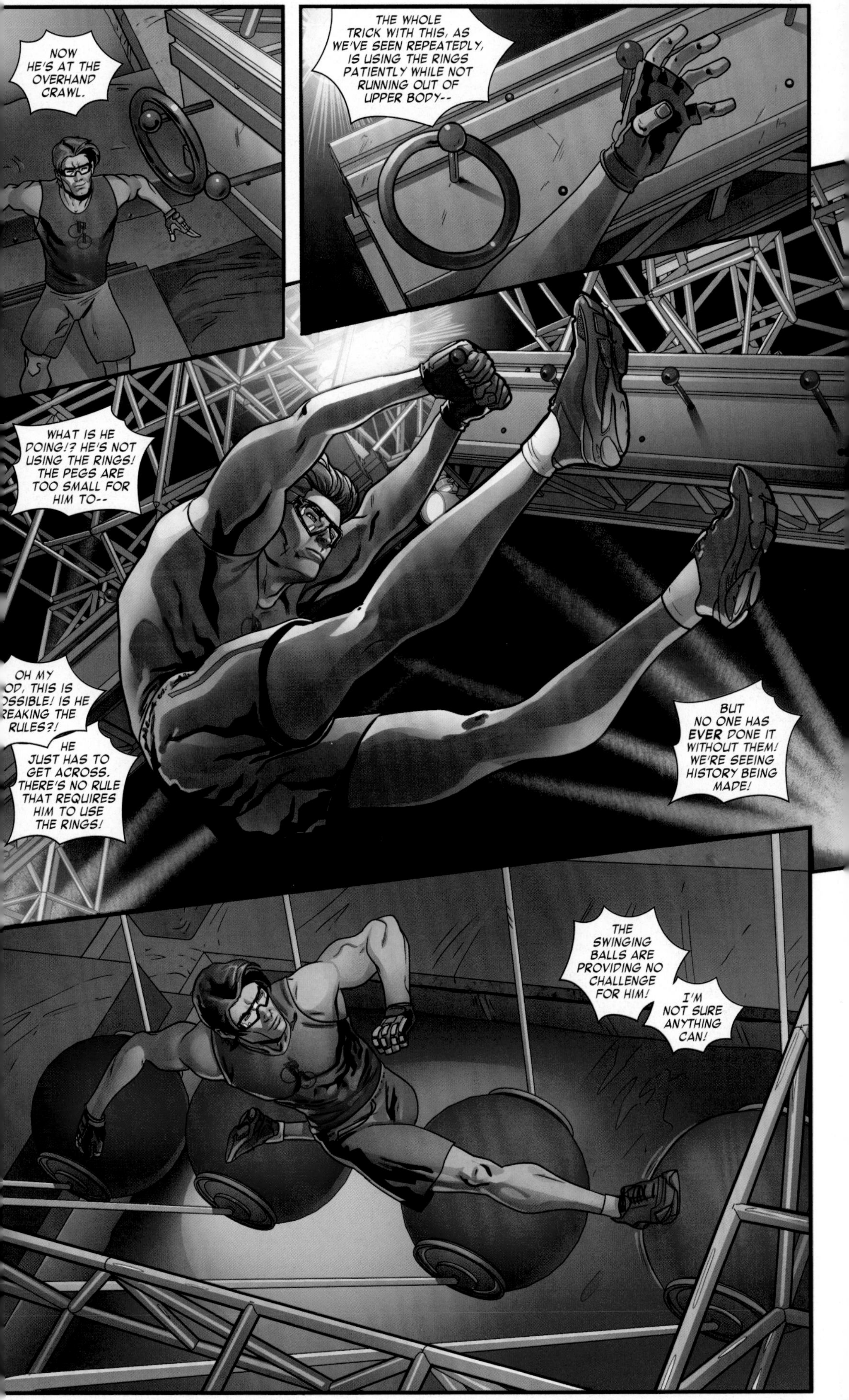
NOW HE'S AT THE OVERHAND CRAWL.
THE WHOLE TRICK WITH THIS, AS WE'VE SEEN REPEATEDLY, IS USING THE RINGS PATIENTLY WHILE NOT RUNNING OUT OF UPPER BODY--
WHAT IS HE DOING!? HE'S NOT USING THE RINGS! THE PEGS ARE TOO SMALL FOR HIM TO--
OH MY
OD, THIS IS
OSSIBLE! IS HE
REAKING THE
RULES?!
HE JUST HAS TO GET ACROSS. THERE'S NO RULE THAT REQUIRES HIM TO USE THE RINGS!
BUT NO ONE HAS **EVER** DONE IT WITHOUT THEM! WE'RE SEEING HISTORY BEING MADE!
THE SWINGING BALLS ARE PROVIDING NO CHALLENGE FOR HIM!
I'M NOT SURE ANYTHING CAN!

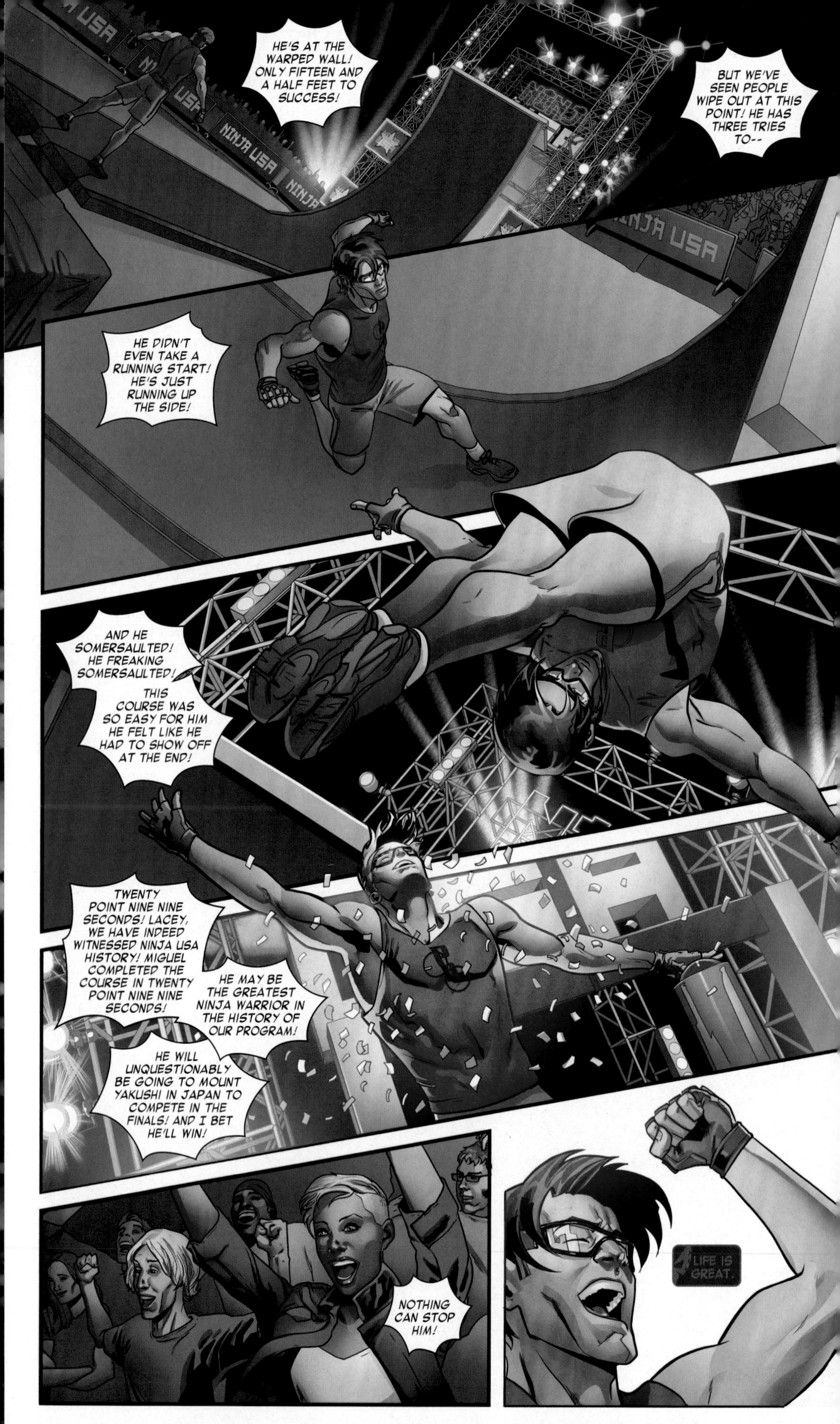

HE'S AT THE WARPED WALL! ONLY FIFTEEN AND A HALF FEET TO SUCCESS!
BUT WE'VE SEEN PEOPLE WIPE OUT AT THIS POINT! HE HAS THREE TRIES TO--
NINJA USA
HE DIDN'T EVEN TAKE A RUNNING START! HE'S JUST RUNNING UP THE SIDE!
AND HE SOMERSAULTED! HE FREAKING SOMERSAULTED!
THIS COURSE WAS SO EASY FOR HIM HE FELT LIKE HE HAD TO SHOW OFF AT THE END!
TWENTY POINT NINE NINE SECONDS! LACEY, WE HAVE INDEED WITNESSED NINJA USA HISTORY! MIGUEL COMPLETED THE COURSE IN TWENTY POINT NINE NINE SECONDS!
HE MAY BE THE GREATEST NINJA WARRIOR IN THE HISTORY OF OUR PROGRAM!
HE WILL UNQUESTIONABLY BE GOING TO MOUNT YAKUSHI IN JAPAN TO COMPETE IN THE FINALS! AND I BET HE'LL WIN!
NOTHING CAN STOP HIM!
LIFE IS GREAT.

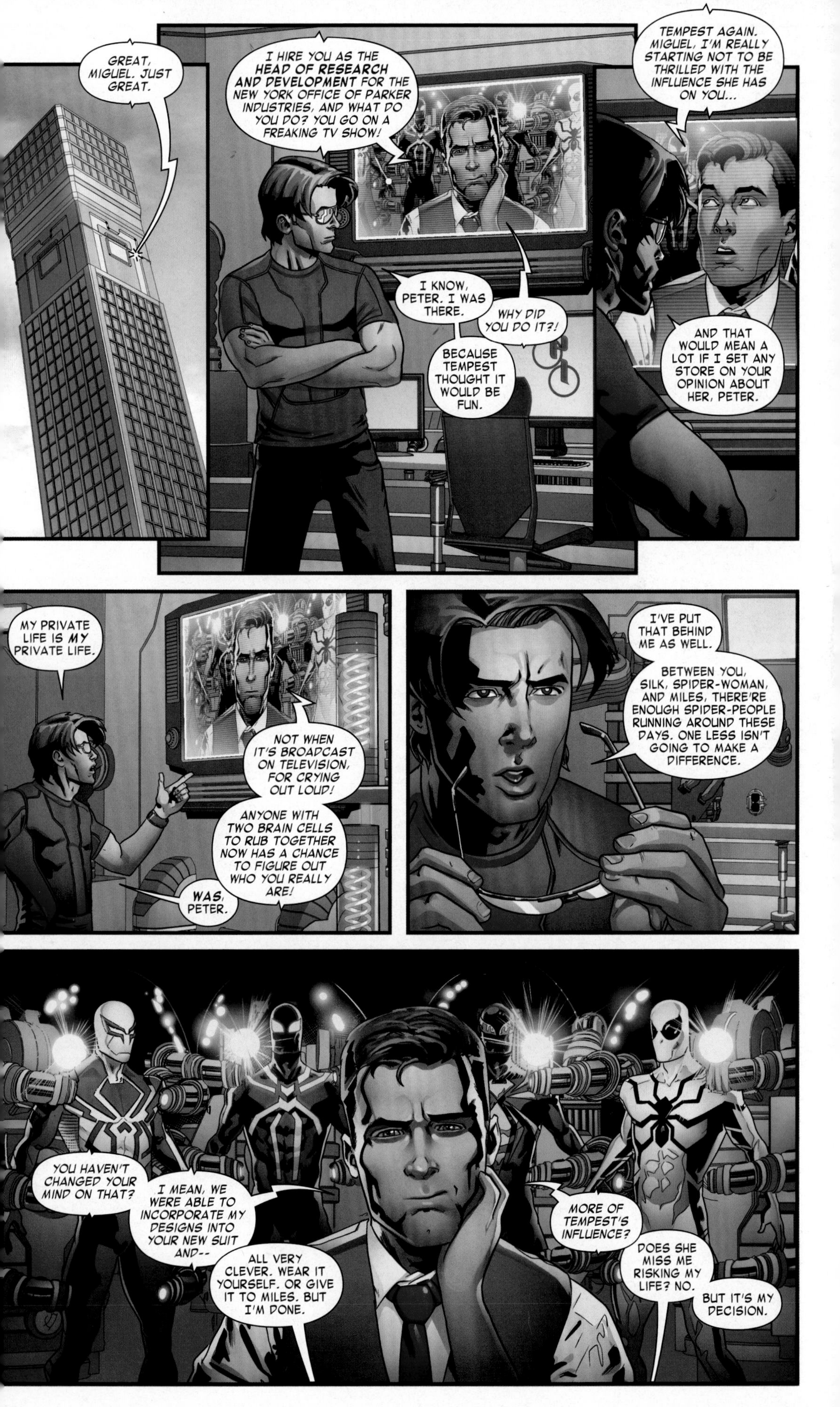
GREAT, MIGUEL. JUST GREAT.
I HIRE YOU AS THE **HEAD OF RESEARCH AND DEVELOPMENT** FOR THE NEW YORK OFFICE OF PARKER INDUSTRIES, AND WHAT DO YOU DO? YOU GO ON A FREAKING TV SHOW!
I KNOW, PETER. I WAS THERE.
WHY DID YOU DO IT?!
BECAUSE TEMPEST THOUGHT IT WOULD BE FUN.
TEMPEST AGAIN. MIGUEL, I'M REALLY STARTING NOT TO BE THRILLED WITH THE INFLUENCE SHE HAS ON YOU...
AND THAT WOULD MEAN A LOT IF I SET ANY STORE ON YOUR OPINION ABOUT HER, PETER.
MY PRIVATE LIFE IS **MY** PRIVATE LIFE.
NOT WHEN IT'S BROADCAST ON TELEVISION, FOR CRYING OUT LOUD!
ANYONE WITH TWO BRAIN CELLS TO RUB TOGETHER NOW HAS A CHANCE TO FIGURE OUT WHO YOU REALLY ARE!
WAS, PETER.
I'VE PUT THAT BEHIND ME AS WELL.
BETWEEN YOU, SILK, SPIDER-WOMAN, AND MILES, THERE'RE ENOUGH SPIDER-PEOPLE RUNNING AROUND THESE DAYS. ONE LESS ISN'T GOING TO MAKE A DIFFERENCE.
YOU HAVEN'T CHANGED YOUR MIND ON THAT?
I MEAN, WE WERE ABLE TO INCORPORATE MY DESIGNS INTO YOUR NEW SUIT AND--
ALL VERY CLEVER. WEAR IT YOURSELF. OR GIVE IT TO MILES. BUT I'M DONE.
MORE OF TEMPEST'S INFLUENCE?
DOES SHE MISS ME RISKING MY LIFE? NO.
BUT IT'S MY DECISION.

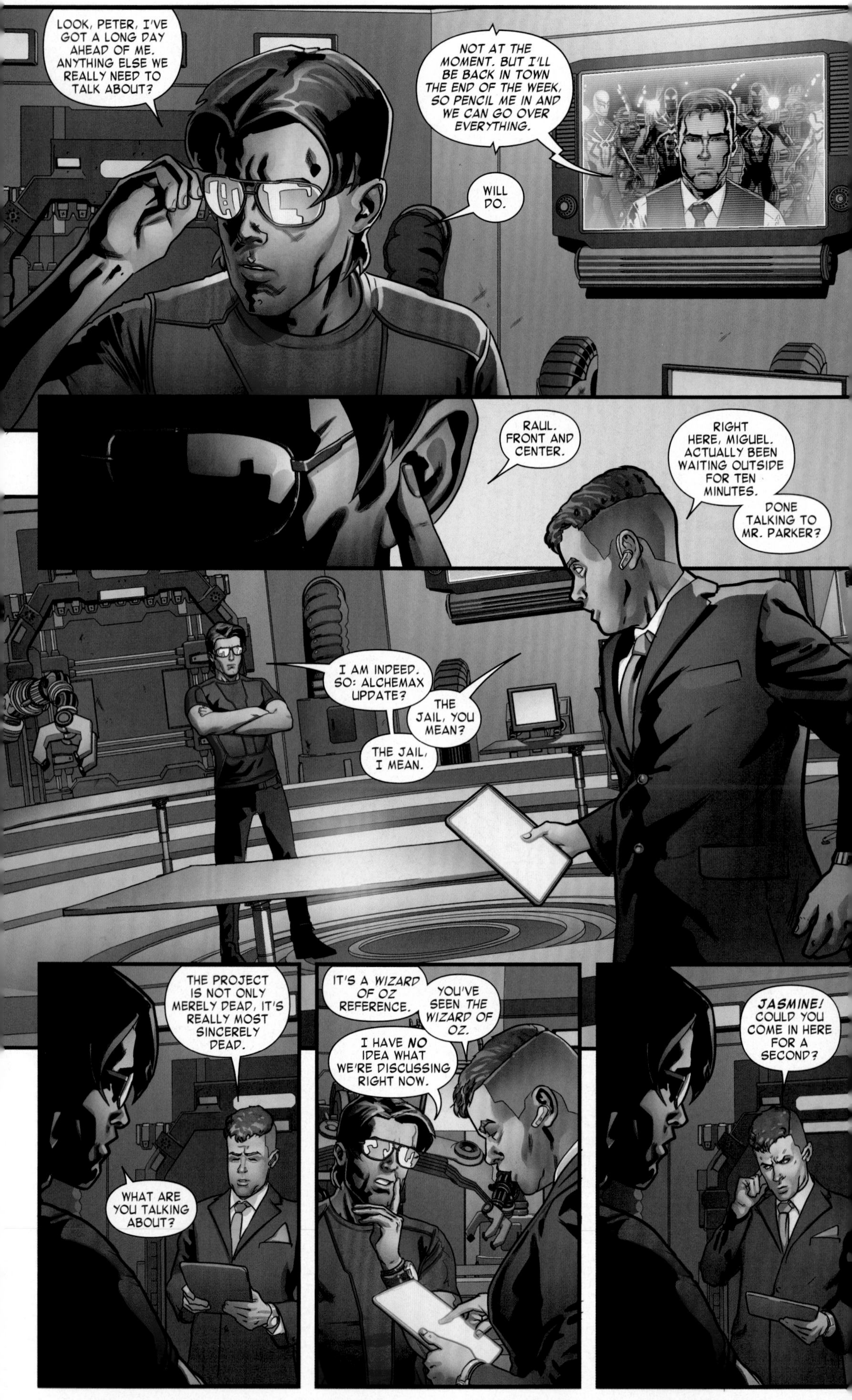
LOOK, PETER, I'VE GOT A LONG DAY AHEAD OF ME. ANYTHING ELSE WE REALLY NEED TO TALK ABOUT?
NOT AT THE MOMENT. BUT I'LL BE BACK IN TOWN THE END OF THE WEEK, SO PENCIL ME IN AND WE CAN GO OVER EVERYTHING.
WILL DO.
RAUL. FRONT AND CENTER.
RIGHT HERE, MIGUEL. ACTUALLY BEEN WAITING OUTSIDE FOR TEN MINUTES.
DONE TALKING TO MR. PARKER?
I AM INDEED. SO: ALCHEMAX UPDATE?
THE JAIL, YOU MEAN?
THE JAIL, I MEAN.
THE PROJECT IS NOT ONLY MERELY DEAD, IT'S REALLY MOST SINCERELY DEAD.
WHAT ARE YOU TALKING ABOUT?
IT'S A *WIZARD OF OZ* REFERENCE.
YOU'VE SEEN *THE WIZARD OF OZ.*
I HAVE **NO** IDEA WHAT WE'RE DISCUSSING RIGHT NOW.
JASMINE! COULD YOU COME IN HERE FOR A SECOND?

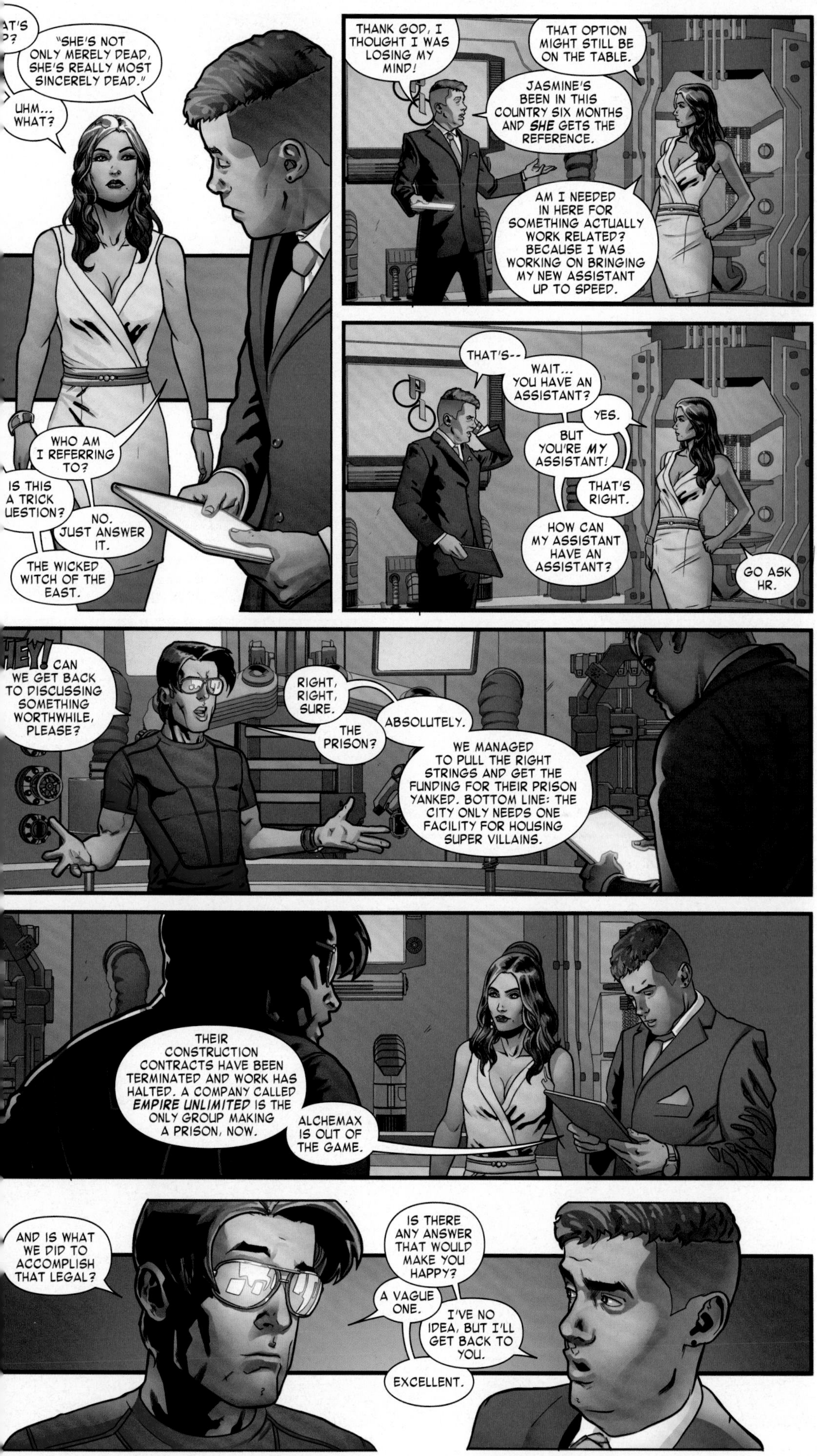

AT'S
?
"SHE'S NOT ONLY MERELY DEAD, SHE'S REALLY MOST SINCERELY DEAD."
UHM... WHAT?
WHO AM I REFERRING TO?
IS THIS A TRICK UESTION?
NO. JUST ANSWER IT.
THE WICKED WITCH OF THE EAST.
THANK GOD, I THOUGHT I WAS LOSING MY MIND!
THAT OPTION MIGHT STILL BE ON THE TABLE.
JASMINE'S BEEN IN THIS COUNTRY SIX MONTHS AND SHE GETS THE REFERENCE.
AM I NEEDED IN HERE FOR SOMETHING ACTUALLY WORK RELATED? BECAUSE I WAS WORKING ON BRINGING MY NEW ASSISTANT UP TO SPEED.
THAT'S--
WAIT... YOU HAVE AN ASSISTANT?
YES.
BUT YOU'RE MY ASSISTANT!
THAT'S RIGHT.
HOW CAN MY ASSISTANT HAVE AN ASSISTANT?
GO ASK HR.
HEY! CAN WE GET BACK TO DISCUSSING SOMETHING WORTHWHILE, PLEASE?
RIGHT, RIGHT, SURE.
ABSOLUTELY.
THE PRISON?
WE MANAGED TO PULL THE RIGHT STRINGS AND GET THE FUNDING FOR THEIR PRISON YANKED. BOTTOM LINE: THE CITY ONLY NEEDS ONE FACILITY FOR HOUSING SUPER VILLAINS.
THEIR CONSTRUCTION CONTRACTS HAVE BEEN TERMINATED AND WORK HAS HALTED. A COMPANY CALLED EMPIRE UNLIMITED IS THE ONLY GROUP MAKING A PRISON, NOW.
ALCHEMAX IS OUT OF THE GAME.
AND IS WHAT WE DID TO ACCOMPLISH THAT LEGAL?
IS THERE ANY ANSWER THAT WOULD MAKE YOU HAPPY?
A VAGUE ONE.
I'VE NO IDEA, BUT I'LL GET BACK TO YOU.
EXCELLENT.

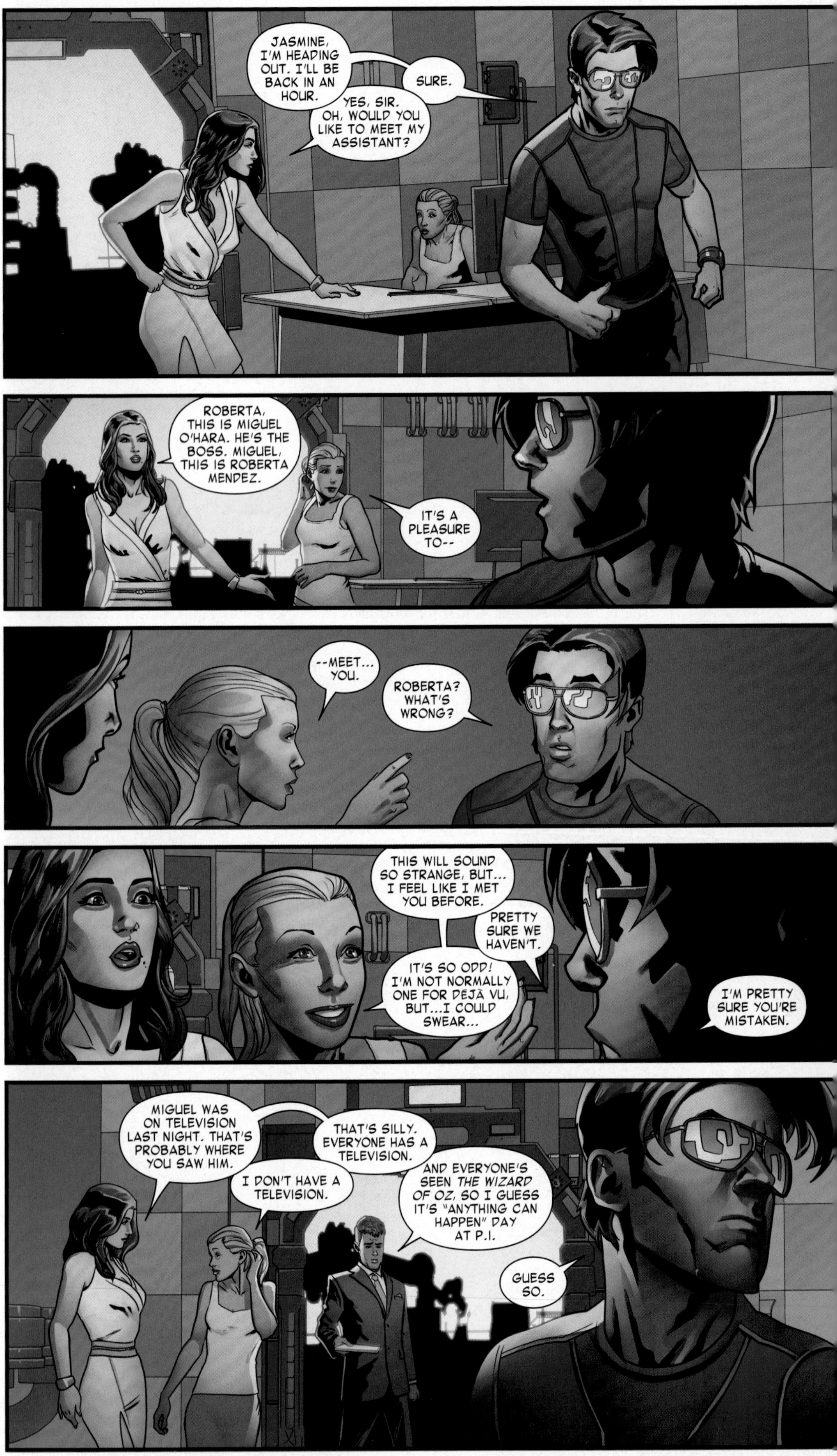
JASMINE, I'M HEADING OUT. I'LL BE BACK IN AN HOUR.
SURE.
YES, SIR. OH, WOULD YOU LIKE TO MEET MY ASSISTANT?
ROBERTA, THIS IS MIGUEL O'HARA. HE'S THE BOSS. MIGUEL, THIS IS ROBERTA MENDEZ.
IT'S A PLEASURE TO--
--MEET... YOU.
ROBERTA? WHAT'S WRONG?
THIS WILL SOUND SO STRANGE, BUT... I FEEL LIKE I MET YOU BEFORE.
PRETTY SURE WE HAVEN'T.
IT'S SO ODD! I'M NOT NORMALLY ONE FOR DÉJÀ VU, BUT...I COULD SWEAR...
I'M PRETTY SURE YOU'RE MISTAKEN.
MIGUEL WAS ON TELEVISION LAST NIGHT. THAT'S PROBABLY WHERE YOU SAW HIM.
THAT'S SILLY. EVERYONE HAS A TELEVISION.
I DON'T HAVE A TELEVISION.
AND EVERYONE'S SEEN *THE WIZARD OF OZ*, SO I GUESS IT'S "ANYTHING CAN HAPPEN" DAY AT P.I.
GUESS SO.

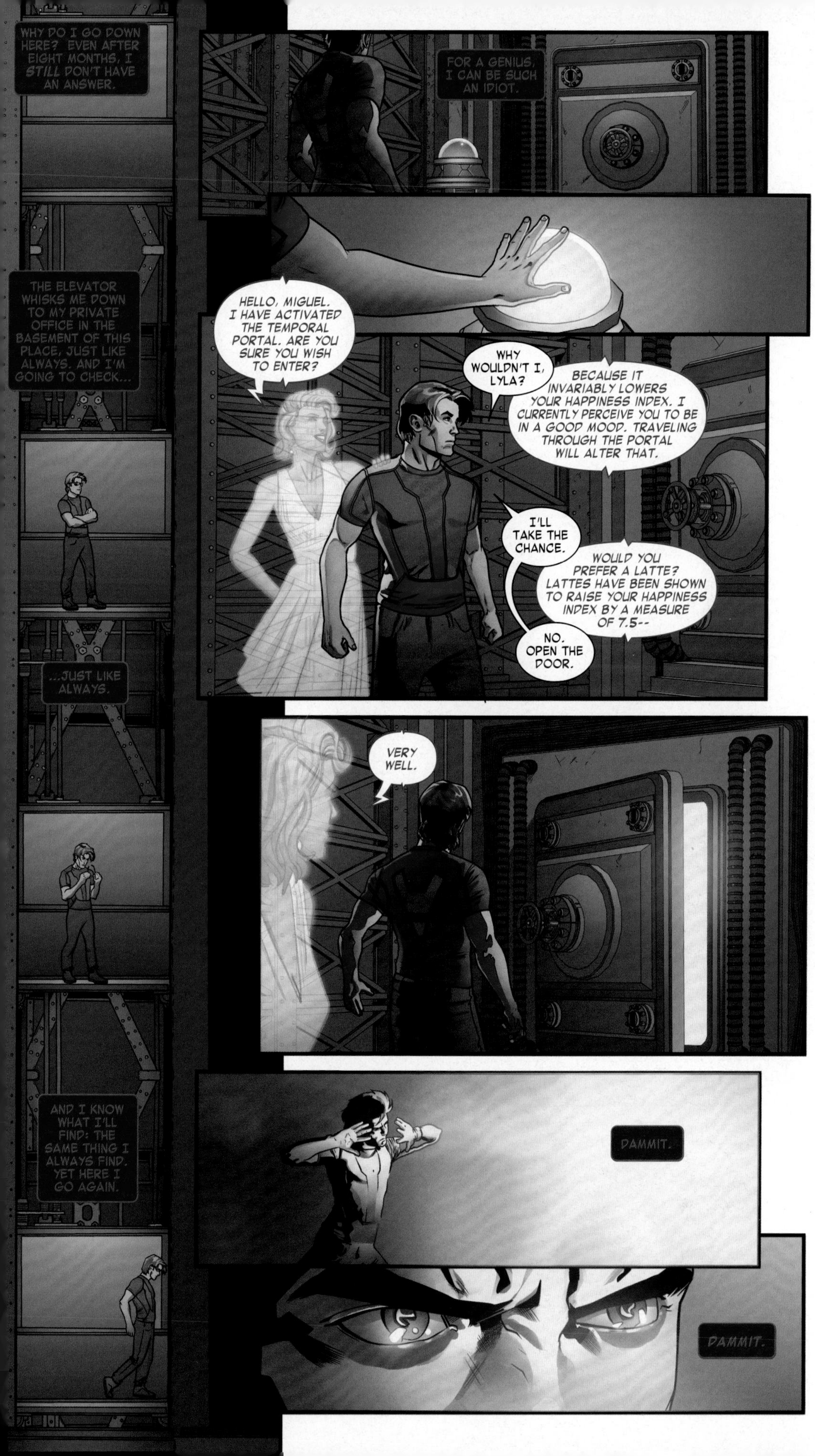
WHY DO I GO DOWN HERE? EVEN AFTER EIGHT MONTHS, I STILL DON'T HAVE AN ANSWER.
FOR A GENIUS, I CAN BE SUCH AN IDIOT.
THE ELEVATOR WHISKS ME DOWN TO MY PRIVATE OFFICE IN THE BASEMENT OF THIS PLACE, JUST LIKE ALWAYS. AND I'M GOING TO CHECK...
HELLO, MIGUEL. I HAVE ACTIVATED THE TEMPORAL PORTAL. ARE YOU SURE YOU WISH TO ENTER?
WHY WOULDN'T I, LYLA?
BECAUSE IT INVARIABLY LOWERS YOUR HAPPINESS INDEX. I CURRENTLY PERCEIVE YOU TO BE IN A GOOD MOOD. TRAVELING THROUGH THE PORTAL WILL ALTER THAT.
I'LL TAKE THE CHANCE.
WOULD YOU PREFER A LATTE? LATTES HAVE BEEN SHOWN TO RAISE YOUR HAPPINESS INDEX BY A MEASURE OF 7.5--
NO. OPEN THE DOOR.
...JUST LIKE ALWAYS.
VERY WELL.
AND I KNOW WHAT I'LL FIND: THE SAME THING I ALWAYS FIND. YET HERE I GO AGAIN.
DAMMIT.
DAMMIT.

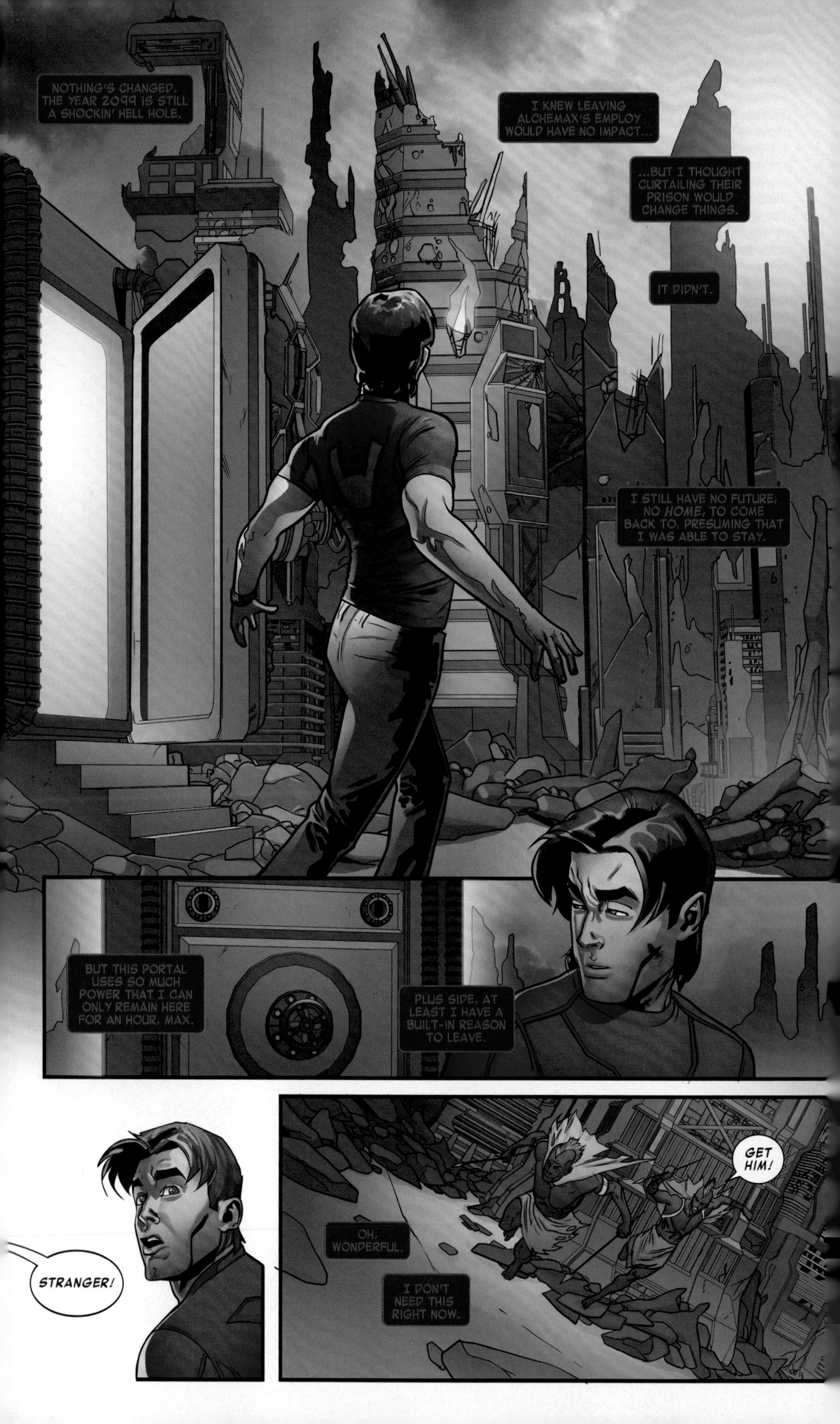
NOTHING'S CHANGED. THE YEAR 2099 IS STILL A SHOCKIN' HELL HOLE.
I KNEW LEAVING ALCHEMAX'S EMPLOY WOULD HAVE NO IMPACT...
...BUT I THOUGHT CURTAILING THEIR PRISON WOULD CHANGE THINGS.
IT DIDN'T.
I STILL HAVE NO FUTURE, NO *HOME*, TO COME BACK TO. PRESUMING THAT I WAS ABLE TO STAY.
BUT THIS PORTAL USES SO MUCH POWER THAT I CAN ONLY REMAIN HERE FOR AN HOUR, MAX.
PLUS SIDE, AT LEAST I HAVE A BUILT-IN REASON TO LEAVE.
STRANGER!
GET HIM!
OH, WONDERFUL.
I DON'T NEED THIS RIGHT NOW.

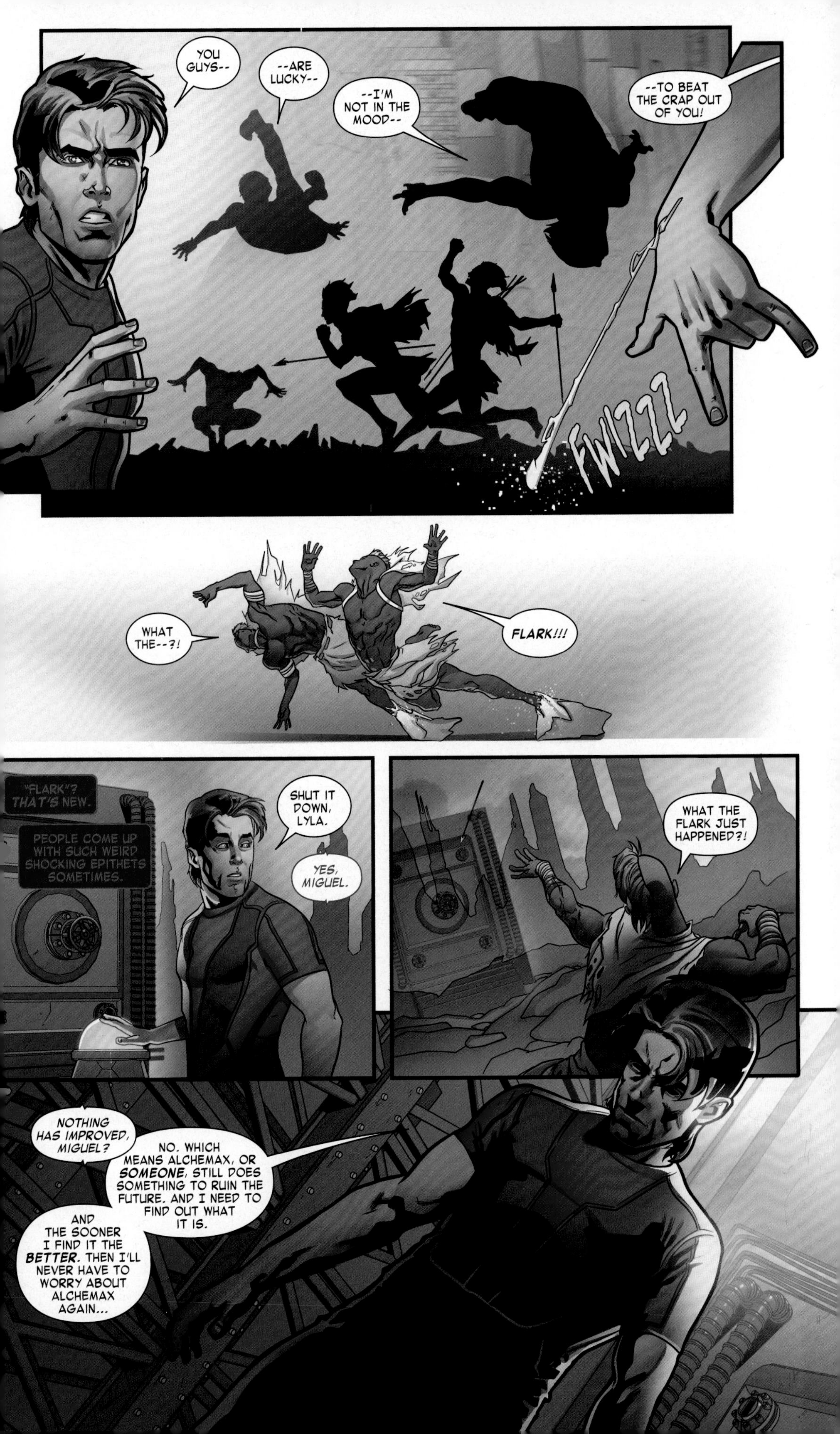
YOU GUYS--
--ARE LUCKY--
--I'M NOT IN THE MOOD--
--TO BEAT THE CRAP OUT OF YOU!
FWIZZZ
WHAT THE--?!
FLARK!!!
"FLARK"? THAT'S NEW.
PEOPLE COME UP WITH SUCH WEIRD SHOCKING EPITHETS SOMETIMES.
SHUT IT DOWN, LYLA.
YES, MIGUEL.
WHAT THE FLARK JUST HAPPENED?!
NOTHING HAS IMPROVED, MIGUEL?
NO. WHICH MEANS ALCHEMAX, OR SOMEONE, STILL DOES SOMETHING TO RUIN THE FUTURE. AND I NEED TO FIND OUT WHAT IT IS.
AND THE SOONER I FIND IT THE BETTER. THEN I'LL NEVER HAVE TO WORRY ABOUT ALCHEMAX AGAIN...

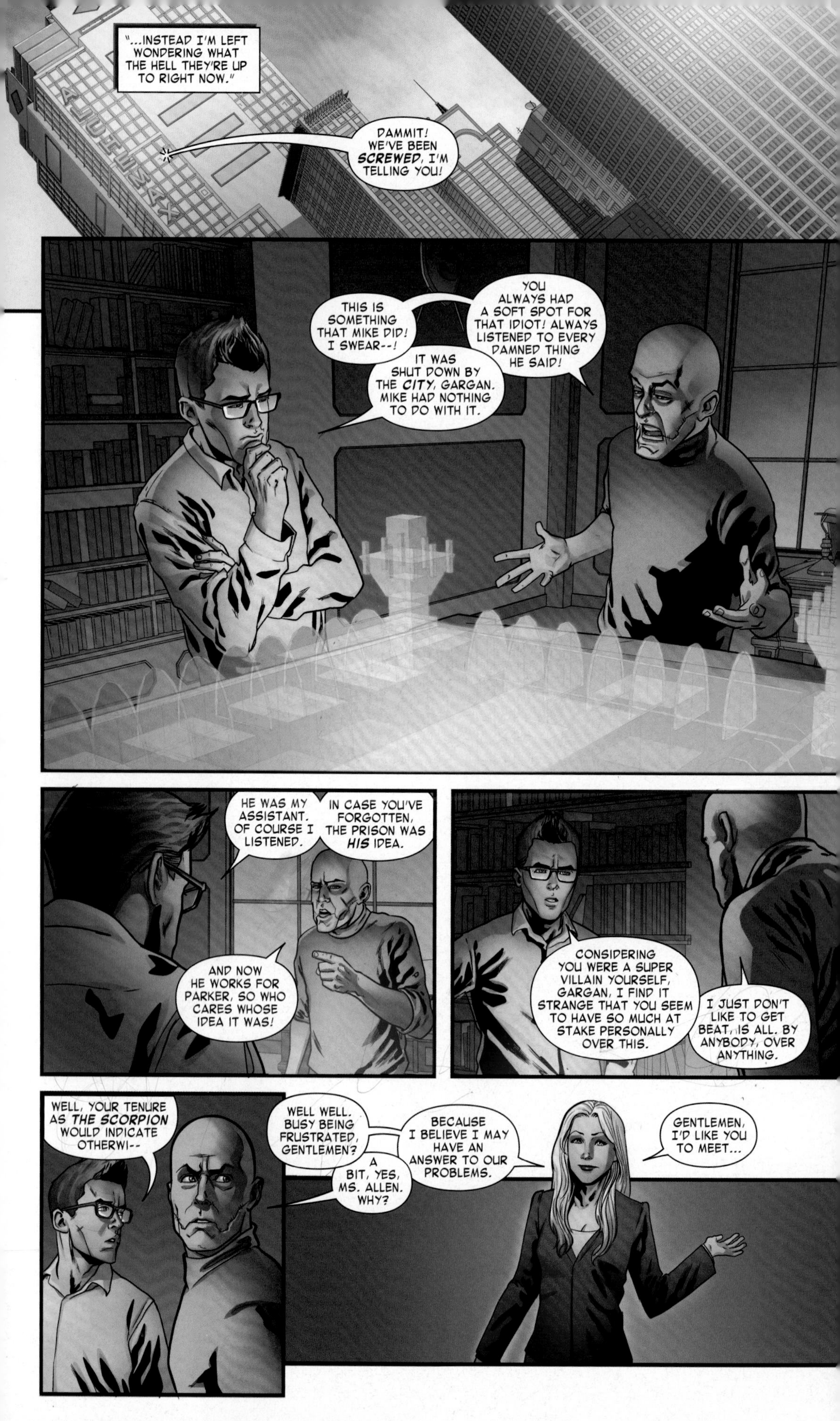
"...INSTEAD I'M LEFT WONDERING WHAT THE HELL THEY'RE UP TO RIGHT NOW."
DAMMIT! WE'VE BEEN SCREWED, I'M TELLING YOU!
THIS IS SOMETHING THAT MIKE DID! I SWEAR--!
YOU ALWAYS HAD A SOFT SPOT FOR THAT IDIOT! ALWAYS LISTENED TO EVERY DAMNED THING HE SAID!
IT WAS SHUT DOWN BY THE CITY, GARGAN. MIKE HAD NOTHING TO DO WITH IT.
HE WAS MY ASSISTANT. OF COURSE I LISTENED.
IN CASE YOU'VE FORGOTTEN, THE PRISON WAS HIS IDEA.
AND NOW HE WORKS FOR PARKER, SO WHO CARES WHOSE IDEA IT WAS!
CONSIDERING YOU WERE A SUPER VILLAIN YOURSELF, GARGAN, I FIND IT STRANGE THAT YOU SEEM TO HAVE SO MUCH AT STAKE PERSONALLY OVER THIS.
I JUST DON'T LIKE TO GET BEAT, IS ALL. BY ANYBODY, OVER ANYTHING.
WELL, YOUR TENURE AS THE SCORPION WOULD INDICATE OTHERWI--
WELL WELL. BUSY BEING FRUSTRATED, GENTLEMEN?
A BIT, YES, MS. ALLEN. WHY?
BECAUSE I BELIEVE I MAY HAVE AN ANSWER TO OUR PROBLEMS.
GENTLEMEN, I'D LIKE YOU TO MEET...

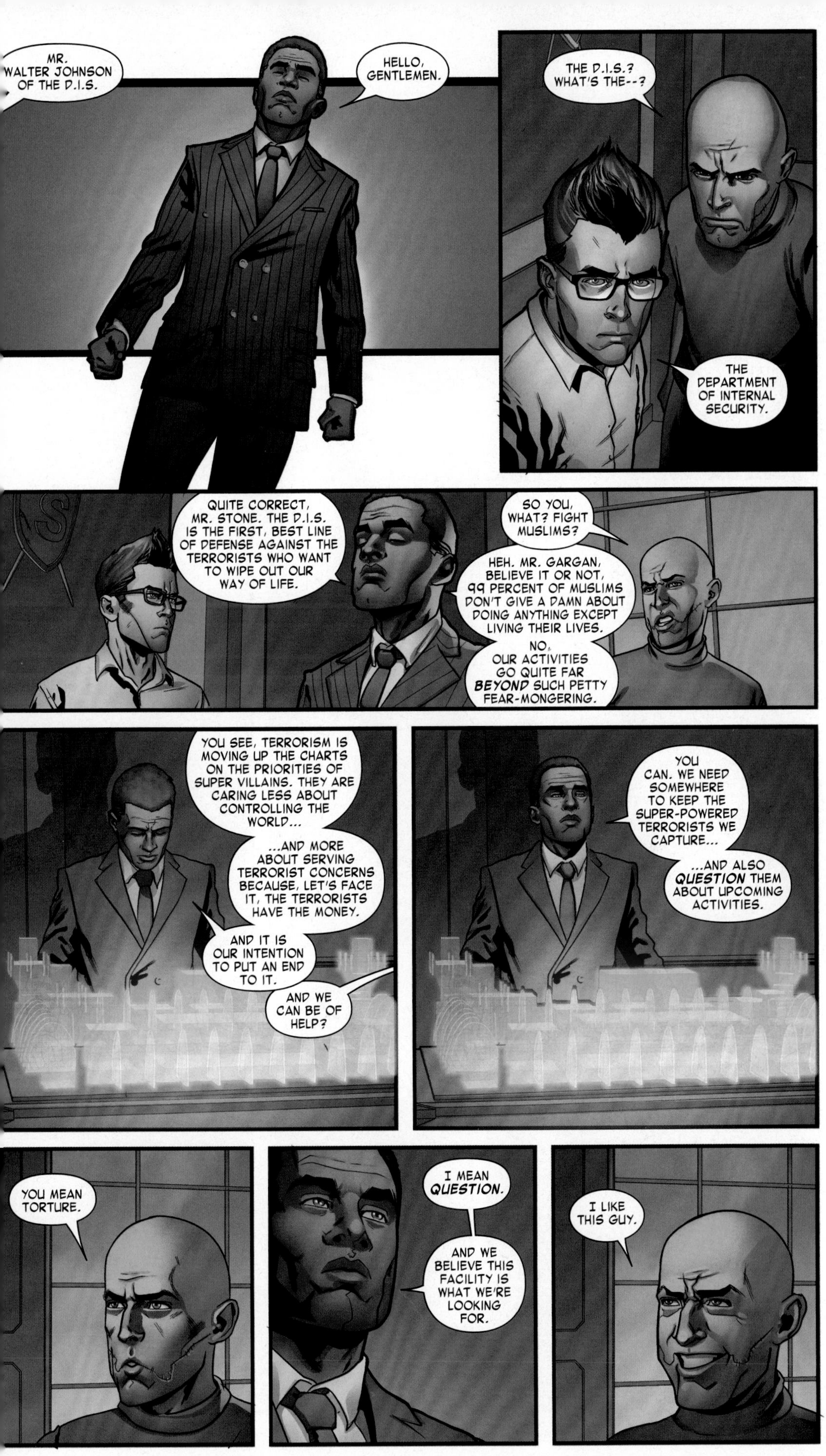
MR. WALTER JOHNSON OF THE D.I.S.
HELLO, GENTLEMEN.
THE D.I.S.? WHAT'S THE--?
THE DEPARTMENT OF INTERNAL SECURITY.
QUITE CORRECT, MR. STONE. THE D.I.S. IS THE FIRST, BEST LINE OF DEFENSE AGAINST THE TERRORISTS WHO WANT TO WIPE OUT OUR WAY OF LIFE.
SO YOU, WHAT? FIGHT MUSLIMS?
HEH. MR. GARGAN, BELIEVE IT OR NOT, 99 PERCENT OF MUSLIMS DON'T GIVE A DAMN ABOUT DOING ANYTHING EXCEPT LIVING THEIR LIVES.
NO. OUR ACTIVITIES GO QUITE FAR BEYOND SUCH PETTY FEAR-MONGERING.
YOU SEE, TERRORISM IS MOVING UP THE CHARTS ON THE PRIORITIES OF SUPER VILLAINS. THEY ARE CARING LESS ABOUT CONTROLLING THE WORLD...
...AND MORE ABOUT SERVING TERRORIST CONCERNS BECAUSE, LET'S FACE IT, THE TERRORISTS HAVE THE MONEY.
AND IT IS OUR INTENTION TO PUT AN END TO IT.
AND WE CAN BE OF HELP?
YOU CAN. WE NEED SOMEWHERE TO KEEP THE SUPER-POWERED TERRORISTS WE CAPTURE...
...AND ALSO QUESTION THEM ABOUT UPCOMING ACTIVITIES.
YOU MEAN TORTURE.
I MEAN QUESTION.
AND WE BELIEVE THIS FACILITY IS WHAT WE'RE LOOKING FOR.
I LIKE THIS GUY.

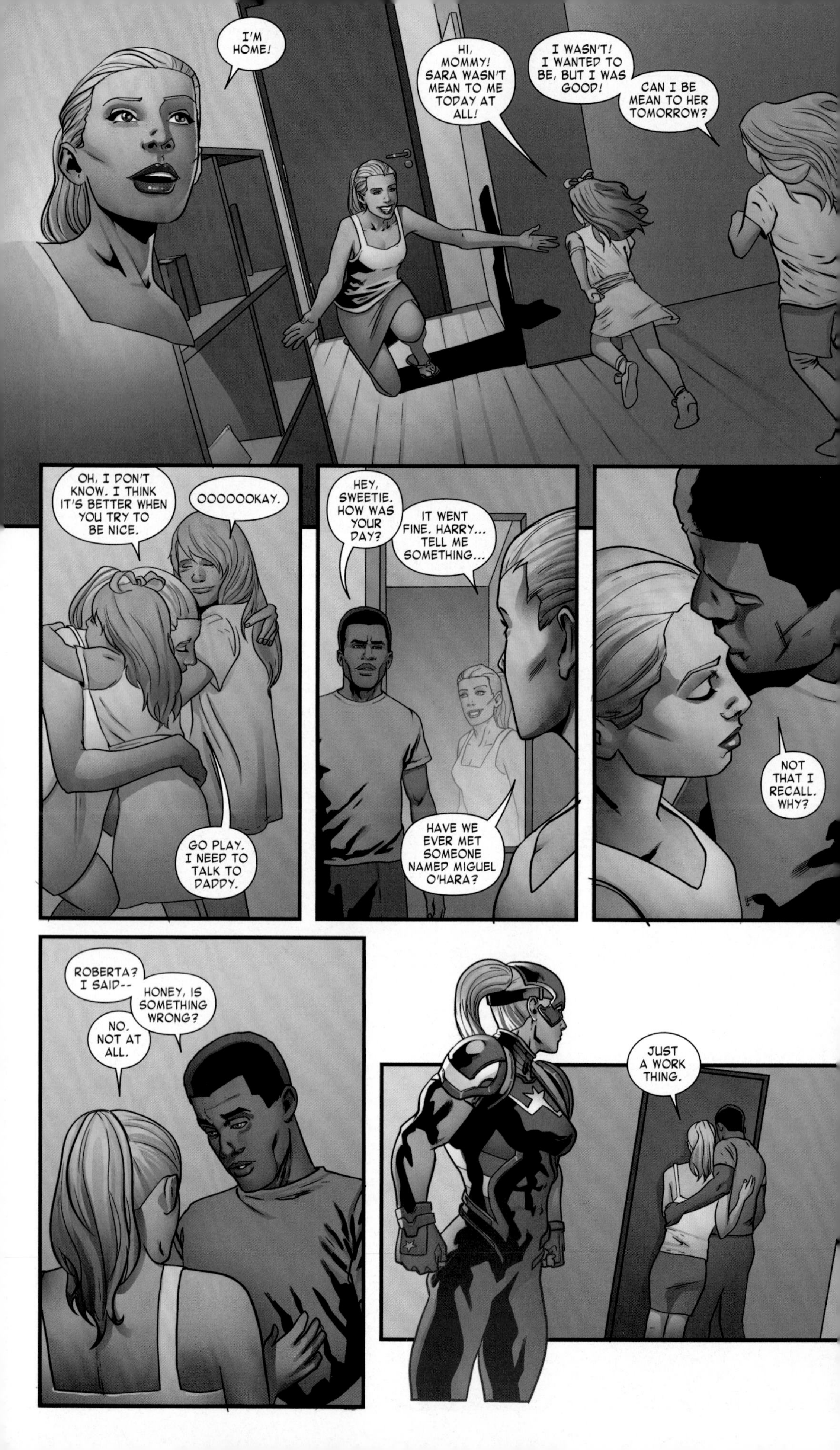
I'M HOME!
HI, MOMMY! SARA WASN'T MEAN TO ME TODAY AT ALL!
I WASN'T! I WANTED TO BE, BUT I WAS GOOD!
CAN I BE MEAN TO HER TOMORROW?
OH, I DON'T KNOW. I THINK IT'S BETTER WHEN YOU TRY TO BE NICE.
OOOOOOKAY.
GO PLAY. I NEED TO TALK TO DADDY.
HEY, SWEETIE. HOW WAS YOUR DAY?
IT WENT FINE. HARRY... TELL ME SOMETHING...
HAVE WE EVER MET SOMEONE NAMED MIGUEL O'HARA?
NOT THAT I RECALL. WHY?
ROBERTA? I SAID--
HONEY, IS SOMETHING WRONG?
NO. NOT AT ALL.
JUST A WORK THING.

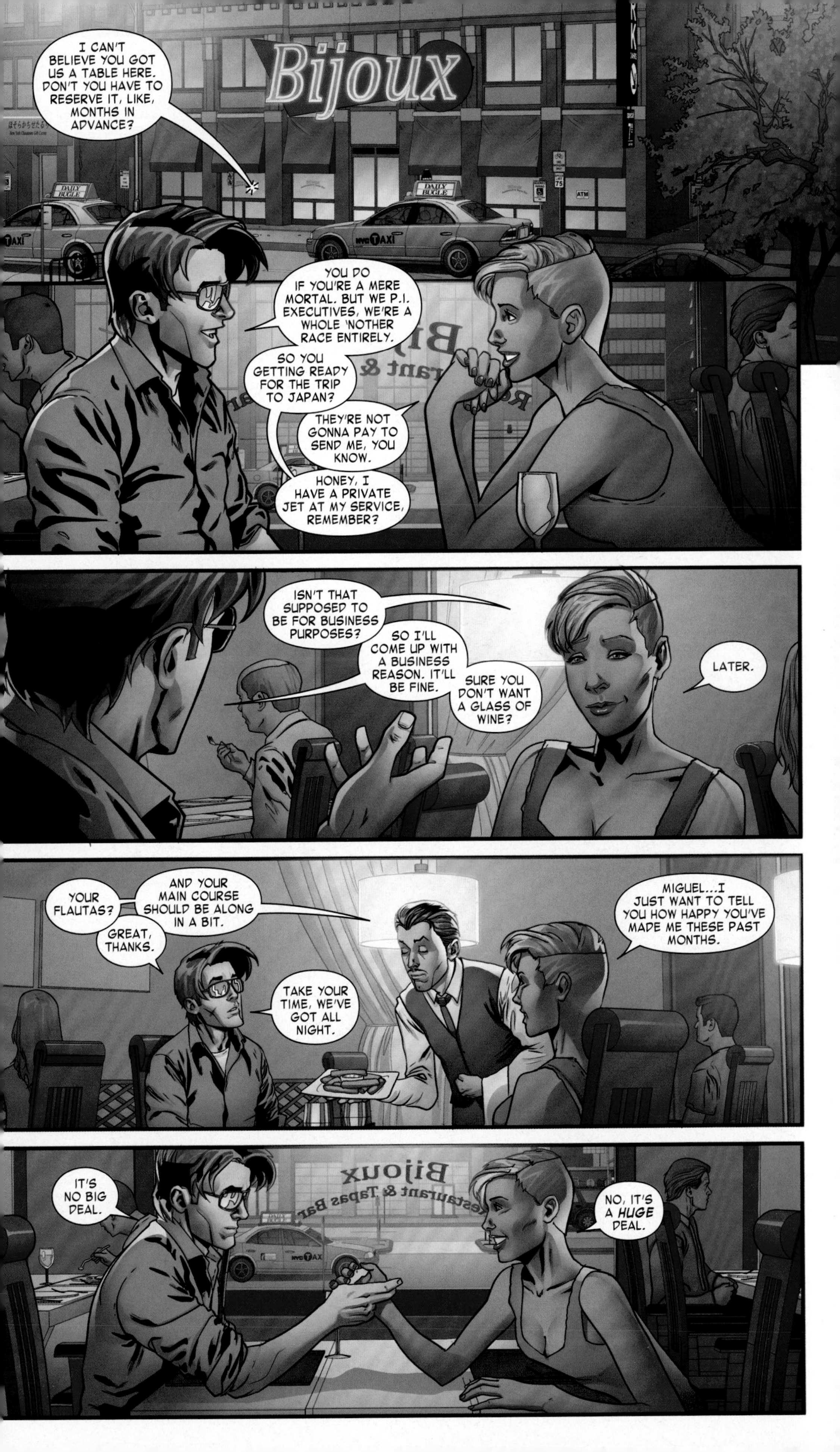

Bijoux
DAILY BUGLE
I CAN'T BELIEVE YOU GOT US A TABLE HERE. DON'T YOU HAVE TO RESERVE IT, LIKE, MONTHS IN ADVANCE?
YOU DO IF YOU'RE A MERE MORTAL. BUT WE P.I. EXECUTIVES, WE'RE A WHOLE 'NOTHER RACE ENTIRELY.
SO YOU GETTING READY FOR THE TRIP TO JAPAN?
THEY'RE NOT GONNA PAY TO SEND ME, YOU KNOW.
HONEY, I HAVE A PRIVATE JET AT MY SERVICE, REMEMBER?
ISN'T THAT SUPPOSED TO BE FOR BUSINESS PURPOSES?
SO I'LL COME UP WITH A BUSINESS REASON. IT'LL BE FINE.
SURE YOU DON'T WANT A GLASS OF WINE?
LATER.
YOUR FLAUTAS?
AND YOUR MAIN COURSE SHOULD BE ALONG IN A BIT.
GREAT, THANKS.
TAKE YOUR TIME, WE'VE GOT ALL NIGHT.
MIGUEL...I JUST WANT TO TELL YOU HOW HAPPY YOU'VE MADE ME THESE PAST MONTHS.
IT'S NO BIG DEAL.
NO, IT'S A *HUGE* DEAL.

I WAS DYING WHEN I MET YOU.

AND THEN YOU CURED ME WITH SOME... SOME MAGIC FORMULA.

WHICH ALSO TURNED YOU INTO A KILLER INSECT WOMAN.

YEAH, WELL, IT'S NOT LIKE CHEMO WOULD HAVE BEEN A LOT OF LAUGHS, EITHER.

I OWE YOU MY LIFE.

YEAH, I KNOW, AND...

AND WHAT?

SOMETIMES I WORRY THAT'S WHY YOU'RE IN LOVE WITH ME. THAT IT'S LESS TO DO WITH HOW YOU FEEL ABOUT ME, AND MORE A SENSE OF GRATITUDE.

YOU REALLY WORRY ABOUT THAT?

KIND OF. ALSO GLOBAL WARMING. AND DONALD TRUMP.

WHO WOULD'VE THOUGHT THAT YOU, OF ALL PEOPLE, WOULD SUFFER FROM CONFIDENCE ISSUES?

I LOVE YOU FOR A HUNDRED REASONS, MIGGY.

AND I'M ABOUT TO GIVE YOU ONE MORE.

YEAH?

YEAH. IT'S THIS:

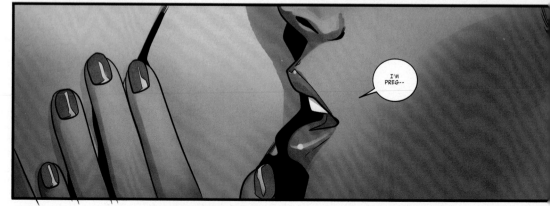

I'M PREG--

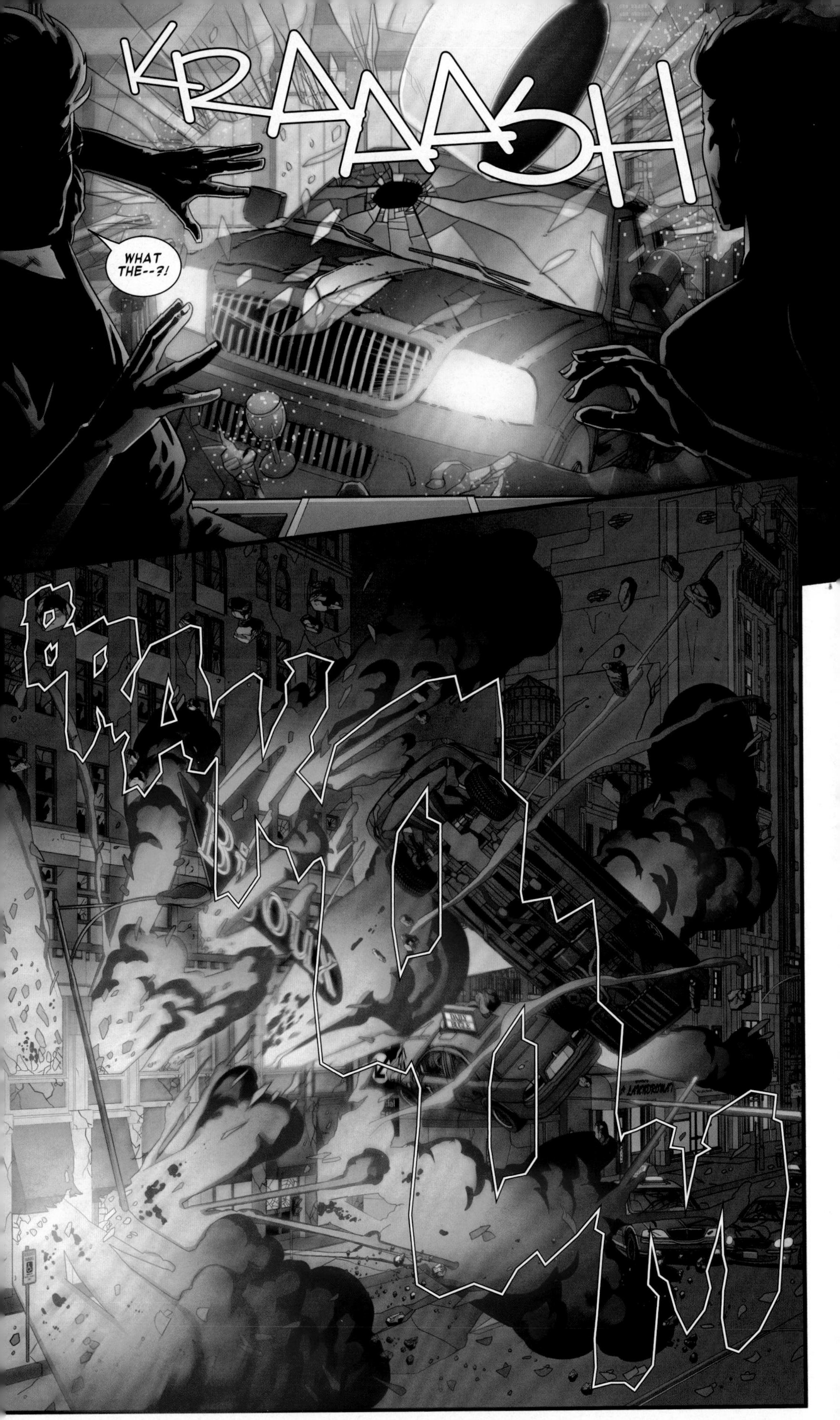
KRAAASH
WHAT THE--?!

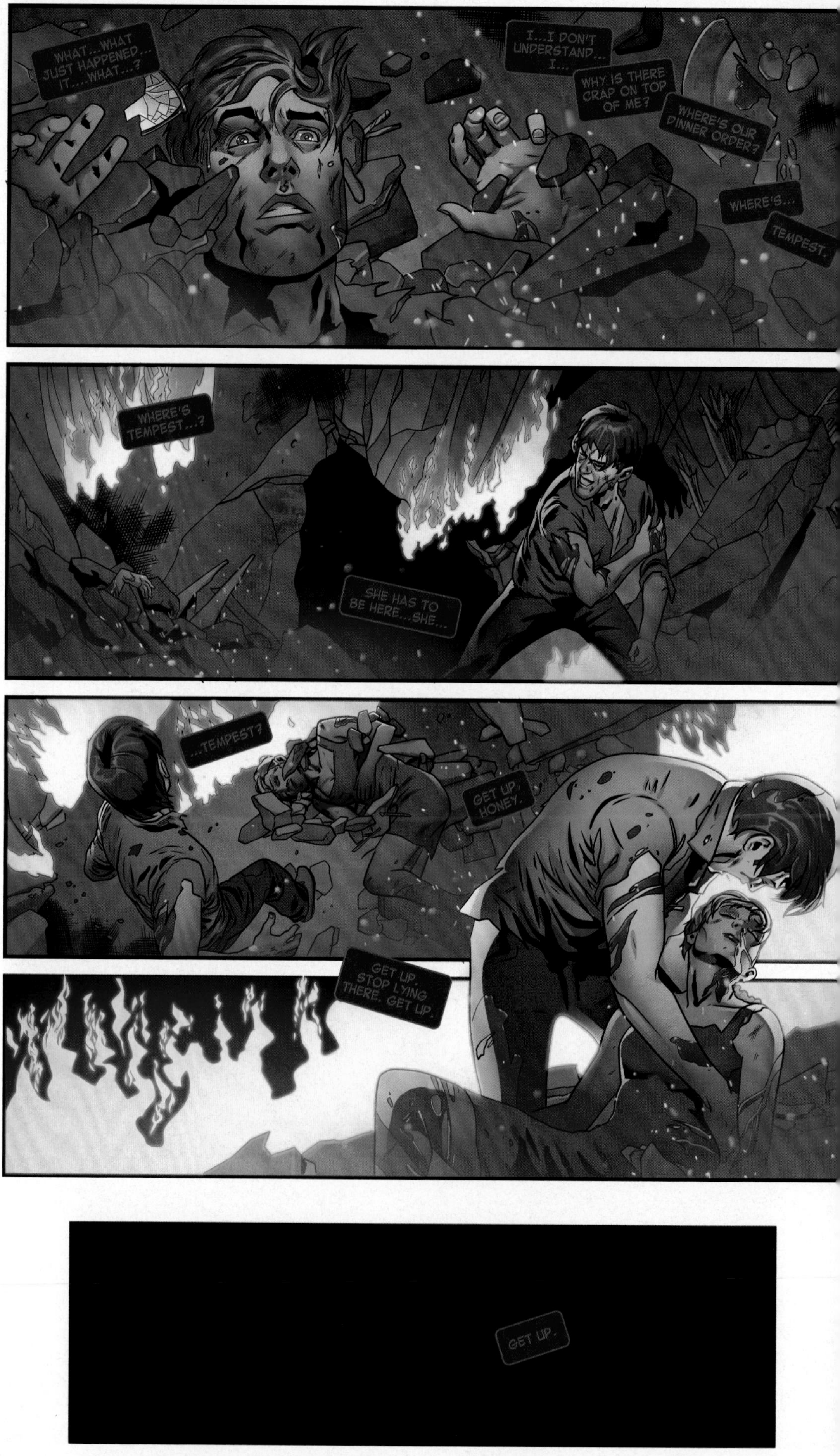
WHAT...WHAT JUST HAPPENED... IT....WHAT...?
I...I DON'T UNDERSTAND... I...
WHY IS THERE CRAP ON TOP OF ME?
WHERE'S OUR DINNER ORDER?
WHERE'S...
TEMPEST.
WHERE'S TEMPEST...?
SHE HAS TO BE HERE...SHE...
...TEMPEST?
GET UP, HONEY.
GET UP. STOP LYING THERE. GET UP.
GET UP.

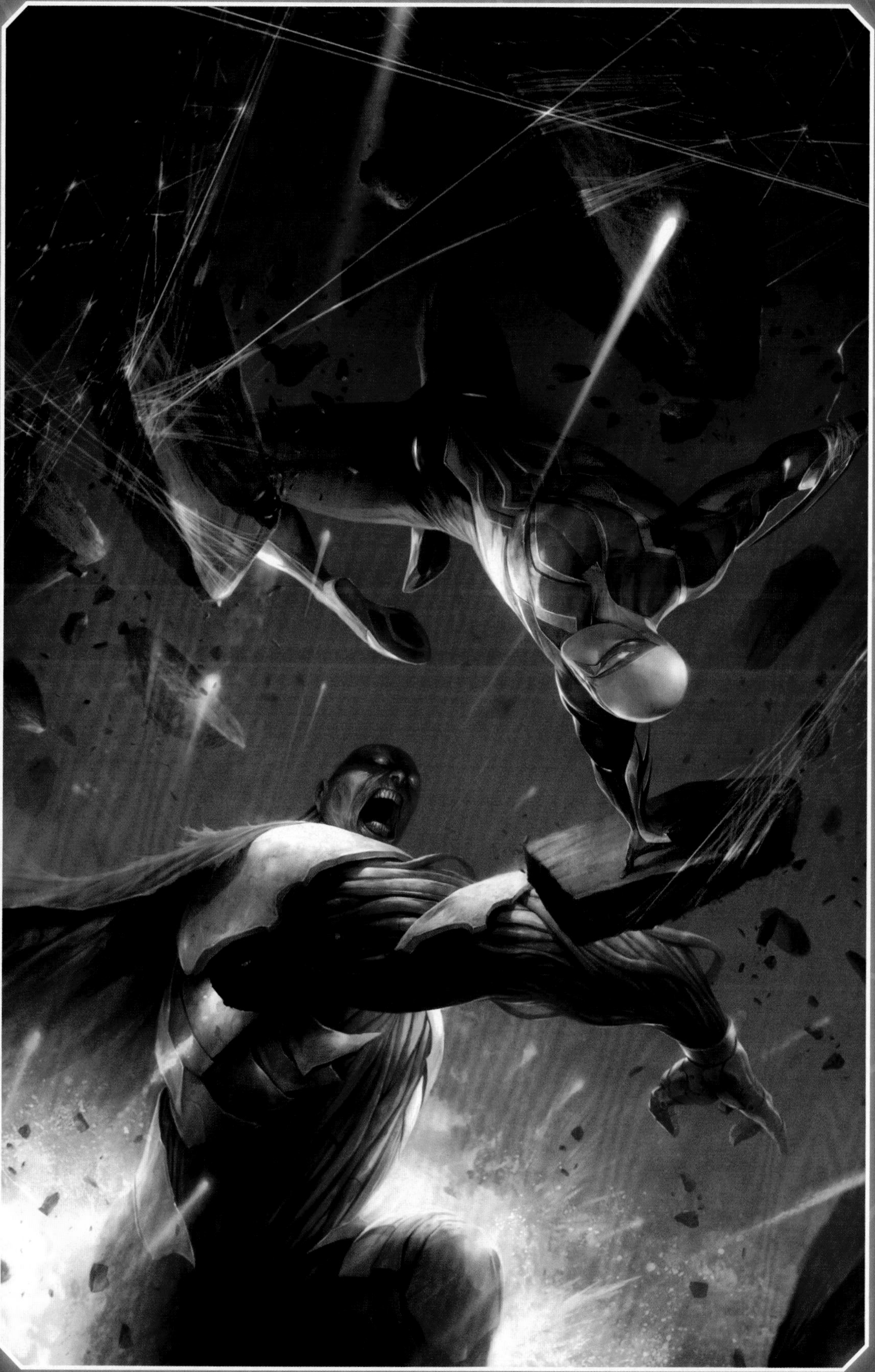

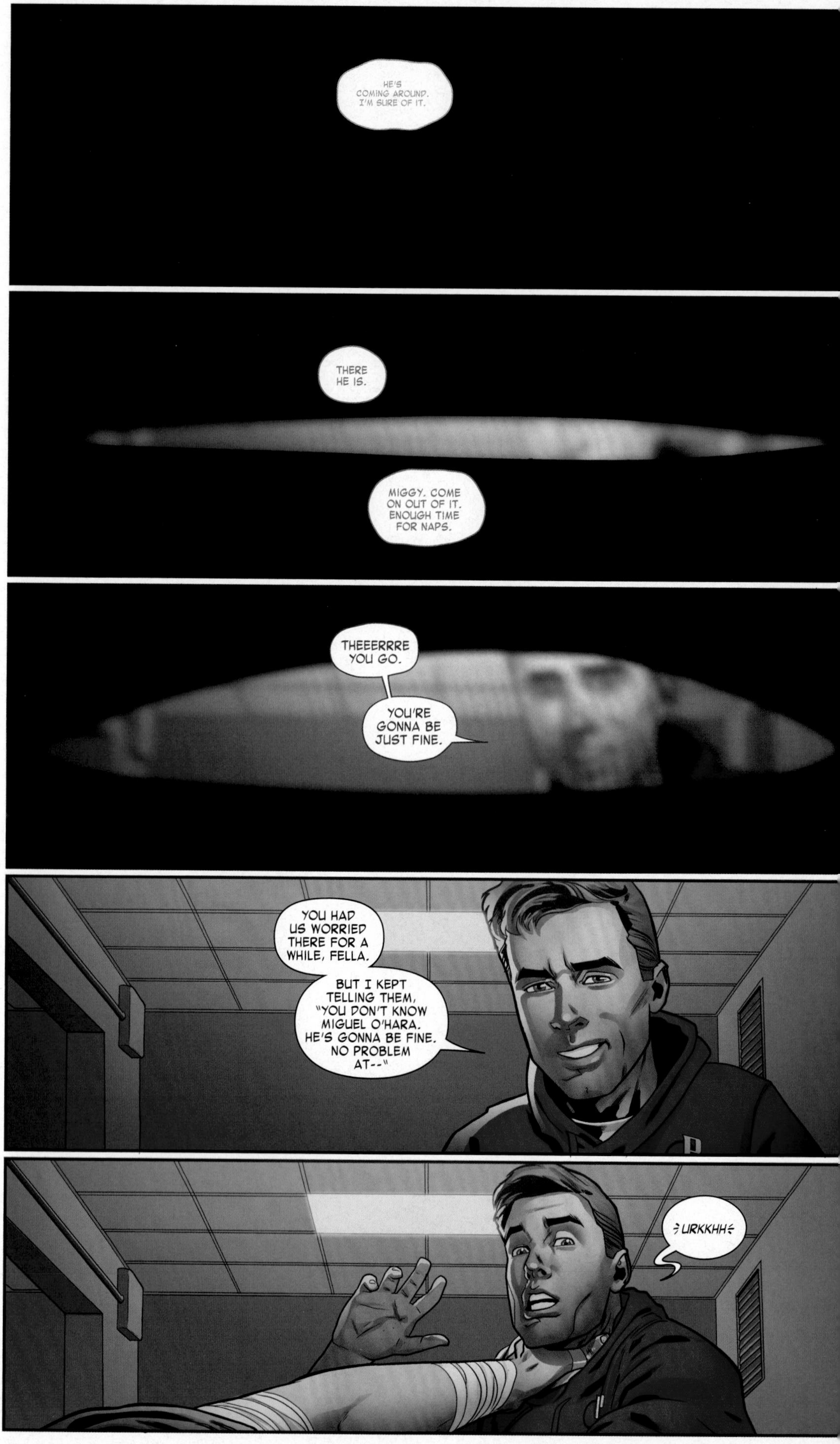
HE'S COMING AROUND. I'M SURE OF IT.
THERE HE IS.
MIGGY. COME ON OUT OF IT. ENOUGH TIME FOR NAPS.
THEEERRRE YOU GO.
YOU'RE GONNA BE JUST FINE.
YOU HAD US WORRIED THERE FOR A WHILE, FELLA.
BUT I KEPT TELLING THEM, "YOU DON'T KNOW MIGUEL O'HARA. HE'S GONNA BE FINE. NO PROBLEM AT--"
URKKHH

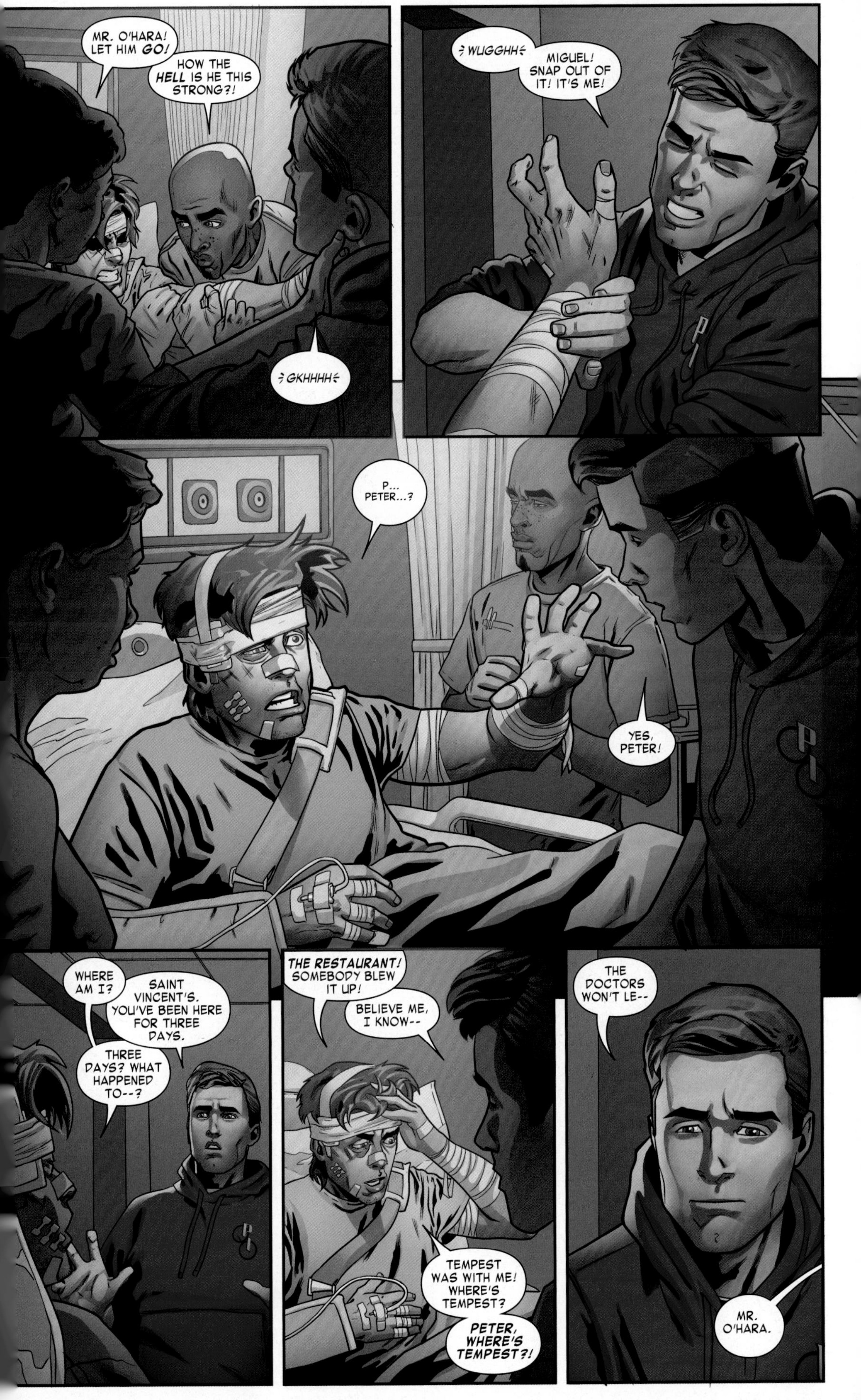
MR. O'HARA! LET HIM *GO!*
HOW THE *HELL* IS HE THIS STRONG?!
GKHHHH
WUGGHH
MIGUEL! SNAP OUT OF IT! IT'S ME!
P... PETER...?
YES, PETER!
WHERE AM I?
SAINT VINCENT'S. YOU'VE BEEN HERE FOR THREE DAYS.
THREE DAYS? WHAT HAPPENED TO--?
THE RESTAURANT! SOMEBODY BLEW IT UP!
BELIEVE ME, I KNOW--
TEMPEST WAS WITH ME! WHERE'S TEMPEST?
PETER, WHERE'S TEMPEST?!
THE DOCTORS WON'T LE--
MR. O'HARA.

YEAH? WHAT?

MY NAME IS CECELIA MONROE.

PERHAPS MY DAUGHTER MENTIONED ME TO YOU.

YES, SHE DID, BUT NOT IN DEPTH. WHERE IS SHE?

WE DID NOT HAVE THE CLOSEST RELATIONSHIP. I HAD PLANS FOR HER, AND SHE TURNED HER BACK ON THEM AND ME WHEN SHE MET YOU. BUT THAT DOESN'T MATTER NOW.

I WOULDN'T KNOW. SH' BARELY EV' MENTIONE' YOU.

WHERE IS TEMPEST?

I DON'T KNOW WHAT TO SAY TO--

WAAP

SHE'S DEAD, MR. O'HARA. AND IT'S *YOUR* FAULT.

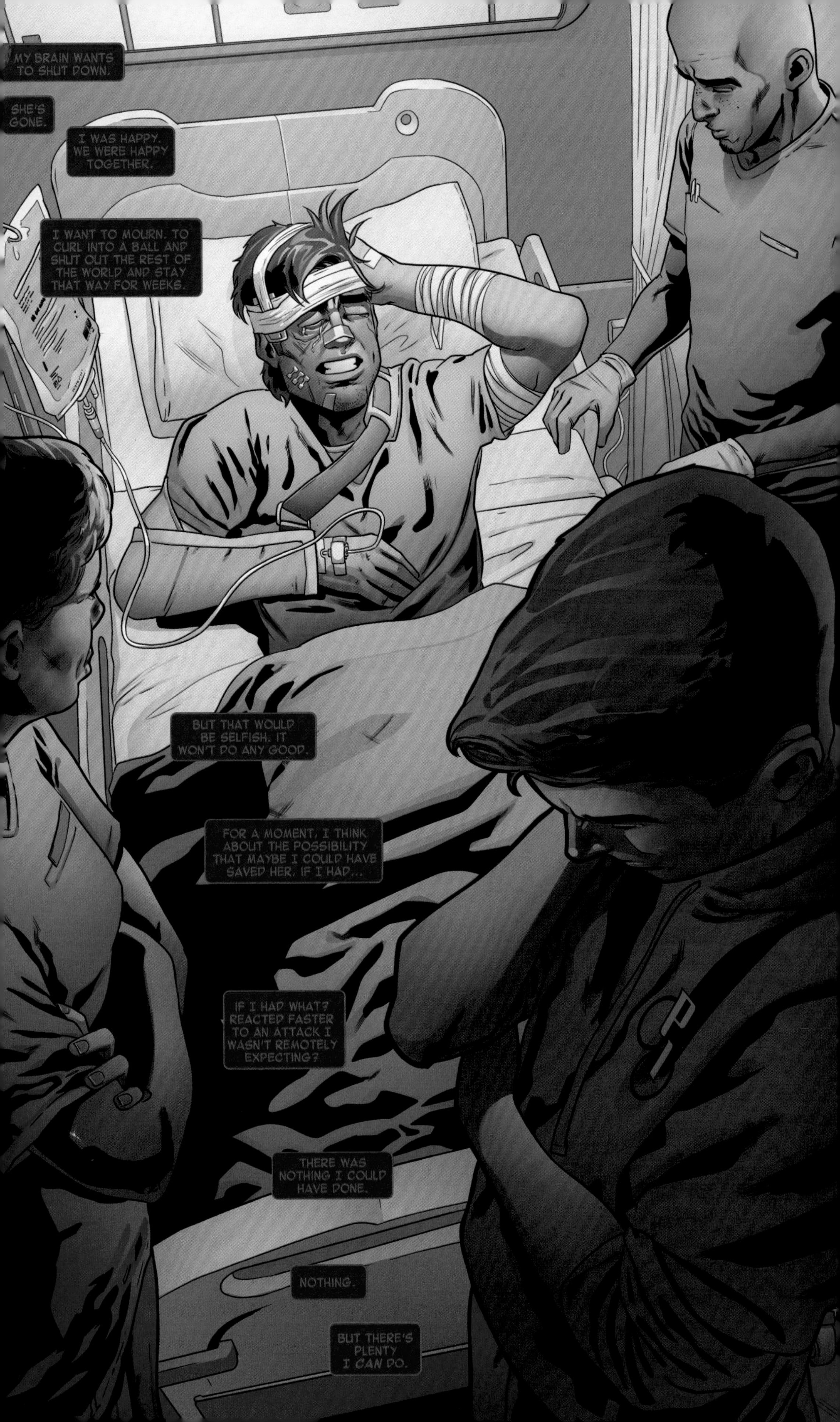
MY BRAIN WANTS TO SHUT DOWN.
SHE'S GONE.
I WAS HAPPY. WE WERE HAPPY TOGETHER.
I WANT TO MOURN. TO CURL INTO A BALL AND SHUT OUT THE REST OF THE WORLD AND STAY THAT WAY FOR WEEKS.
BUT THAT WOULD BE SELFISH. IT WON'T DO ANY GOOD.
FOR A MOMENT, I THINK ABOUT THE POSSIBILITY THAT MAYBE I COULD HAVE SAVED HER, IF I HAD...
IF I HAD WHAT? REACTED FASTER TO AN ATTACK I WASN'T REMOTELY EXPECTING?
THERE WAS NOTHING I COULD HAVE DONE.
NOTHING.
BUT THERE'S PLENTY I CAN DO.

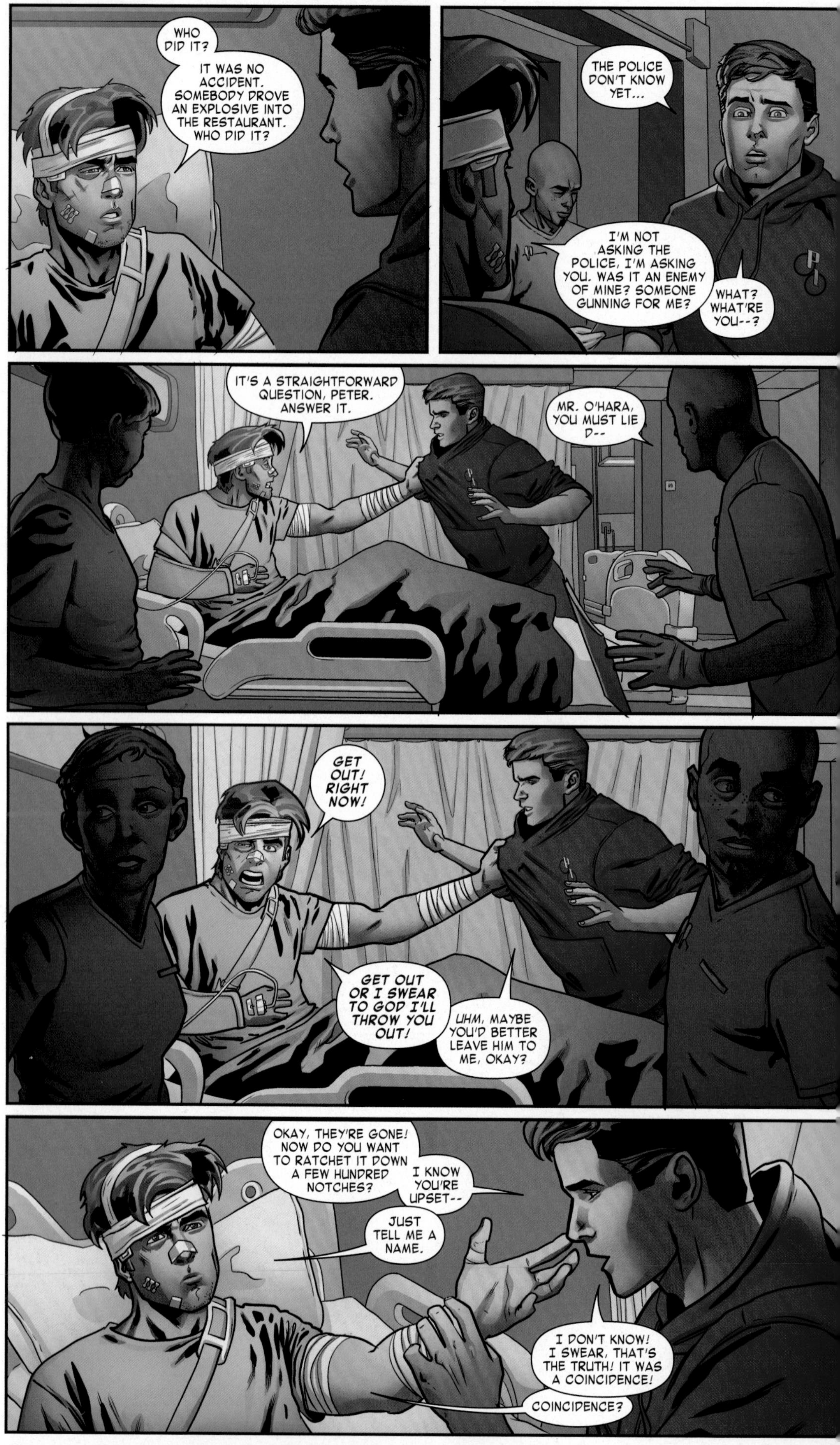
WHO DID IT?
IT WAS NO ACCIDENT. SOMEBODY DROVE AN EXPLOSIVE INTO THE RESTAURANT. WHO DID IT?
THE POLICE DON'T KNOW YET...
I'M NOT ASKING THE POLICE, I'M ASKING YOU. WAS IT AN ENEMY OF MINE? SOMEONE GUNNING FOR ME?
WHAT? WHAT'RE YOU--?
IT'S A STRAIGHTFORWARD QUESTION, PETER. ANSWER IT.
MR. O'HARA, YOU MUST LIE D--
GET OUT! RIGHT NOW!
GET OUT OR I SWEAR TO GOD I'LL THROW YOU OUT!
UHM, MAYBE YOU'D BETTER LEAVE HIM TO ME, OKAY?
OKAY, THEY'RE GONE! NOW DO YOU WANT TO RATCHET IT DOWN A FEW HUNDRED NOTCHES?
I KNOW YOU'RE UPSET--
JUST TELL ME A NAME.
I DON'T KNOW! I SWEAR, THAT'S THE TRUTH! IT WAS A COINCIDENCE!
COINCIDENCE?

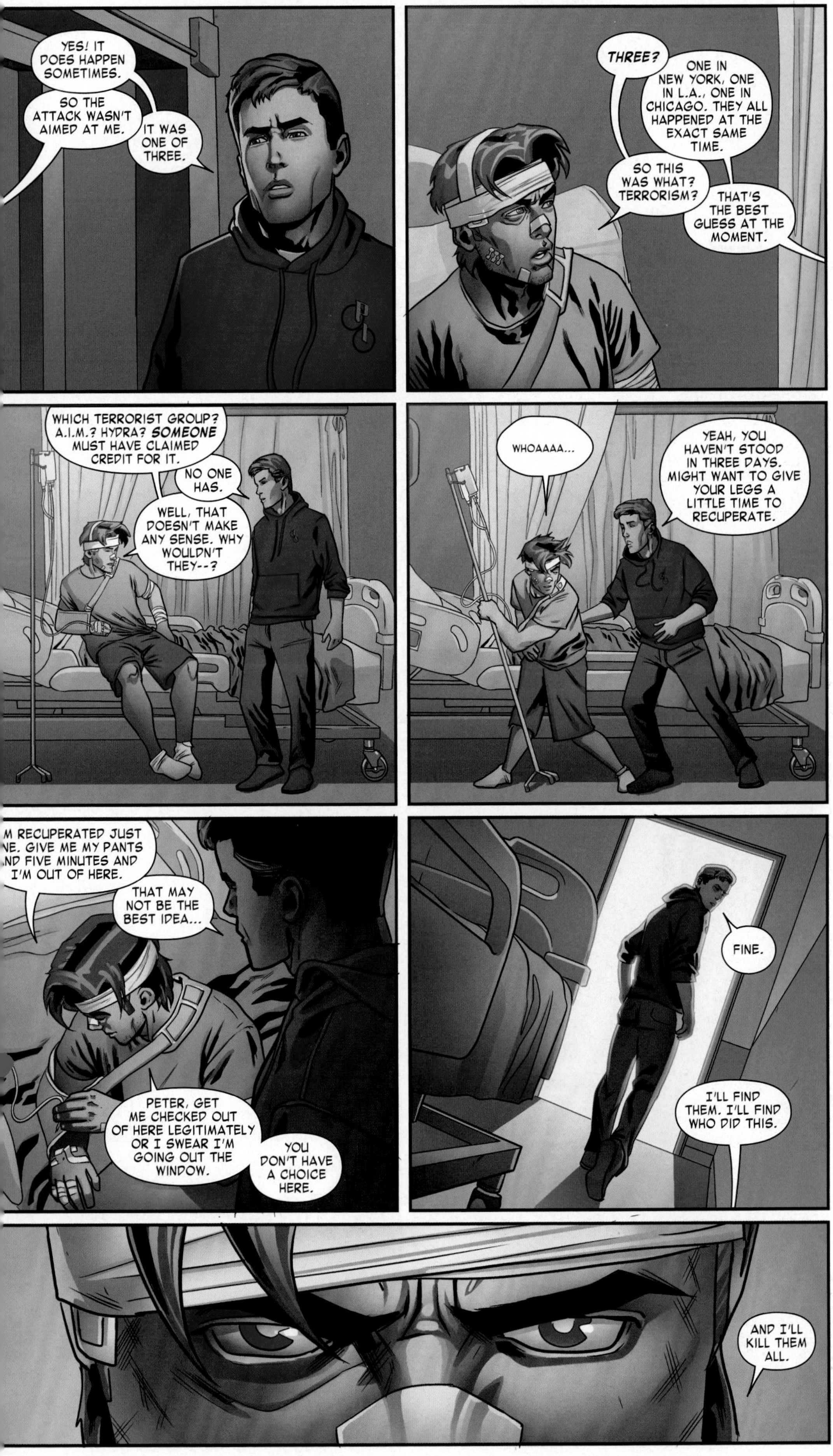

YES! IT DOES HAPPEN SOMETIMES.
SO THE ATTACK WASN'T AIMED AT ME.
IT WAS ONE OF THREE.
THREE?
ONE IN NEW YORK, ONE IN L.A., ONE IN CHICAGO. THEY ALL HAPPENED AT THE EXACT SAME TIME.
SO THIS WAS WHAT? TERRORISM?
THAT'S THE BEST GUESS AT THE MOMENT.
WHICH TERRORIST GROUP? A.I.M.? HYDRA? SOMEONE MUST HAVE CLAIMED CREDIT FOR IT.
NO ONE HAS.
WELL, THAT DOESN'T MAKE ANY SENSE. WHY WOULDN'T THEY--?
WHOAAAA...
YEAH, YOU HAVEN'T STOOD IN THREE DAYS. MIGHT WANT TO GIVE YOUR LEGS A LITTLE TIME TO RECUPERATE.
M RECUPERATED JUST NE. GIVE ME MY PANTS ND FIVE MINUTES AND I'M OUT OF HERE.
THAT MAY NOT BE THE BEST IDEA...
PETER, GET ME CHECKED OUT OF HERE LEGITIMATELY OR I SWEAR I'M GOING OUT THE WINDOW.
YOU DON'T HAVE A CHOICE HERE.
FINE.
I'LL FIND THEM. I'LL FIND WHO DID THIS.
AND I'LL KILL THEM ALL.

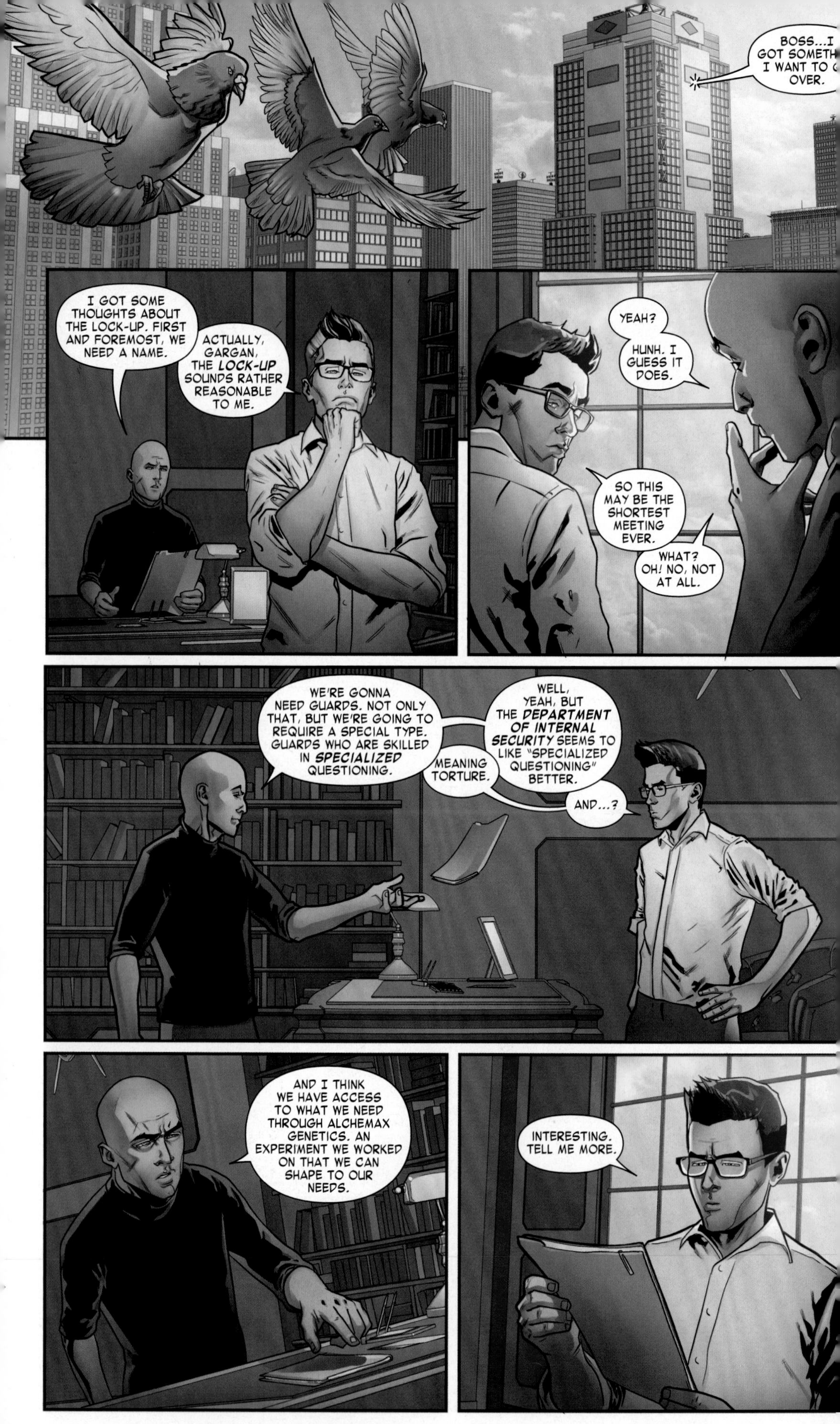
BOSS...I GOT SOMETH I WANT TO OVER.
I GOT SOME THOUGHTS ABOUT THE LOCK-UP. FIRST AND FOREMOST, WE NEED A NAME.
ACTUALLY, GARGAN, THE LOCK-UP SOUNDS RATHER REASONABLE TO ME.
YEAH?
HUNH. I GUESS IT DOES.
SO THIS MAY BE THE SHORTEST MEETING EVER.
WHAT? OH! NO, NOT AT ALL.
WE'RE GONNA NEED GUARDS. NOT ONLY THAT, BUT WE'RE GOING TO REQUIRE A SPECIAL TYPE. GUARDS WHO ARE SKILLED IN SPECIALIZED QUESTIONING.
MEANING TORTURE.
WELL, YEAH, BUT THE DEPARTMENT OF INTERNAL SECURITY SEEMS TO LIKE "SPECIALIZED QUESTIONING" BETTER.
AND...?
AND I THINK WE HAVE ACCESS TO WHAT WE NEED THROUGH ALCHEMAX GENETICS. AN EXPERIMENT WE WORKED ON THAT WE CAN SHAPE TO OUR NEEDS.
INTERESTING. TELL ME MORE.

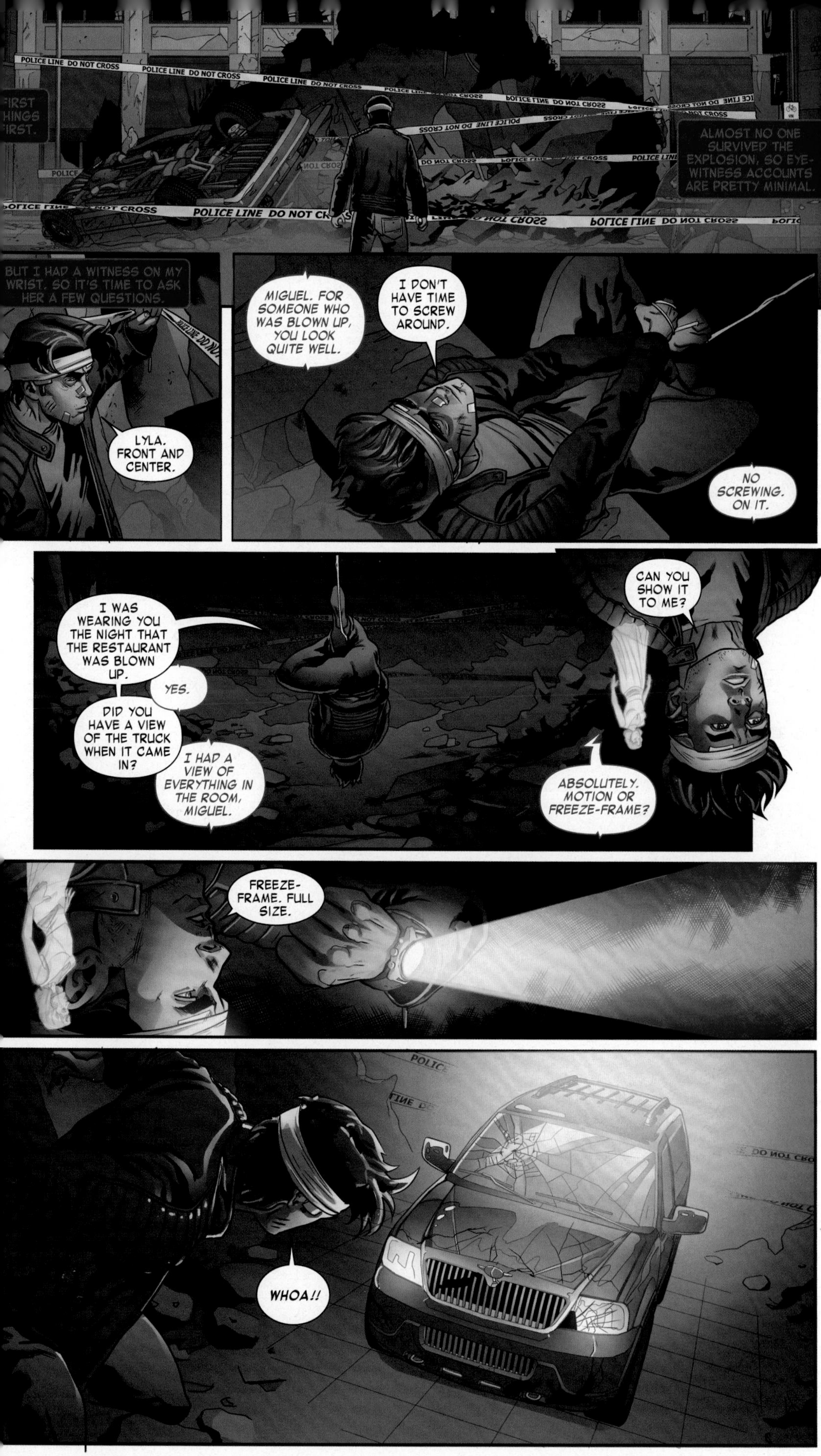
POLICE LINE DO NOT CROSS
FIRST THINGS FIRST.
ALMOST NO ONE SURVIVED THE EXPLOSION, SO EYE-WITNESS ACCOUNTS ARE PRETTY MINIMAL.
BUT I HAD A WITNESS ON MY WRIST. SO IT'S TIME TO ASK HER A FEW QUESTIONS.
LYLA. FRONT AND CENTER.
MIGUEL. FOR SOMEONE WHO WAS BLOWN UP, YOU LOOK QUITE WELL.
I DON'T HAVE TIME TO SCREW AROUND.
NO SCREWING. ON IT.
I WAS WEARING YOU THE NIGHT THAT THE RESTAURANT WAS BLOWN UP.
YES.
DID YOU HAVE A VIEW OF THE TRUCK WHEN IT CAME IN?
I HAD A VIEW OF EVERYTHING IN THE ROOM, MIGUEL.
CAN YOU SHOW IT TO ME?
ABSOLUTELY. MOTION OR FREEZE-FRAME?
FREEZE-FRAME. FULL SIZE.
WHOA!!

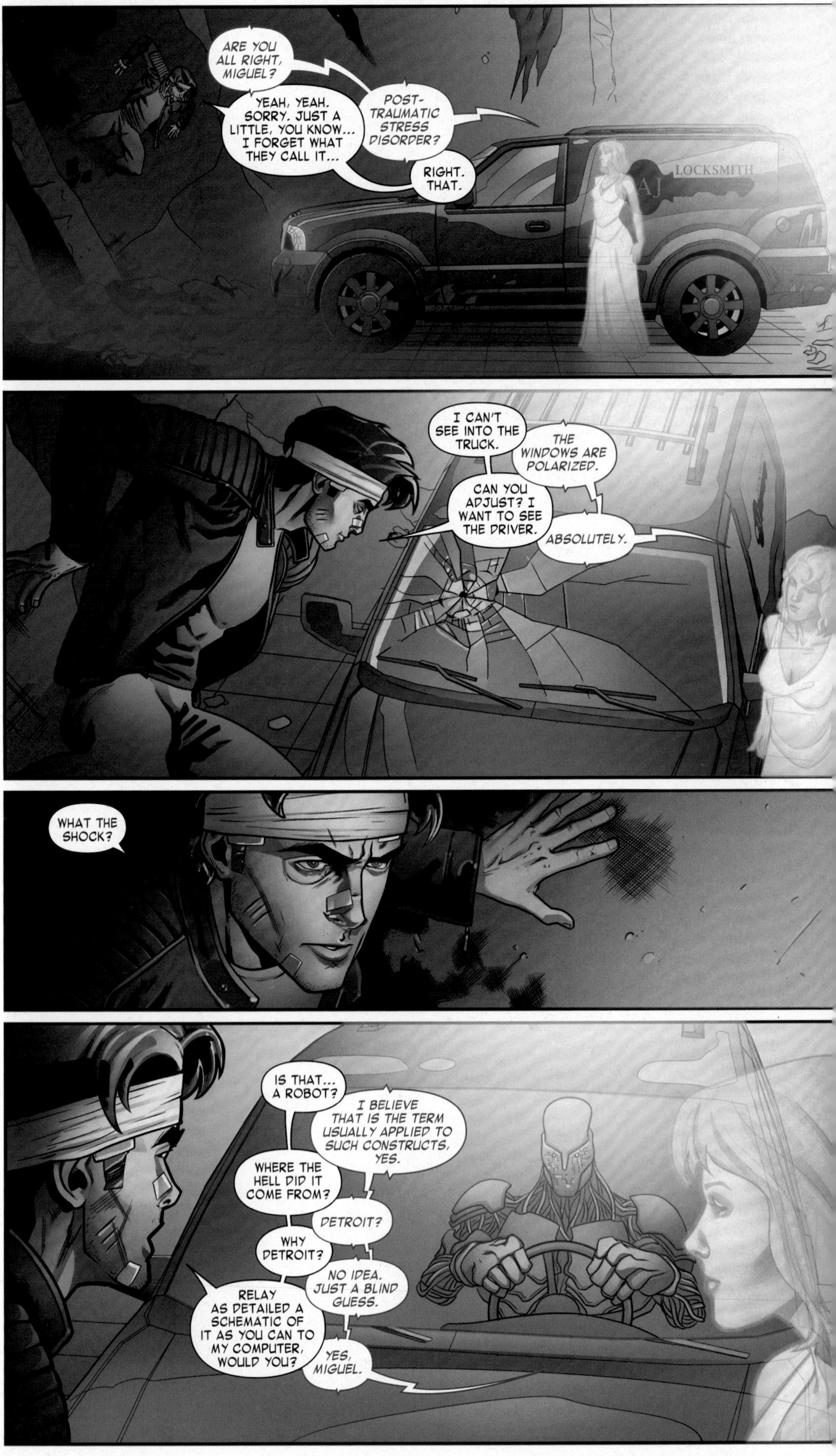
ARE YOU ALL RIGHT, MIGUEL?
YEAH, YEAH. SORRY. JUST A LITTLE, YOU KNOW... I FORGET WHAT THEY CALL IT...
POST-TRAUMATIC STRESS DISORDER?
RIGHT. THAT.
AJ LOCKSMITH
I CAN'T SEE INTO THE TRUCK.
THE WINDOWS ARE POLARIZED.
CAN YOU ADJUST? I WANT TO SEE THE DRIVER.
ABSOLUTELY.
WHAT THE SHOCK?
IS THAT... A ROBOT?
I BELIEVE THAT IS THE TERM USUALLY APPLIED TO SUCH CONSTRUCTS, YES.
WHERE THE HELL DID IT COME FROM?
DETROIT?
WHY DETROIT?
NO IDEA. JUST A BLIND GUESS.
RELAY AS DETAILED A SCHEMATIC OF IT AS YOU CAN TO MY COMPUTER, WOULD YOU?
YES, MIGUEL.

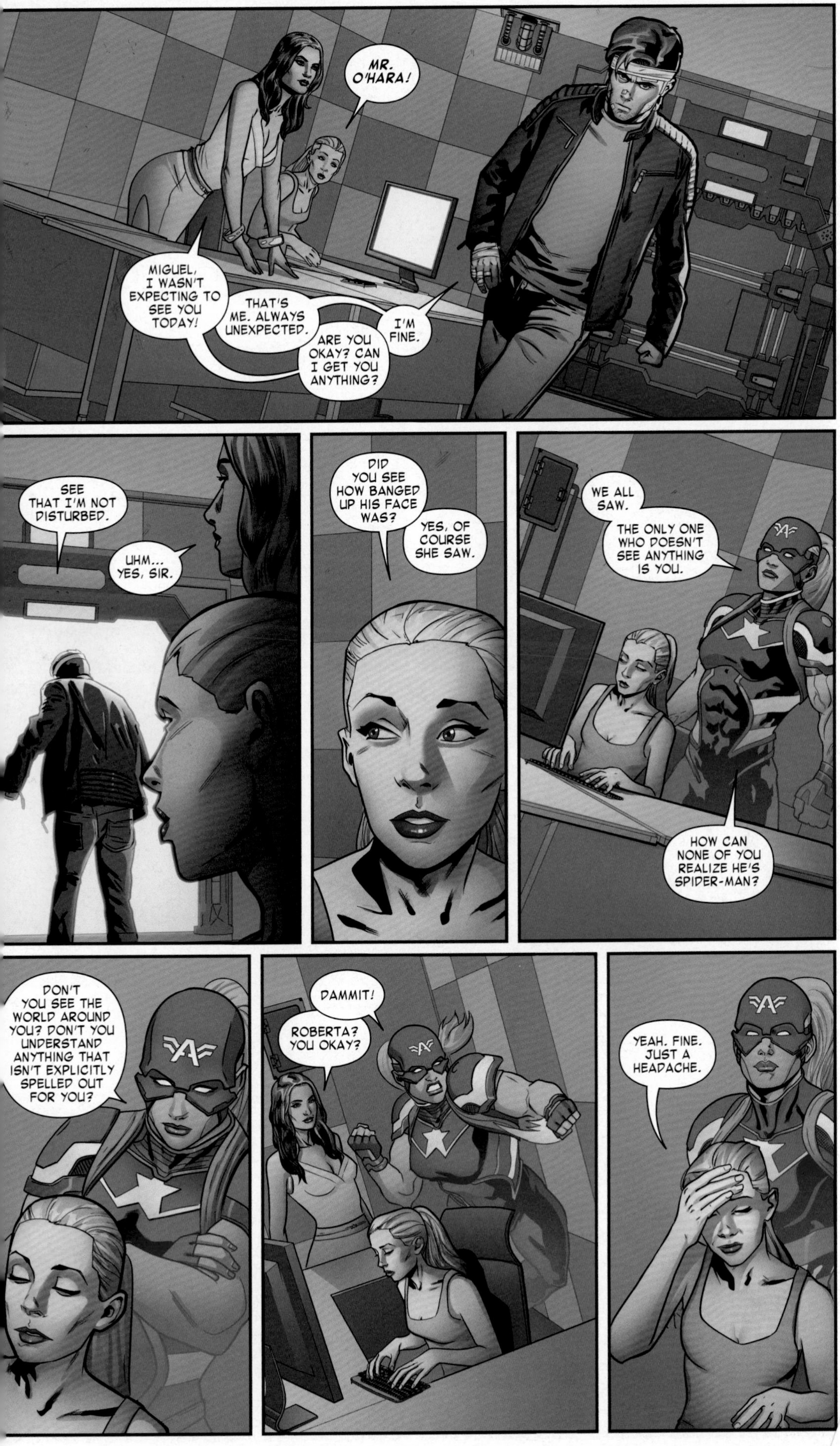
MR. O'HARA!
MIGUEL, I WASN'T EXPECTING TO SEE YOU TODAY!
THAT'S ME. ALWAYS UNEXPECTED.
ARE YOU OKAY? CAN I GET YOU ANYTHING?
I'M FINE.
SEE THAT I'M NOT DISTURBED.
UHM... YES, SIR.
DID YOU SEE HOW BANGED UP HIS FACE WAS?
YES, OF COURSE SHE SAW.
WE ALL SAW.
THE ONLY ONE WHO DOESN'T SEE ANYTHING IS YOU.
HOW CAN NONE OF YOU REALIZE HE'S SPIDER-MAN?
DON'T YOU SEE THE WORLD AROUND YOU? DON'T YOU UNDERSTAND ANYTHING THAT ISN'T EXPLICITLY SPELLED OUT FOR YOU?
DAMMIT!
ROBERTA? YOU OKAY?
YEAH. FINE. JUST A HEADACHE.

A ROBOT. SOMEONE BUILT A ROBOT TO DELIVER A BOMB.

AND IT'S PERFECT, OF COURSE. THE ROBOT GETS BLOWN UP AND ALL THAT'S LEFT IS SCRAP THAT'S INDISTINGUISHABLE FROM ALL THE OTHER REMAINS THAT RESULTED.

NEWS REPORTS SAID TWENTY-THREE PEOPLE DIED IN THAT EXPLOSION, AND THAT WAS JUST IN NEW YORK.

MIGUEL! YOU'RE BACK!

YES, EVERYONE SEEMS TO AGREE ON THAT.

ARE YOU SURE YOU'RE UP FOR RETURNING SO SOON?

WHETHER I AM OR NOT, HERE I AM.

YOU KNOW, WE COULD MANAGE A FEW DAYS WITHOUT YOU...

YOU'RE NOT MY MOTHER, RAUL, SO HOW ABOUT YOU BACK OFF?

RIGHT, SURE.

UHM...ARE YOU THINKING OF HIRING DOCTOR CRONOS?

WHO?

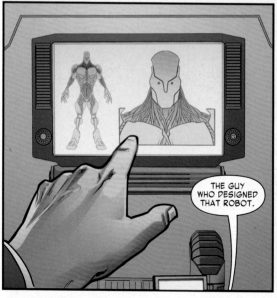

THE GUY WHO DESIGNED THAT ROBOT.

WHAT?

YOU KNOW WHO DESIGNED THIS?

PRETTY SURE, YEAH.

HIS DESIGNS ARE PRETTY DISTINCTIVE.

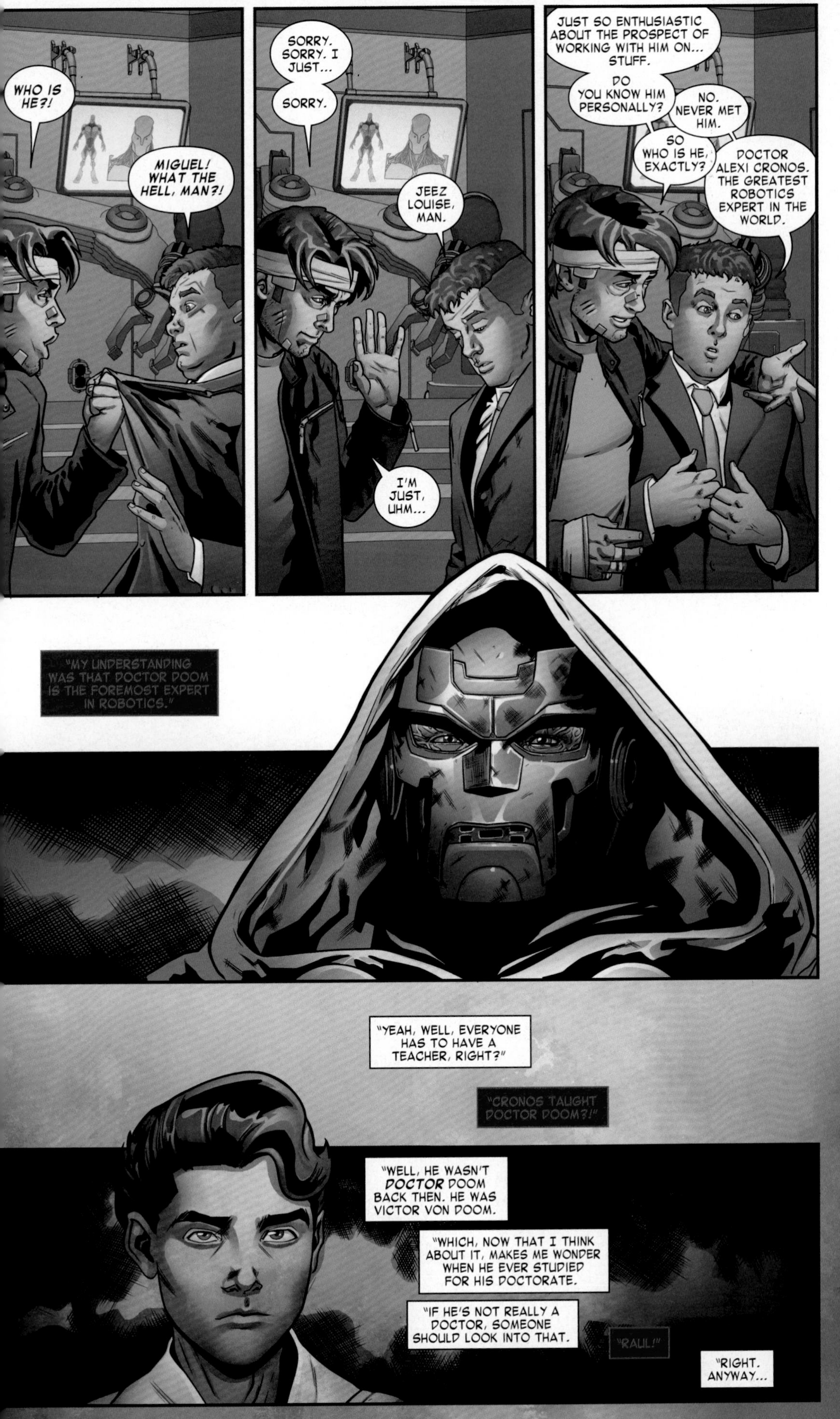

WHO IS HE?!
MIGUEL! WHAT THE HELL, MAN?!
SORRY. SORRY. I JUST...
SORRY.
JEEZ LOUISE, MAN.
I'M JUST, UHM...
JUST SO ENTHUSIASTIC ABOUT THE PROSPECT OF WORKING WITH HIM ON... STUFF.
DO YOU KNOW HIM PERSONALLY?
NO. NEVER MET HIM.
SO WHO IS HE, EXACTLY?
DOCTOR ALEXI CRONOS. THE GREATEST ROBOTICS EXPERT IN THE WORLD.
"MY UNDERSTANDING WAS THAT DOCTOR DOOM IS THE FOREMOST EXPERT IN ROBOTICS."
"YEAH, WELL, EVERYONE HAS TO HAVE A TEACHER, RIGHT?"
"CRONOS TAUGHT DOCTOR DOOM?!"
"WELL, HE WASN'T DOCTOR DOOM BACK THEN. HE WAS VICTOR VON DOOM.
"WHICH, NOW THAT I THINK ABOUT IT, MAKES ME WONDER WHEN HE EVER STUDIED FOR HIS DOCTORATE.
"IF HE'S NOT REALLY A DOCTOR, SOMEONE SHOULD LOOK INTO THAT.
"RAUL!"
"RIGHT. ANYWAY...

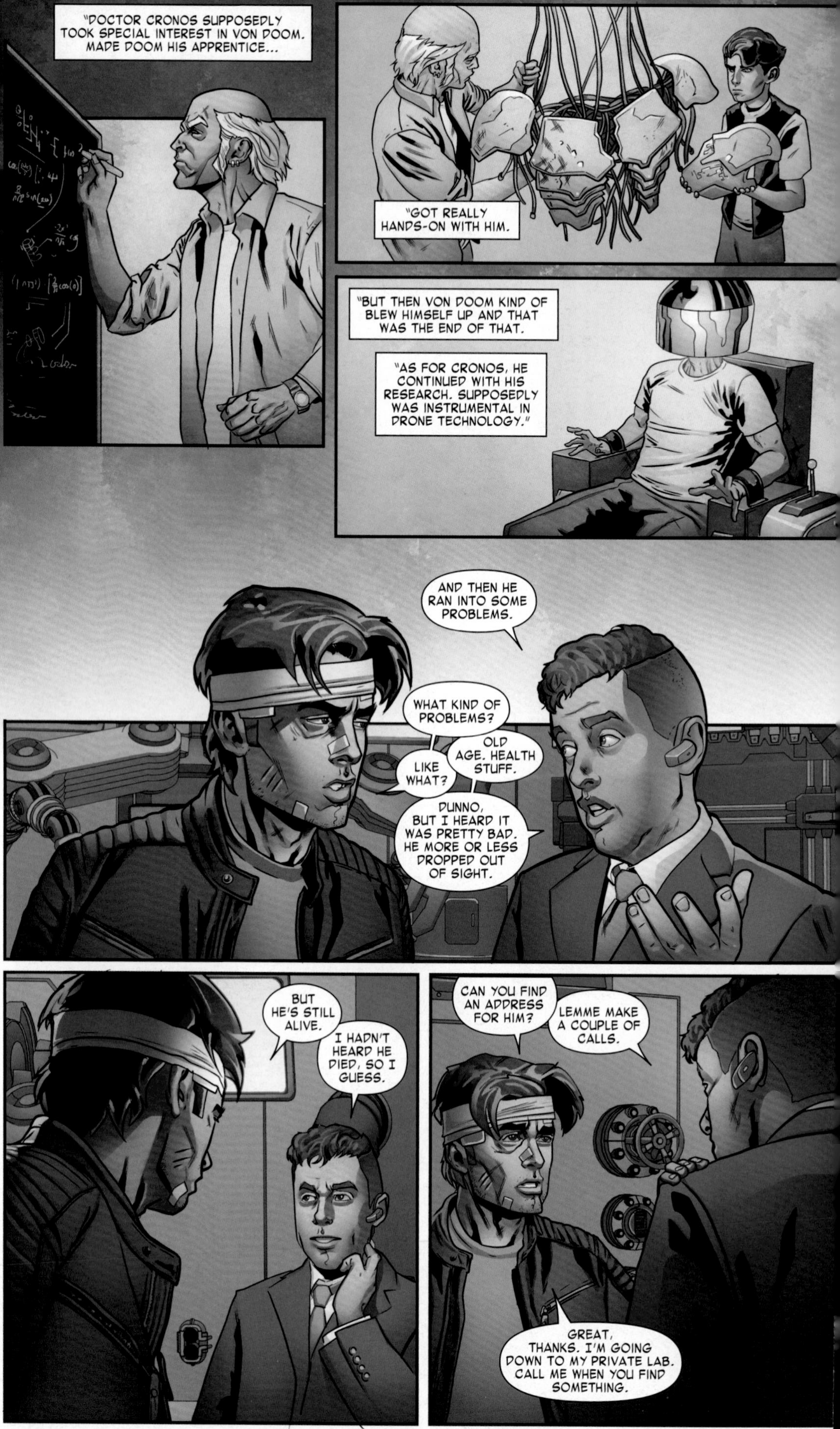
"DOCTOR CRONOS SUPPOSEDLY TOOK SPECIAL INTEREST IN VON DOOM. MADE DOOM HIS APPRENTICE...
"GOT REALLY HANDS-ON WITH HIM.
"BUT THEN VON DOOM KIND OF BLEW HIMSELF UP AND THAT WAS THE END OF THAT.
"AS FOR CRONOS, HE CONTINUED WITH HIS RESEARCH. SUPPOSEDLY WAS INSTRUMENTAL IN DRONE TECHNOLOGY."
AND THEN HE RAN INTO SOME PROBLEMS.
WHAT KIND OF PROBLEMS?
OLD AGE. HEALTH STUFF.
LIKE WHAT?
DUNNO, BUT I HEARD IT WAS PRETTY BAD. HE MORE OR LESS DROPPED OUT OF SIGHT.
BUT HE'S STILL ALIVE.
I HADN'T HEARD HE DIED, SO I GUESS.
CAN YOU FIND AN ADDRESS FOR HIM?
LEMME MAKE A COUPLE OF CALLS.
GREAT, THANKS. I'M GOING DOWN TO MY PRIVATE LAB. CALL ME WHEN YOU FIND SOMETHING.

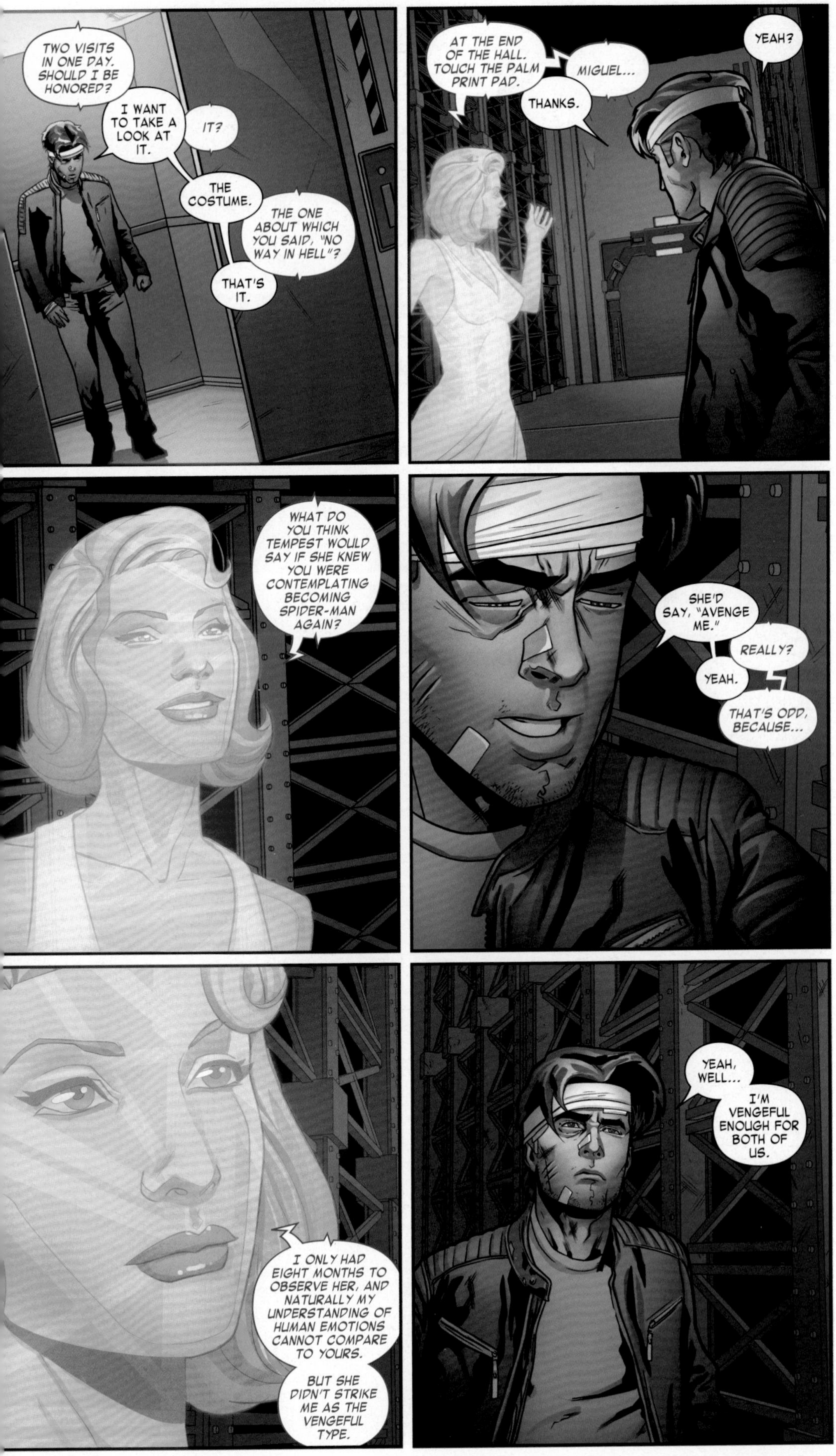
TWO VISITS IN ONE DAY. SHOULD I BE HONORED?
I WANT TO TAKE A LOOK AT IT.
IT?
THE COSTUME.
THE ONE ABOUT WHICH YOU SAID, "NO WAY IN HELL"?
THAT'S IT.
AT THE END OF THE HALL. TOUCH THE PALM PRINT PAD.
THANKS.
MIGUEL...
YEAH?
WHAT DO YOU THINK TEMPEST WOULD SAY IF SHE KNEW YOU WERE CONTEMPLATING BECOMING SPIDER-MAN AGAIN?
SHE'D SAY, "AVENGE ME."
REALLY?
YEAH.
THAT'S ODD, BECAUSE...
I ONLY HAD EIGHT MONTHS TO OBSERVE HER, AND NATURALLY MY UNDERSTANDING OF HUMAN EMOTIONS CANNOT COMPARE TO YOURS.
BUT SHE DIDN'T STRIKE ME AS THE VENGEFUL TYPE.
YEAH, WELL...
I'M VENGEFUL ENOUGH FOR BOTH OF US.

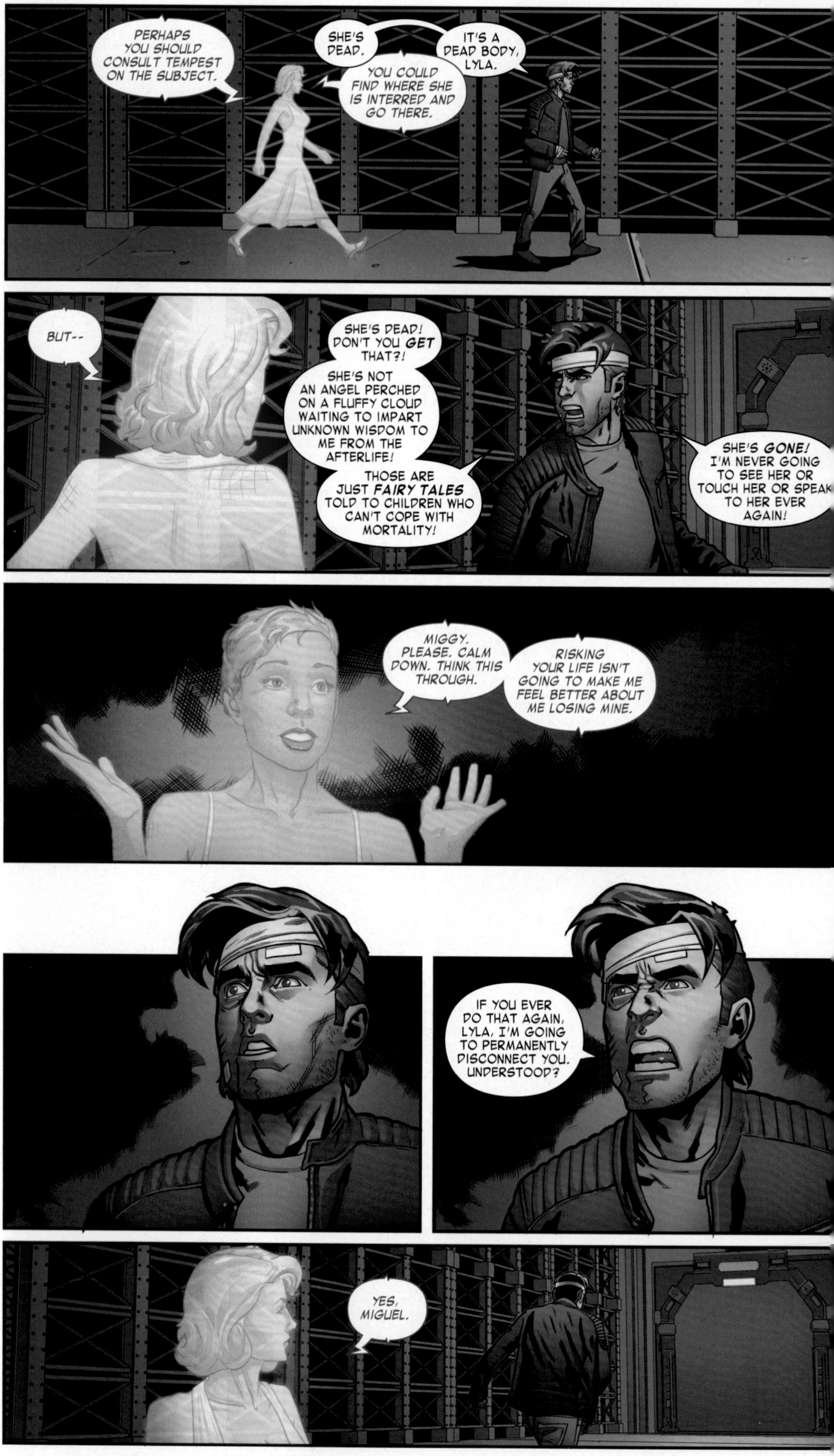

PERHAPS YOU SHOULD CONSULT TEMPEST ON THE SUBJECT.
SHE'S DEAD.
IT'S A DEAD BODY, LYLA.
YOU COULD FIND WHERE SHE IS INTERRED AND GO THERE.
BUT--
SHE'S DEAD! DON'T YOU GET THAT?!
SHE'S NOT AN ANGEL PERCHED ON A FLUFFY CLOUD WAITING TO IMPART UNKNOWN WISDOM TO ME FROM THE AFTERLIFE!
THOSE ARE JUST FAIRY TALES TOLD TO CHILDREN WHO CAN'T COPE WITH MORTALITY!
SHE'S GONE! I'M NEVER GOING TO SEE HER OR TOUCH HER OR SPEAK TO HER EVER AGAIN!
MIGGY. PLEASE. CALM DOWN. THINK THIS THROUGH.
RISKING YOUR LIFE ISN'T GOING TO MAKE ME FEEL BETTER ABOUT ME LOSING MINE.
IF YOU EVER DO THAT AGAIN, LYLA, I'M GOING TO PERMANENTLY DISCONNECT YOU. UNDERSTOOD?
YES, MIGUEL.

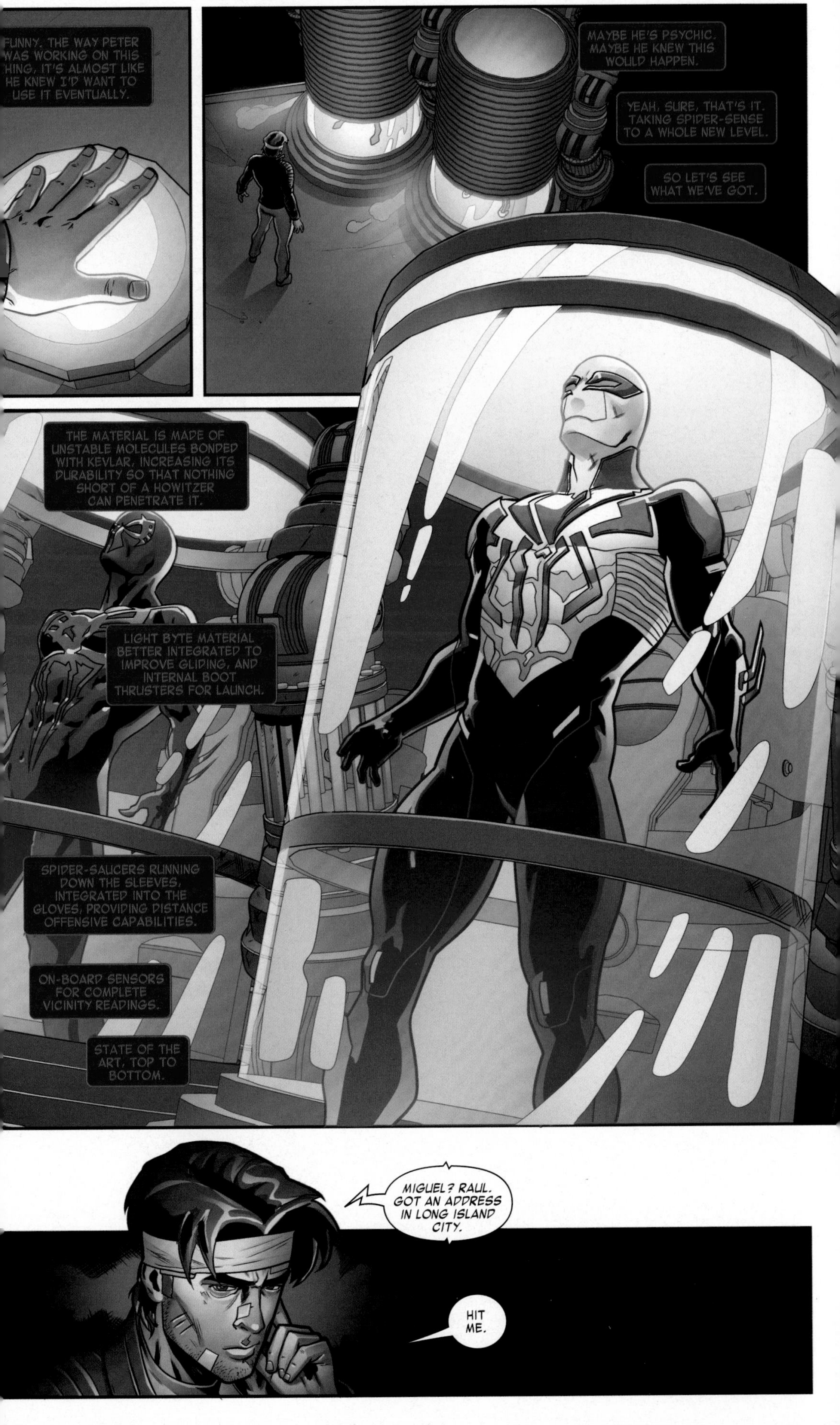
FUNNY. THE WAY PETER WAS WORKING ON THIS THING, IT'S ALMOST LIKE HE KNEW I'D WANT TO USE IT EVENTUALLY.
MAYBE HE'S PSYCHIC. MAYBE HE KNEW THIS WOULD HAPPEN.
YEAH, SURE, THAT'S IT. TAKING SPIDER-SENSE TO A WHOLE NEW LEVEL.
SO LET'S SEE WHAT WE'VE GOT.
THE MATERIAL IS MADE OF UNSTABLE MOLECULES BONDED WITH KEVLAR, INCREASING ITS DURABILITY SO THAT NOTHING SHORT OF A HOWITZER CAN PENETRATE IT.
LIGHT BYTE MATERIAL BETTER INTEGRATED TO IMPROVE GLIDING, AND INTERNAL BOOT THRUSTERS FOR LAUNCH.
SPIDER-SAUCERS RUNNING DOWN THE SLEEVES, INTEGRATED INTO THE GLOVES, PROVIDING DISTANCE OFFENSIVE CAPABILITIES.
ON-BOARD SENSORS FOR COMPLETE VICINITY READINGS.
STATE OF THE ART, TOP TO BOTTOM.
MIGUEL? RAUL. GOT AN ADDRESS IN LONG ISLAND CITY.
HIT ME.

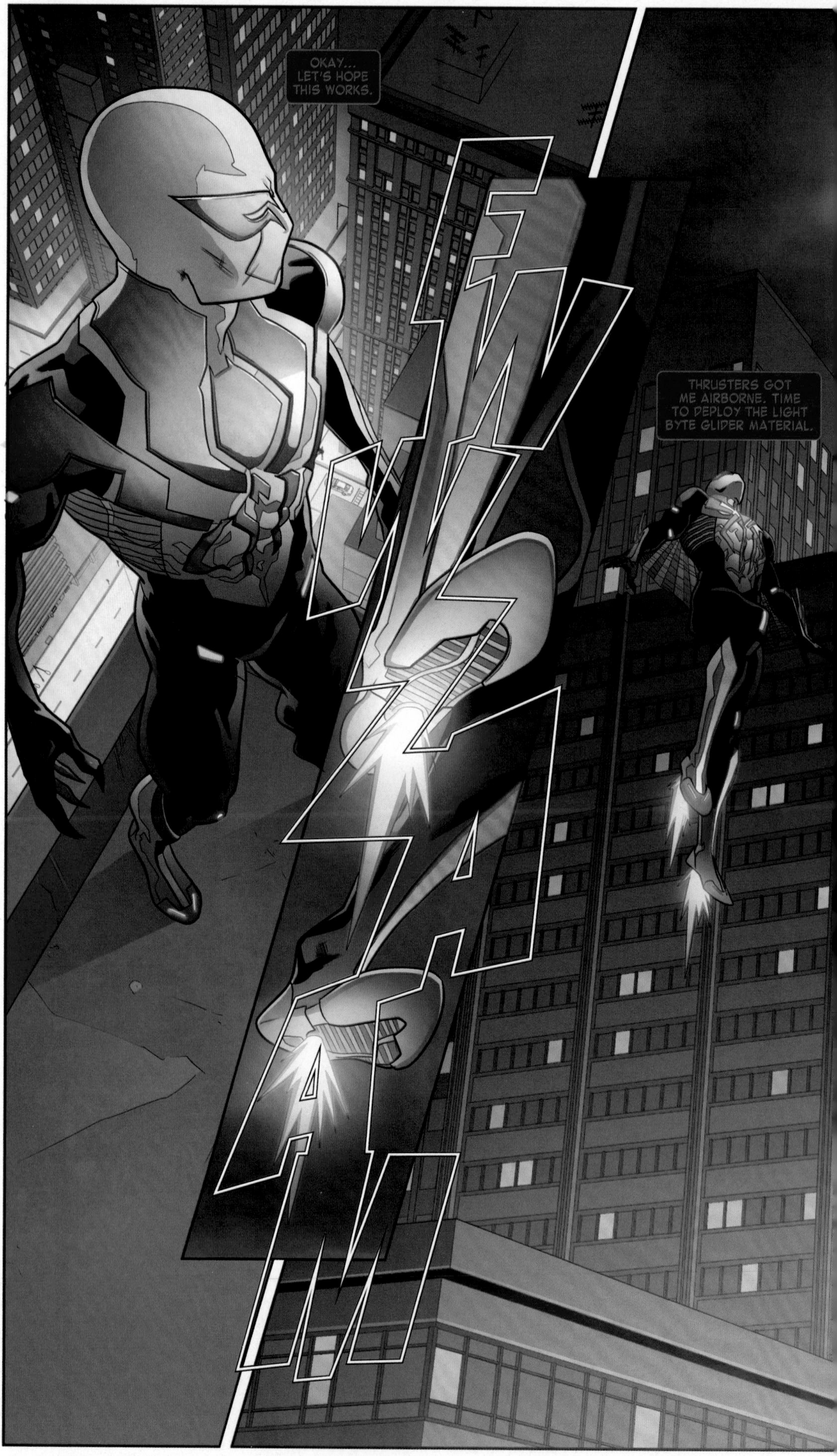
OKAY... LET'S HOPE THIS WORKS.
FWOOSHHH
THRUSTERS GOT ME AIRBORNE. TIME TO DEPLOY THE LIGHT BYTE GLIDER MATERIAL.

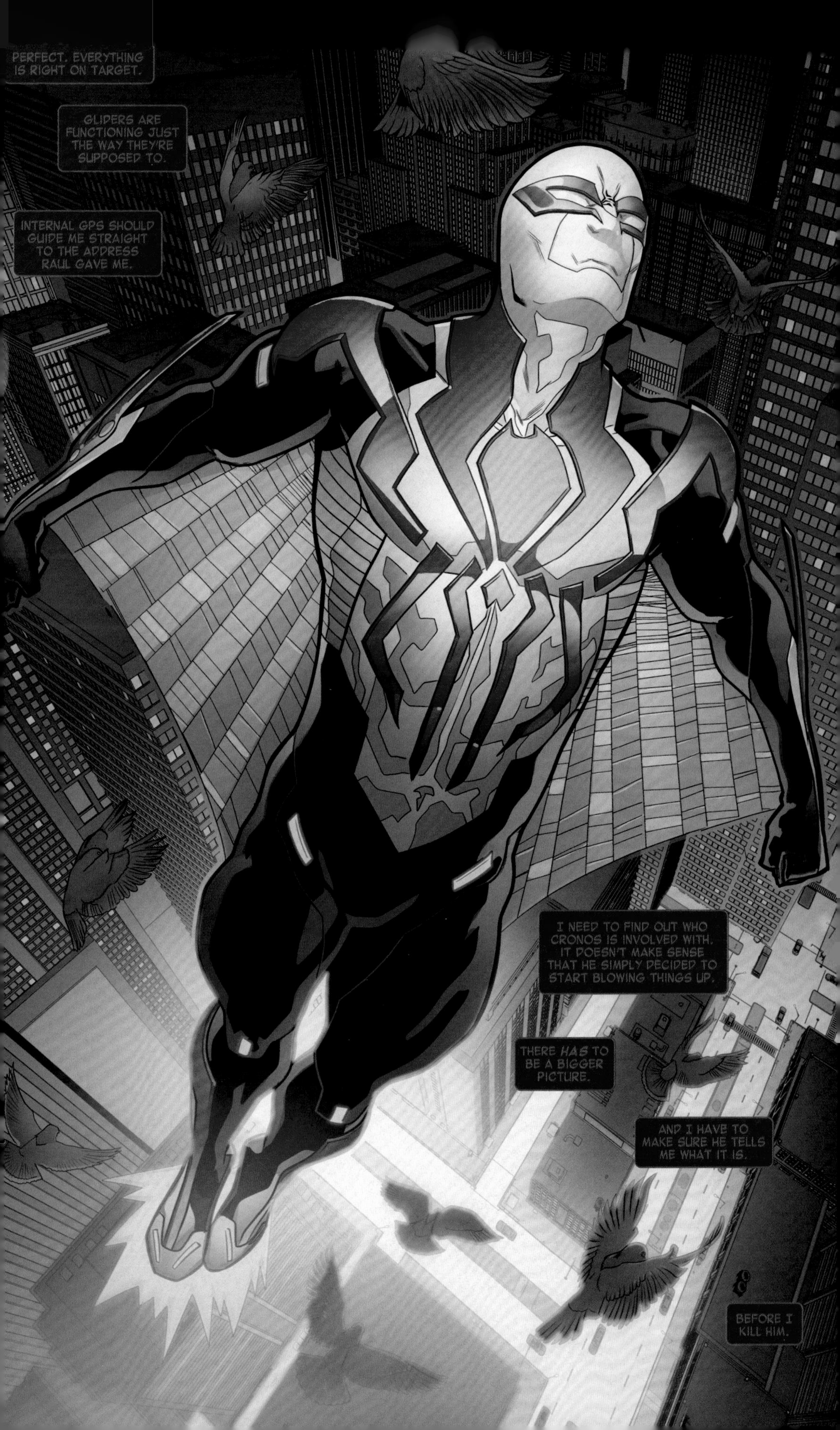
PERFECT. EVERYTHING IS RIGHT ON TARGET.
GLIDERS ARE FUNCTIONING JUST THE WAY THEY'RE SUPPOSED TO.
INTERNAL GPS SHOULD GUIDE ME STRAIGHT TO THE ADDRESS RAUL GAVE ME.
I NEED TO FIND OUT WHO CRONOS IS INVOLVED WITH. IT DOESN'T MAKE SENSE THAT HE SIMPLY DECIDED TO START BLOWING THINGS UP.
THERE *HAS* TO BE A BIGGER PICTURE.
AND I HAVE TO MAKE SURE HE TELLS ME WHAT IT IS.
BEFORE I KILL HIM.

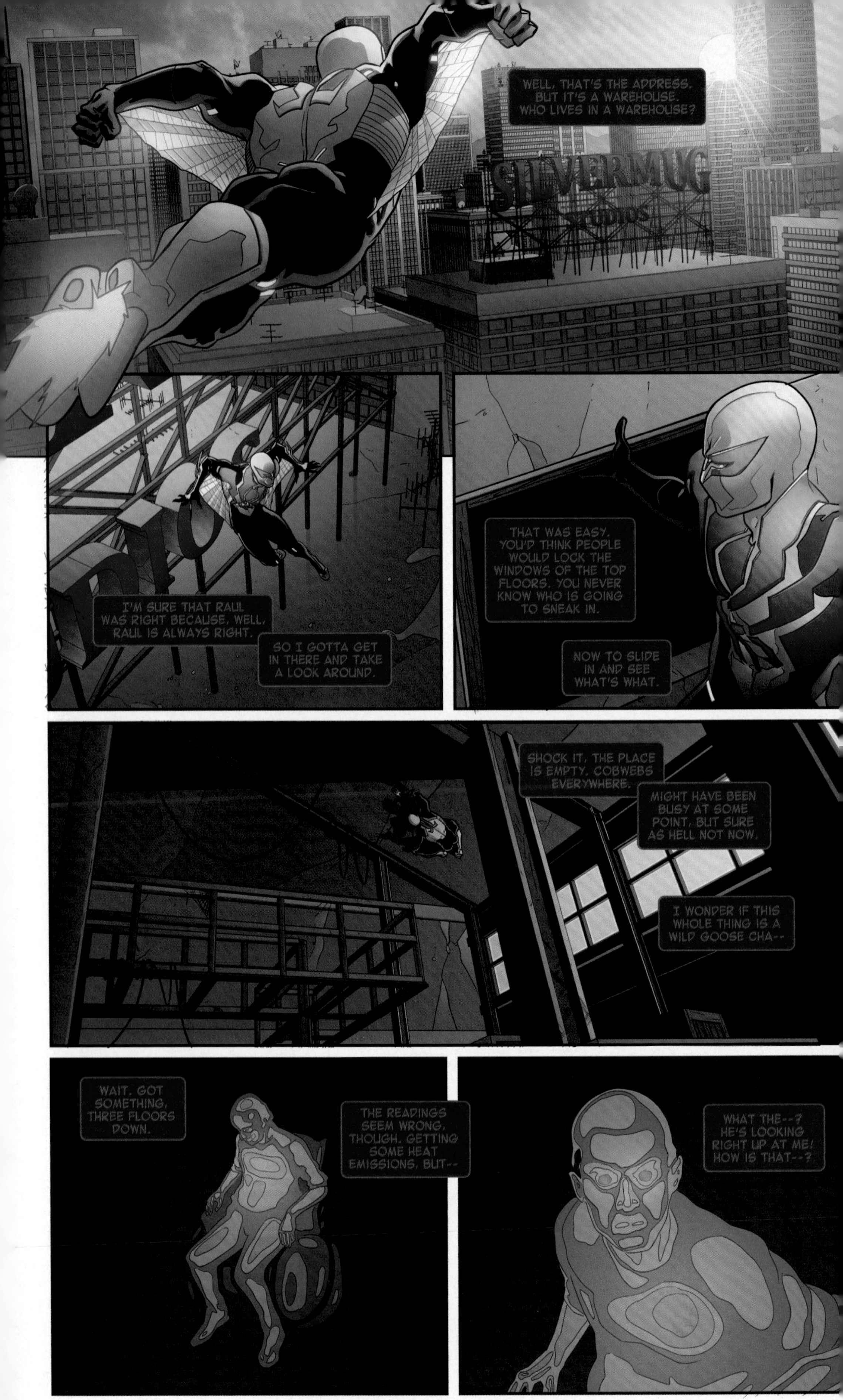
WELL, THAT'S THE ADDRESS. BUT IT'S A WAREHOUSE. WHO LIVES IN A WAREHOUSE?
SILVERMUG STUDIOS
I'M SURE THAT RAUL WAS RIGHT BECAUSE, WELL, RAUL IS ALWAYS RIGHT.
SO I GOTTA GET IN THERE AND TAKE A LOOK AROUND.
THAT WAS EASY. YOU'D THINK PEOPLE WOULD LOCK THE WINDOWS OF THE TOP FLOORS. YOU NEVER KNOW WHO IS GOING TO SNEAK IN.
NOW TO SLIDE IN AND SEE WHAT'S WHAT.
SHOCK IT, THE PLACE IS EMPTY. COBWEBS EVERYWHERE.
MIGHT HAVE BEEN BUSY AT SOME POINT, BUT SURE AS HELL NOT NOW.
I WONDER IF THIS WHOLE THING IS A WILD GOOSE CHA--
WAIT. GOT SOMETHING, THREE FLOORS DOWN.
THE READINGS SEEM WRONG, THOUGH. GETTING SOME HEAT EMISSIONS, BUT--
WHAT THE--? HE'S LOOKING RIGHT UP AT ME! HOW IS THAT--?

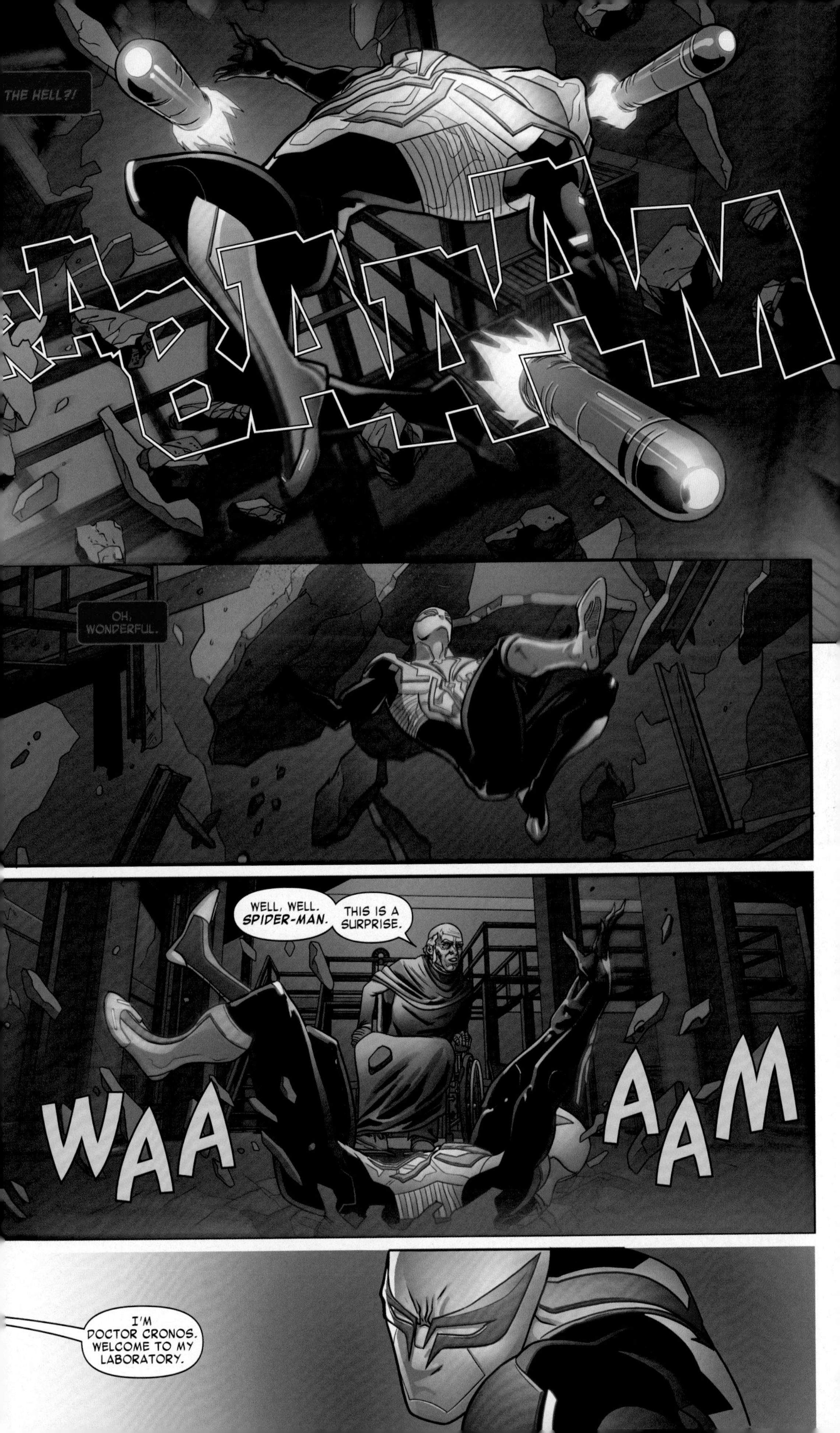
THE HELL?!
OH, WONDERFUL.
WELL, WELL. SPIDER-MAN.
THIS IS A SURPRISE.
WAA AAM
I'M DOCTOR CRONOS. WELCOME TO MY LABORATORY.

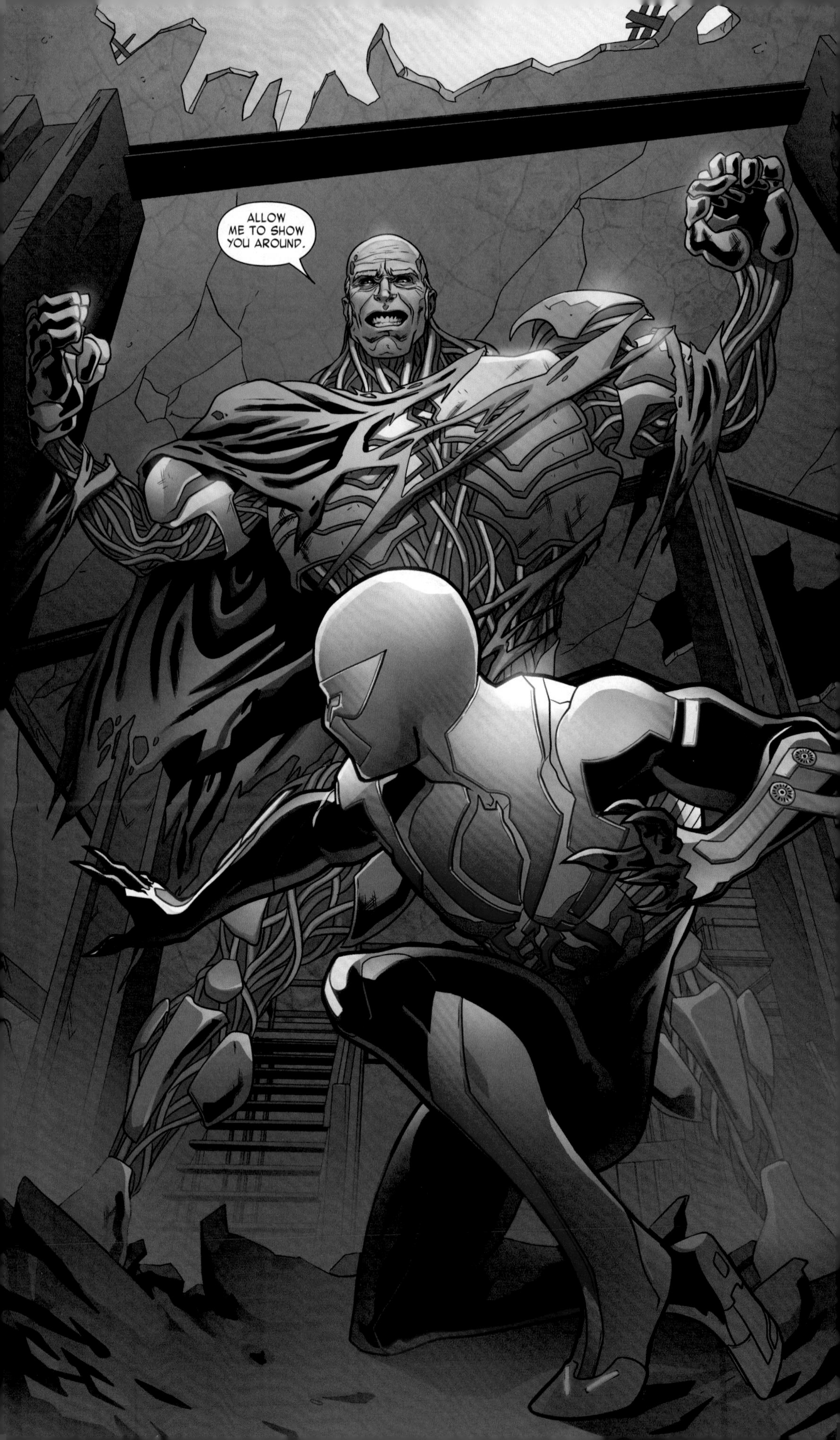
ALLOW ME TO SHOW YOU AROUND.

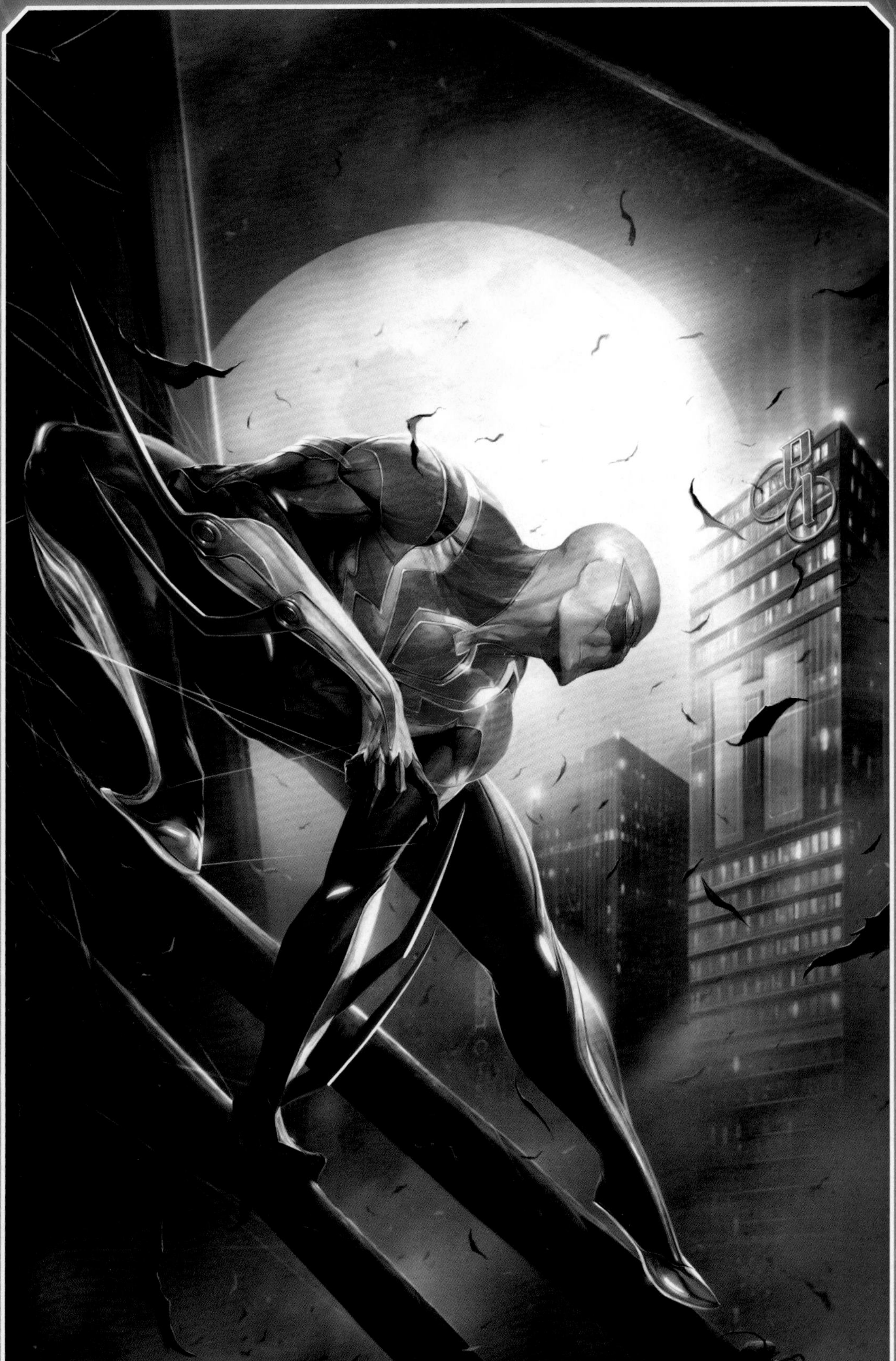

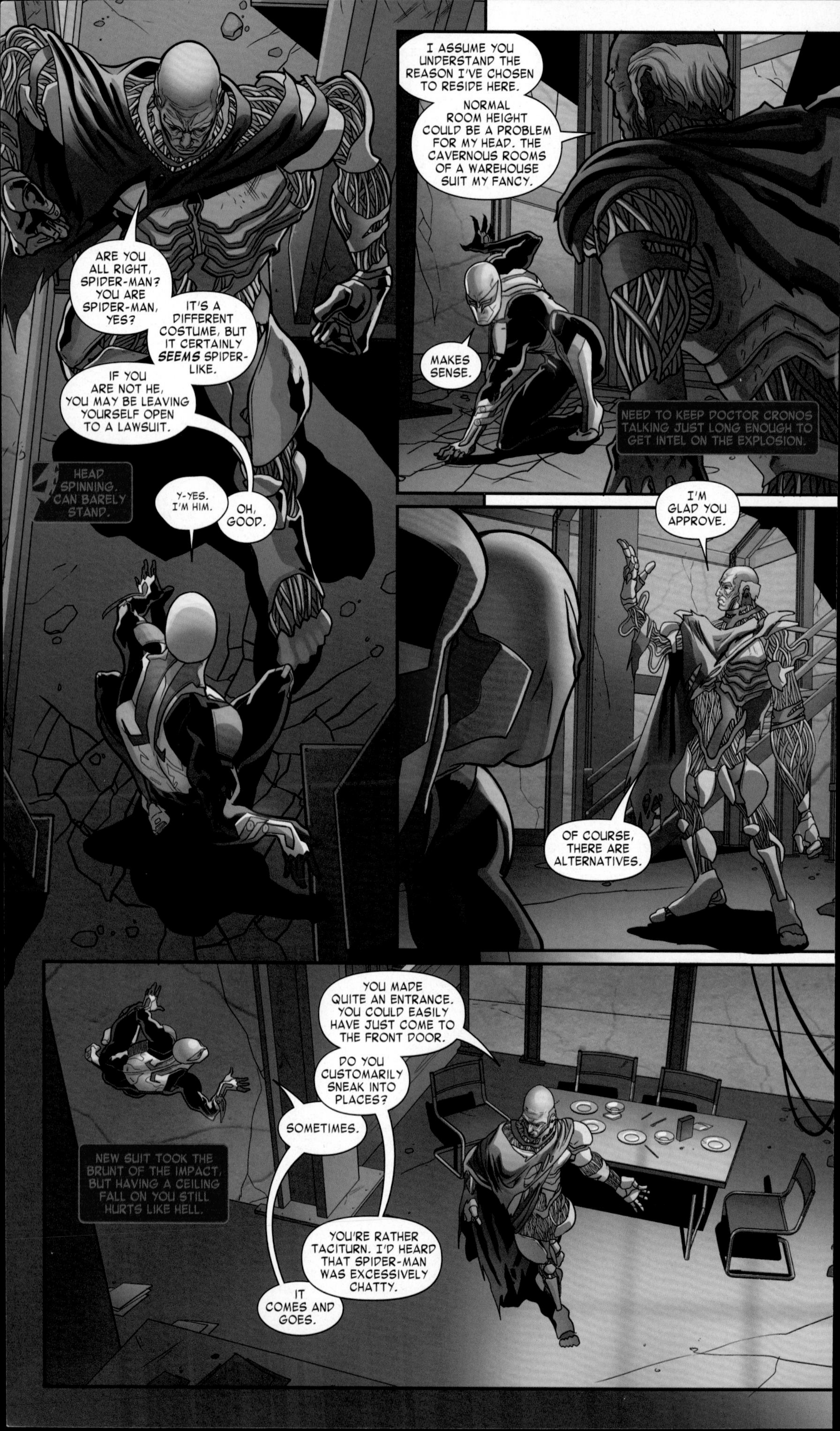
ARE YOU ALL RIGHT, SPIDER-MAN? YOU ARE SPIDER-MAN, YES?
IT'S A DIFFERENT COSTUME, BUT IT CERTAINLY **SEEMS** SPIDER-LIKE.
IF YOU ARE NOT HE, YOU MAY BE LEAVING YOURSELF OPEN TO A LAWSUIT.
HEAD SPINNING. CAN BARELY STAND.
Y-YES. I'M HIM.
OH, GOOD.
I ASSUME YOU UNDERSTAND THE REASON I'VE CHOSEN TO RESIDE HERE.
NORMAL ROOM HEIGHT COULD BE A PROBLEM FOR MY HEAD. THE CAVERNOUS ROOMS OF A WAREHOUSE SUIT MY FANCY.
MAKES SENSE.
NEED TO KEEP DOCTOR CRONOS TALKING JUST LONG ENOUGH TO GET INTEL ON THE EXPLOSION.
I'M GLAD YOU APPROVE.
OF COURSE, THERE ARE ALTERNATIVES.
NEW SUIT TOOK THE BRUNT OF THE IMPACT, BUT HAVING A CEILING FALL ON YOU STILL HURTS LIKE HELL.
YOU MADE QUITE AN ENTRANCE. YOU COULD EASILY HAVE JUST COME TO THE FRONT DOOR.
DO YOU CUSTOMARILY SNEAK INTO PLACES?
SOMETIMES.
YOU'RE RATHER TACITURN. I'D HEARD THAT SPIDER-MAN WAS EXCESSIVELY CHATTY.
IT COMES AND GOES.

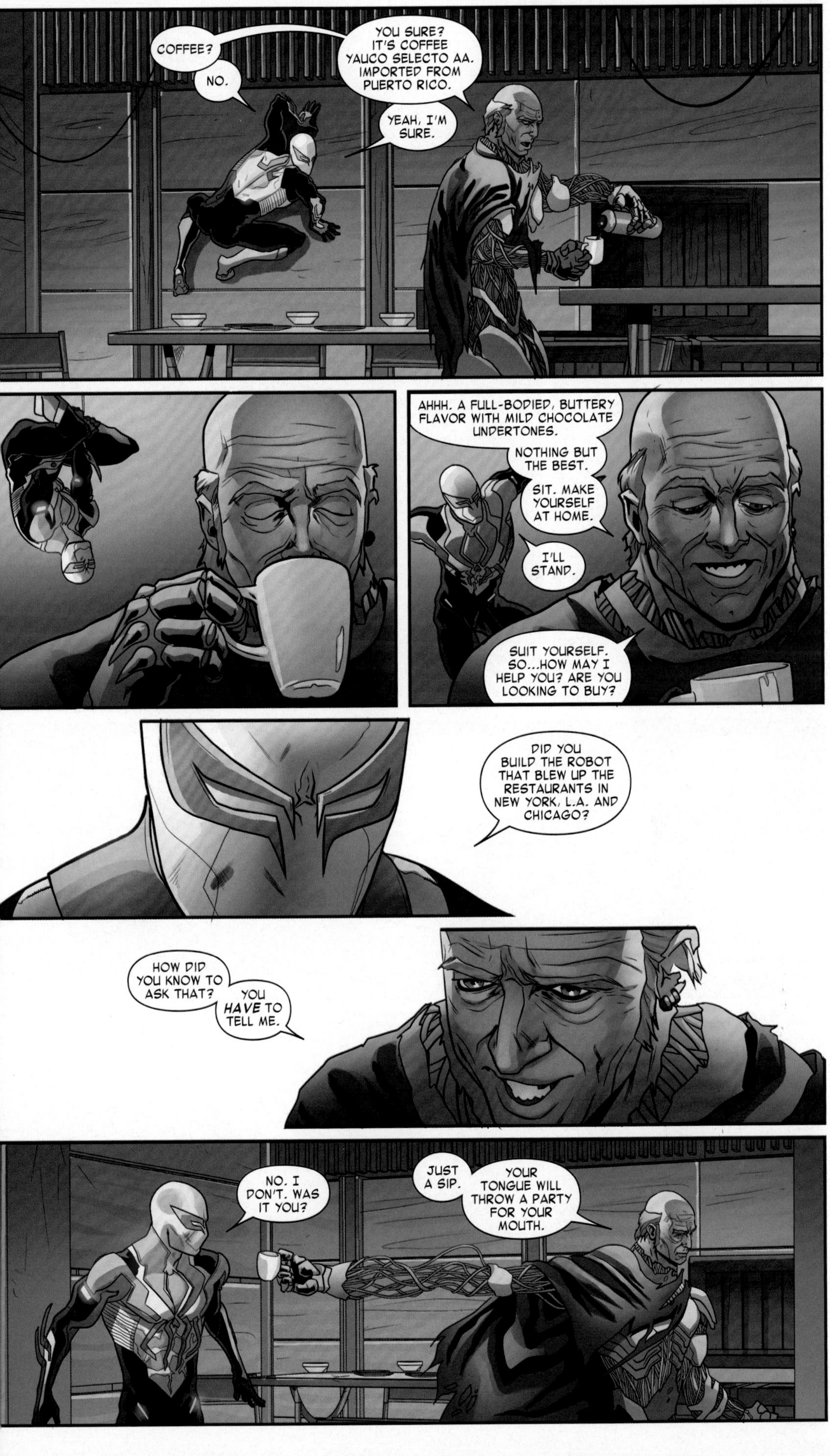
COFFEE?
NO.
YOU SURE? IT'S COFFEE YAUCO SELECTO AA. IMPORTED FROM PUERTO RICO.
YEAH, I'M SURE.
AHHH. A FULL-BODIED, BUTTERY FLAVOR WITH MILD CHOCOLATE UNDERTONES.
NOTHING BUT THE BEST.
SIT. MAKE YOURSELF AT HOME.
I'LL STAND.
SUIT YOURSELF. SO...HOW MAY I HELP YOU? ARE YOU LOOKING TO BUY?
DID YOU BUILD THE ROBOT THAT BLEW UP THE RESTAURANTS IN NEW YORK, L.A. AND CHICAGO?
HOW DID YOU KNOW TO ASK THAT?
YOU HAVE TO TELL ME.
NO. I DON'T. WAS IT YOU?
JUST A SIP.
YOUR TONGUE WILL THROW A PARTY FOR YOUR MOUTH.

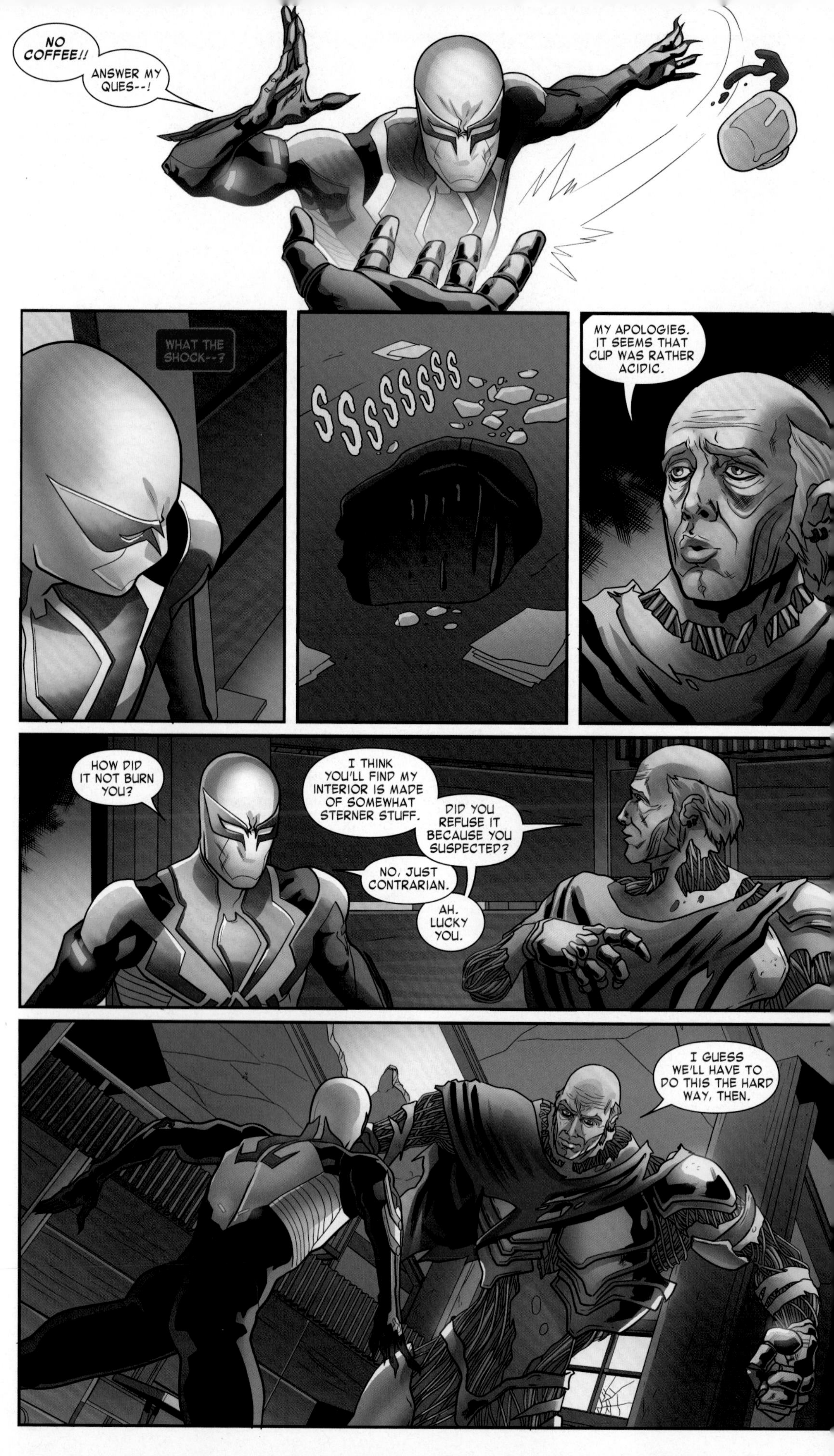
NO COFFEE!!
ANSWER MY QUES--!
WHAT THE SHOCK--?
SSSSSSSS
MY APOLOGIES. IT SEEMS THAT CUP WAS RATHER ACIDIC.
HOW DID IT NOT BURN YOU?
I THINK YOU'LL FIND MY INTERIOR IS MADE OF SOMEWHAT STERNER STUFF.
DID YOU REFUSE IT BECAUSE YOU SUSPECTED?
NO, JUST CONTRARIAN.
AH. LUCKY YOU.
I GUESS WE'LL HAVE TO DO THIS THE HARD WAY, THEN.

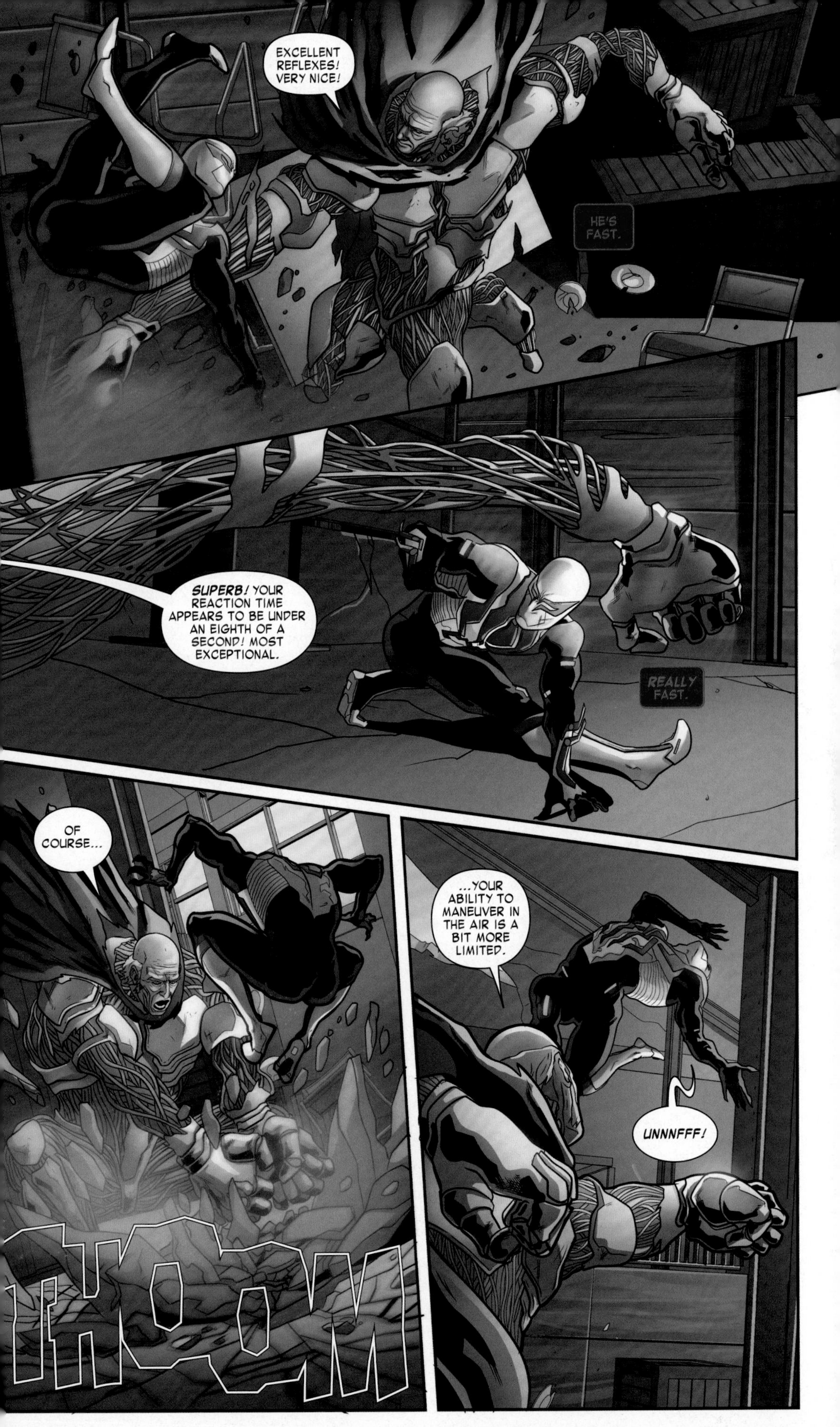

EXCELLENT REFLEXES! VERY NICE!
HE'S FAST.
SUPERB! YOUR REACTION TIME APPEARS TO BE UNDER AN EIGHTH OF A SECOND! MOST EXCEPTIONAL.
REALLY FAST.
OF COURSE...
THOOM
...YOUR ABILITY TO MANEUVER IN THE AIR IS A BIT MORE LIMITED.
UNNNFFF!

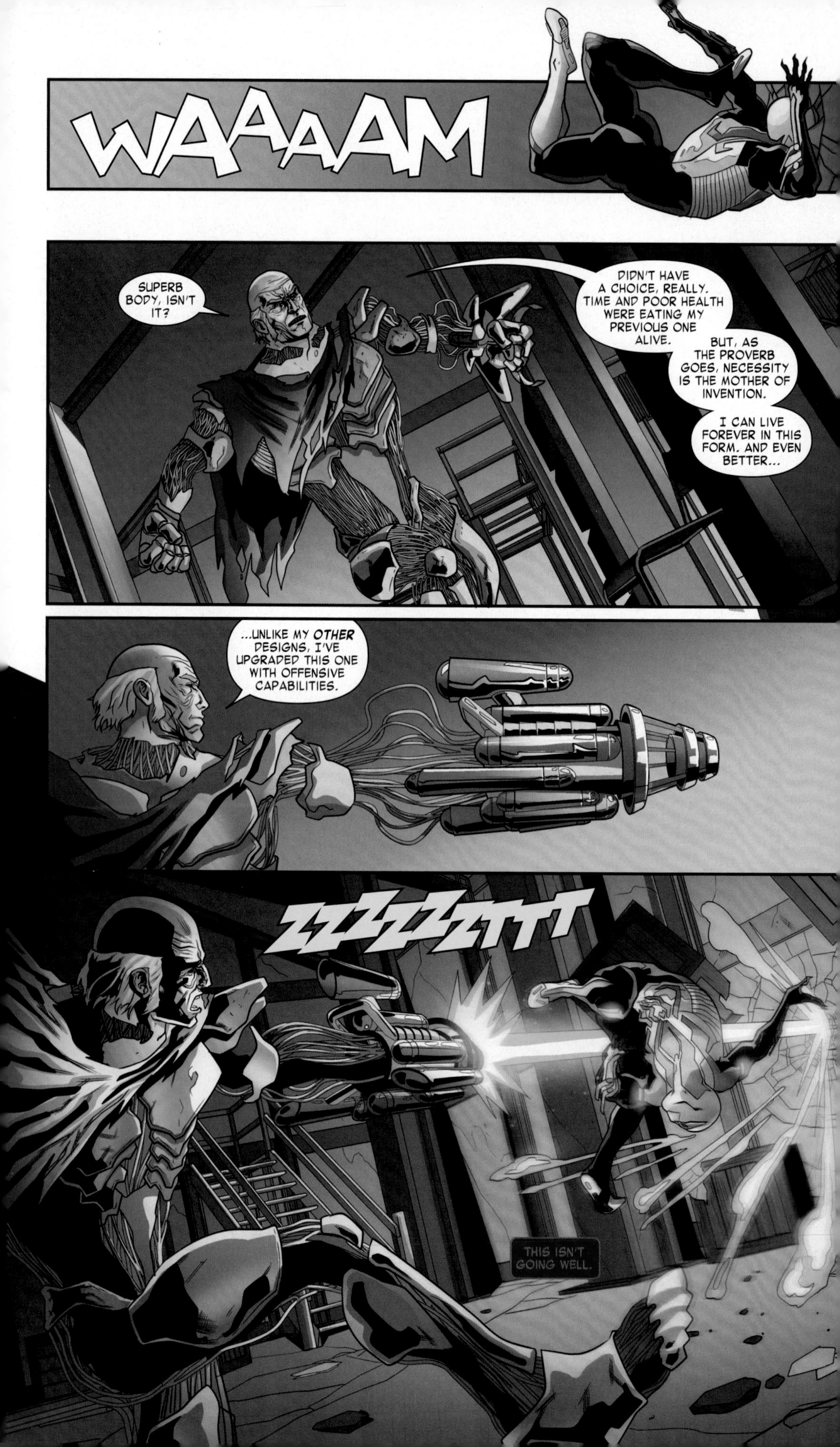

WAAAAM
SUPERB BODY, ISN'T IT?
DIDN'T HAVE A CHOICE, REALLY. TIME AND POOR HEALTH WERE EATING MY PREVIOUS ONE ALIVE.
BUT, AS THE PROVERB GOES, NECESSITY IS THE MOTHER OF INVENTION.
I CAN LIVE FOREVER IN THIS FORM. AND EVEN BETTER...
...UNLIKE MY OTHER DESIGNS, I'VE UPGRADED THIS ONE WITH OFFENSIVE CAPABILITIES.
ZZZZZZTTT
THIS ISN'T GOING WELL.

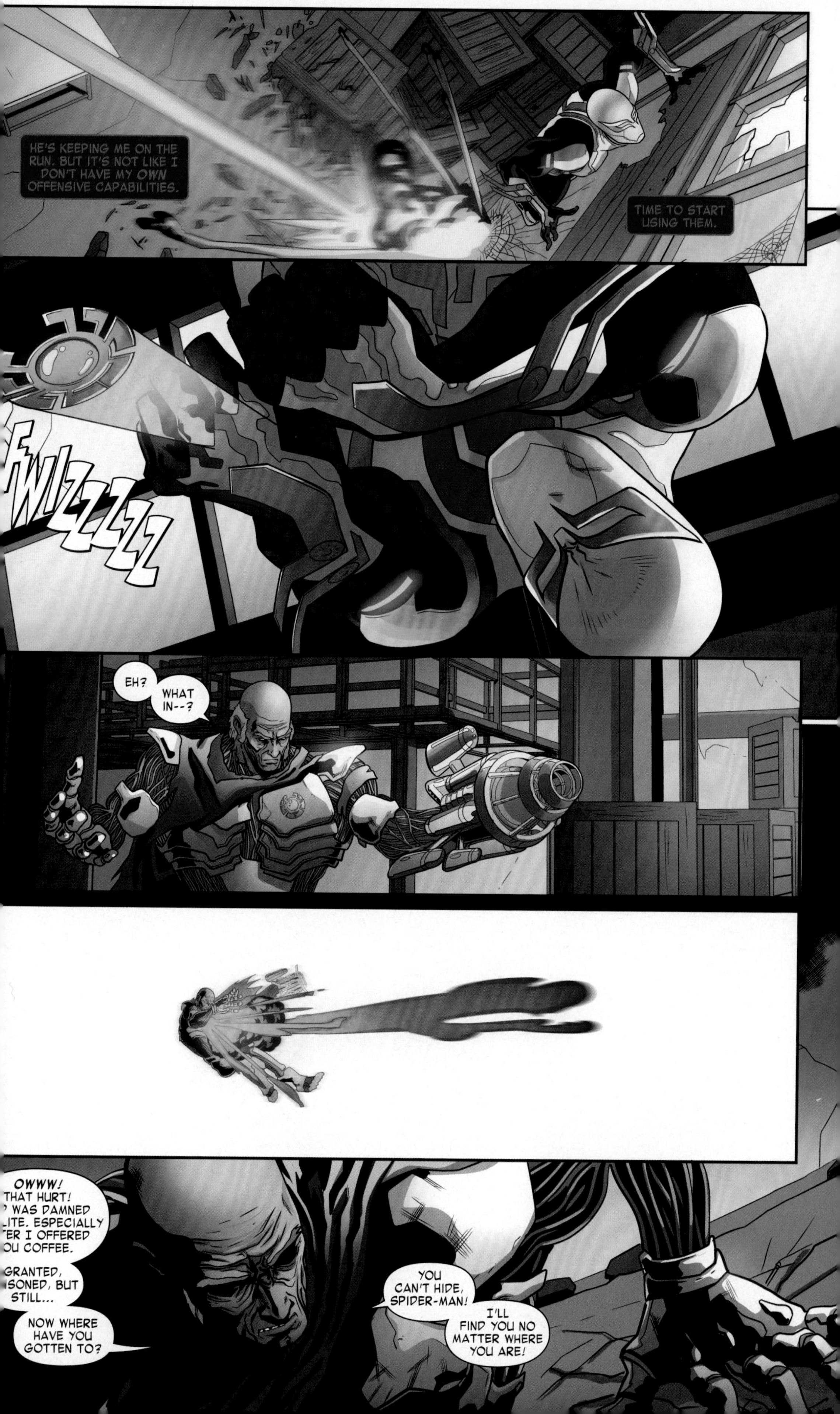
HE'S KEEPING ME ON THE RUN. BUT IT'S NOT LIKE I DON'T HAVE MY *OWN* OFFENSIVE CAPABILITIES.
TIME TO START USING THEM.
FWIZZZZZZ
EH?
WHAT IN--?
OWWW!
THAT HURT!
' WAS DAMNED
LITE. ESPECIALLY
TER I OFFERED
OU COFFEE.
GRANTED,
SONED, BUT
STILL...
NOW WHERE HAVE YOU GOTTEN TO?
YOU CAN'T HIDE, SPIDER-MAN!
I'LL FIND YOU NO MATTER WHERE YOU ARE!

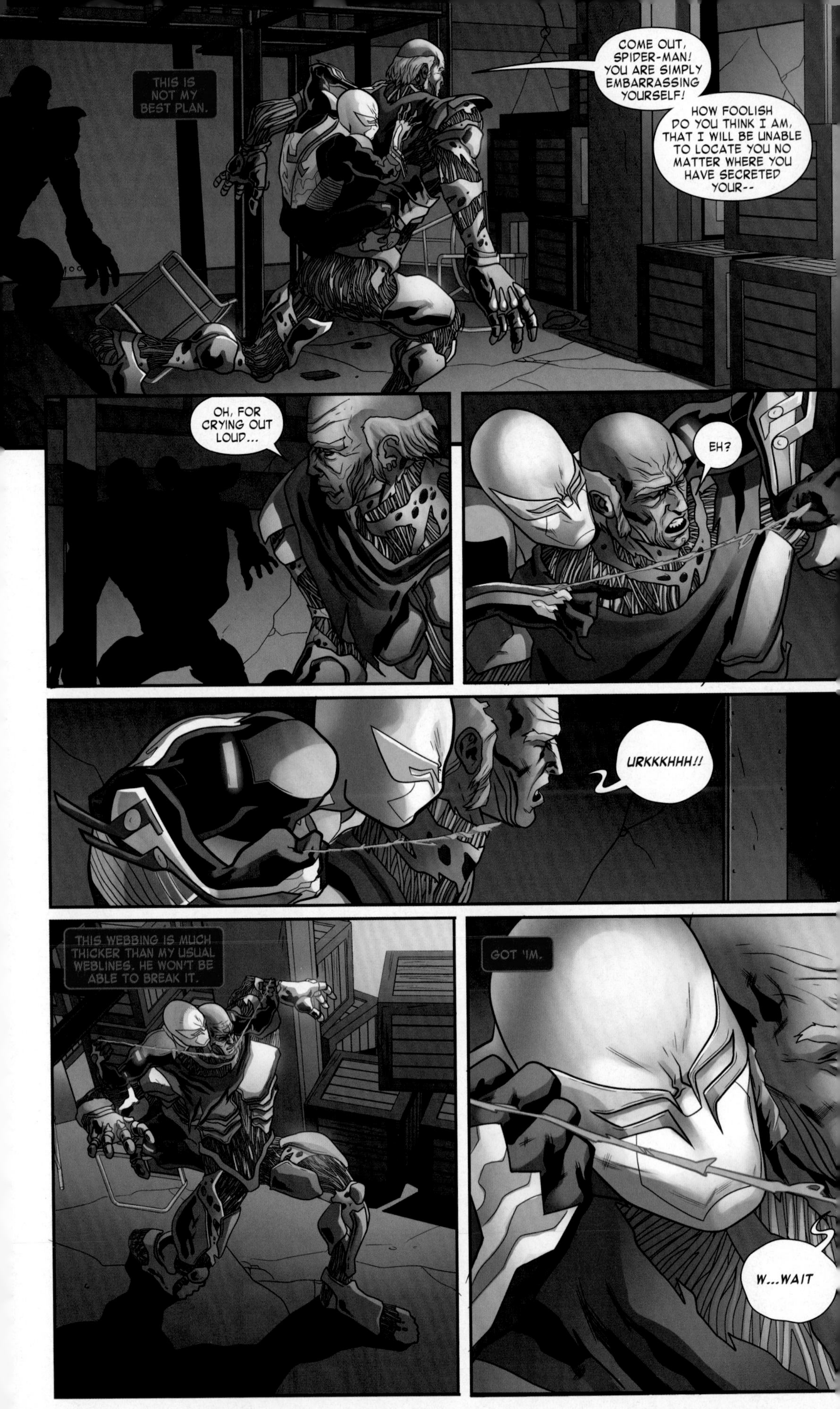
THIS IS NOT MY BEST PLAN.
COME OUT, SPIDER-MAN! YOU ARE SIMPLY EMBARRASSING YOURSELF!
HOW FOOLISH DO YOU THINK I AM, THAT I WILL BE UNABLE TO LOCATE YOU NO MATTER WHERE YOU HAVE SECRETED YOUR--
OH, FOR CRYING OUT LOUD...
EH?
URKKKHHH!!
THIS WEBBING IS MUCH THICKER THAN MY USUAL WEBLINES. HE WON'T BE ABLE TO BREAK IT.
GOT 'IM.
W...WAIT

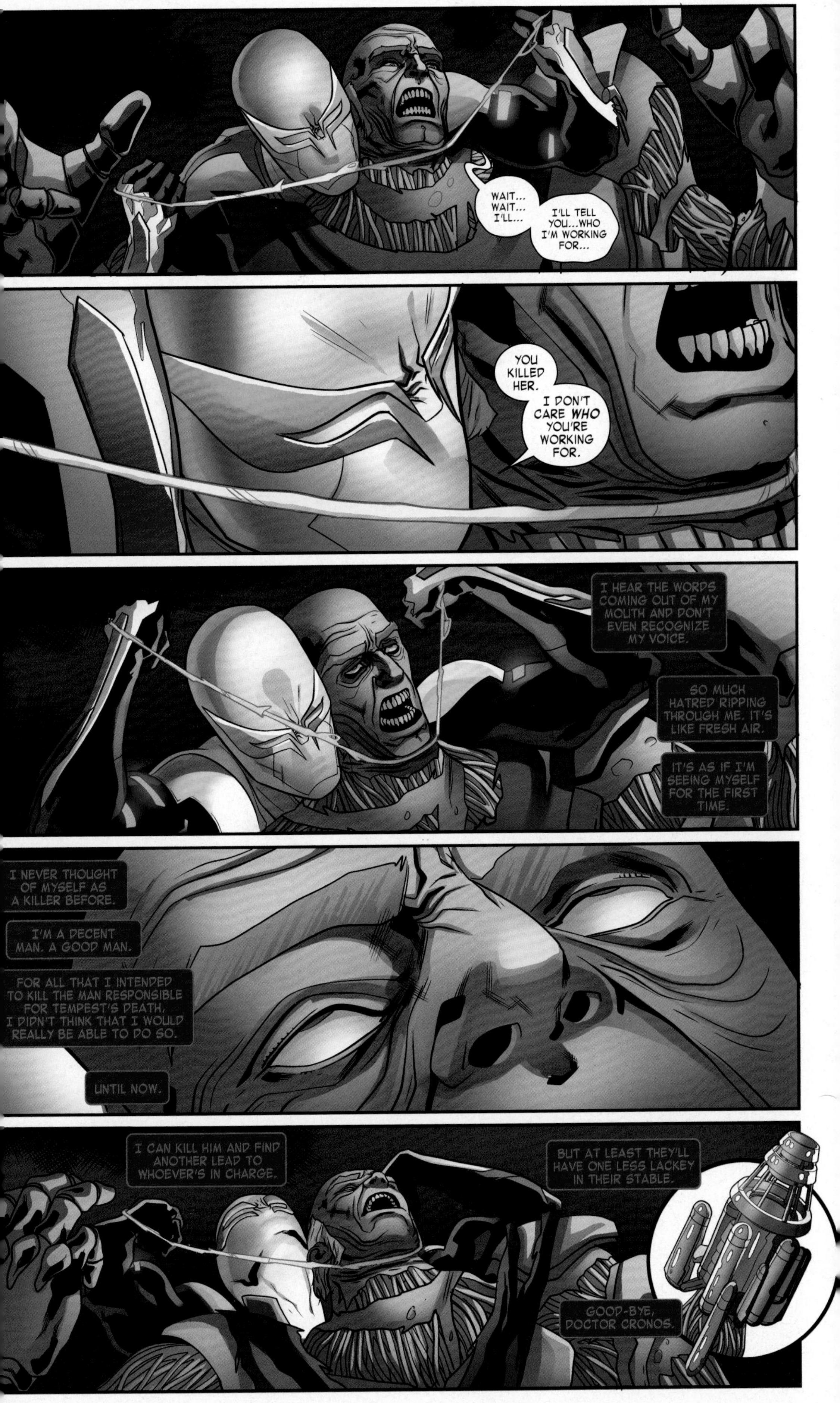
WAIT... WAIT... I'LL...
I'LL TELL YOU...WHO I'M WORKING FOR...
YOU KILLED HER.
I DON'T CARE **WHO** YOU'RE WORKING FOR.
I HEAR THE WORDS COMING OUT OF MY MOUTH AND DON'T EVEN RECOGNIZE MY VOICE.
SO MUCH HATRED RIPPING THROUGH ME. IT'S LIKE FRESH AIR.
IT'S AS IF I'M SEEING MYSELF FOR THE FIRST TIME.
I NEVER THOUGHT OF MYSELF AS A KILLER BEFORE.
I'M A DECENT MAN. A GOOD MAN.
FOR ALL THAT I INTENDED TO KILL THE MAN RESPONSIBLE FOR TEMPEST'S DEATH, I DIDN'T THINK THAT I WOULD REALLY BE ABLE TO DO SO.
UNTIL NOW.
I CAN KILL HIM AND FIND ANOTHER LEAD TO WHOEVER'S IN CHARGE.
BUT AT LEAST THEY'LL HAVE ONE LESS LACKEY IN THEIR STABLE.
GOOD-BYE, DOCTOR CRONOS.

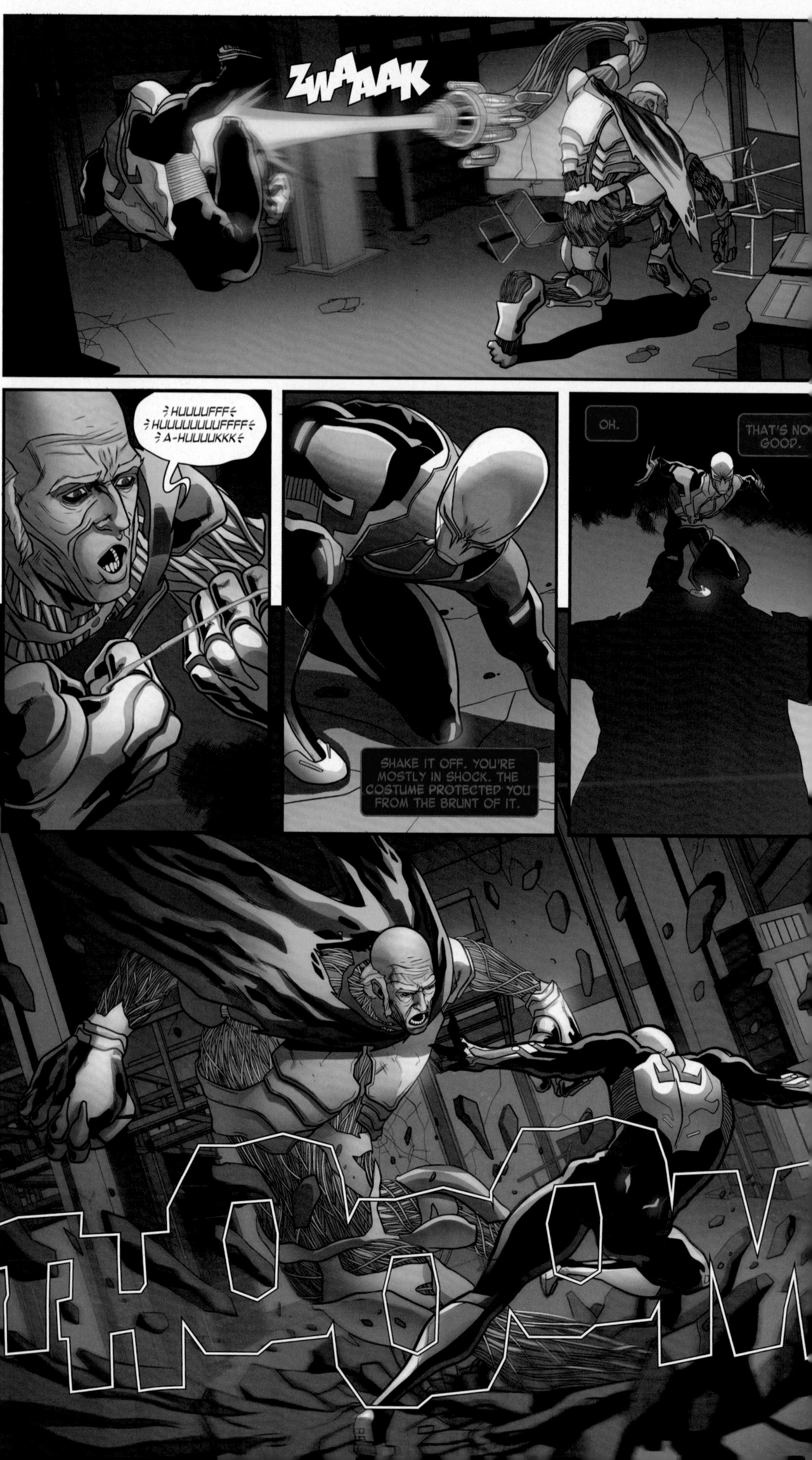
ZWAAAK
HUUUUFFF
HUUUUUUUUFFFF
A-HUUUUKKK
SHAKE IT OFF. YOU'RE MOSTLY IN SHOCK. THE COSTUME PROTECTED YOU FROM THE BRUNT OF IT.
OH.
THAT'S NO GOOD.
THOOOOM

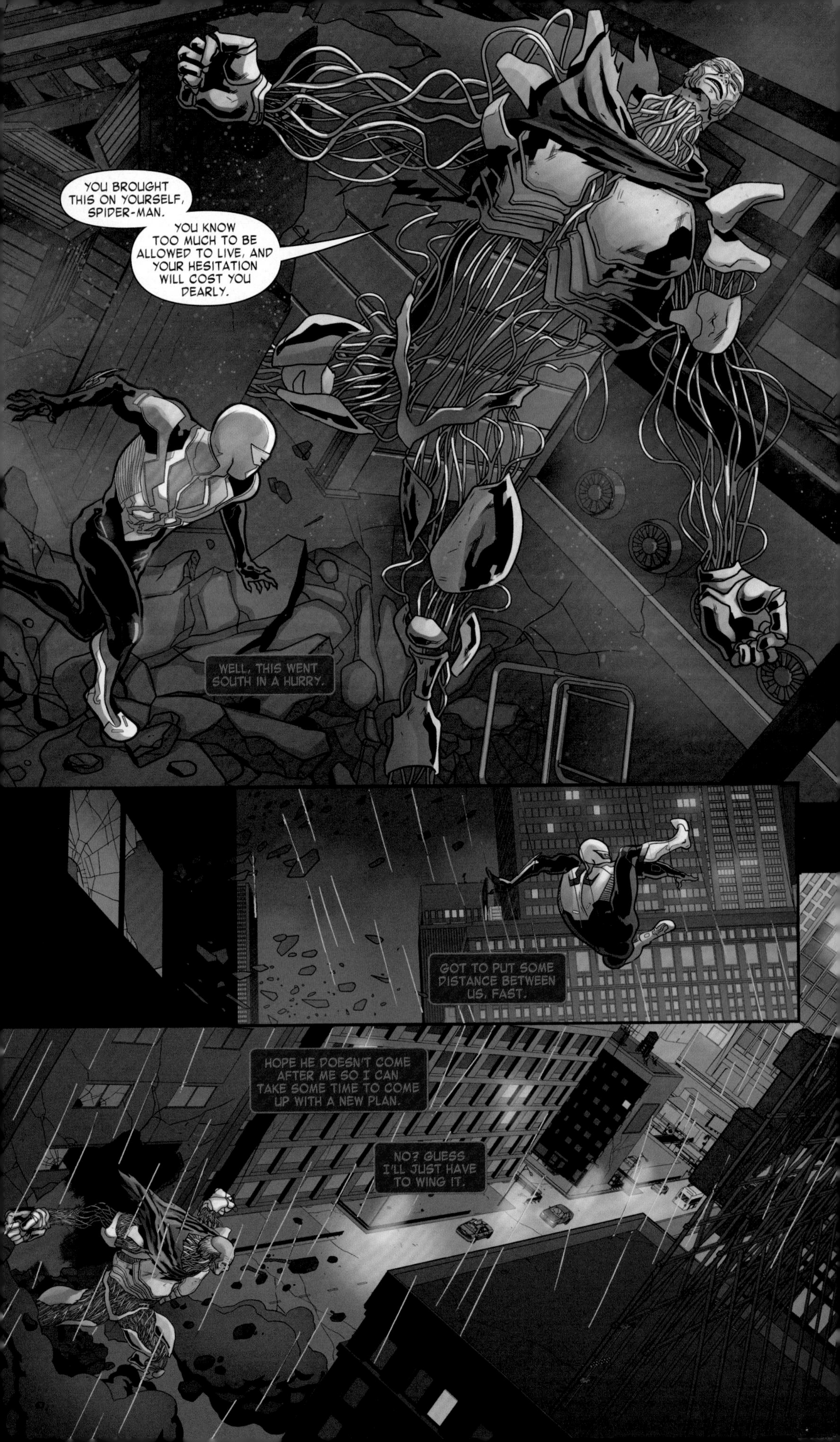
YOU BROUGHT THIS ON YOURSELF, SPIDER-MAN.
YOU KNOW TOO MUCH TO BE ALLOWED TO LIVE, AND YOUR HESITATION WILL COST YOU DEARLY.
WELL, THIS WENT SOUTH IN A HURRY.
GOT TO PUT SOME DISTANCE BETWEEN US, FAST.
HOPE HE DOESN'T COME AFTER ME SO I CAN TAKE SOME TIME TO COME UP WITH A NEW PLAN.
NO? GUESS I'LL JUST HAVE TO WING IT.

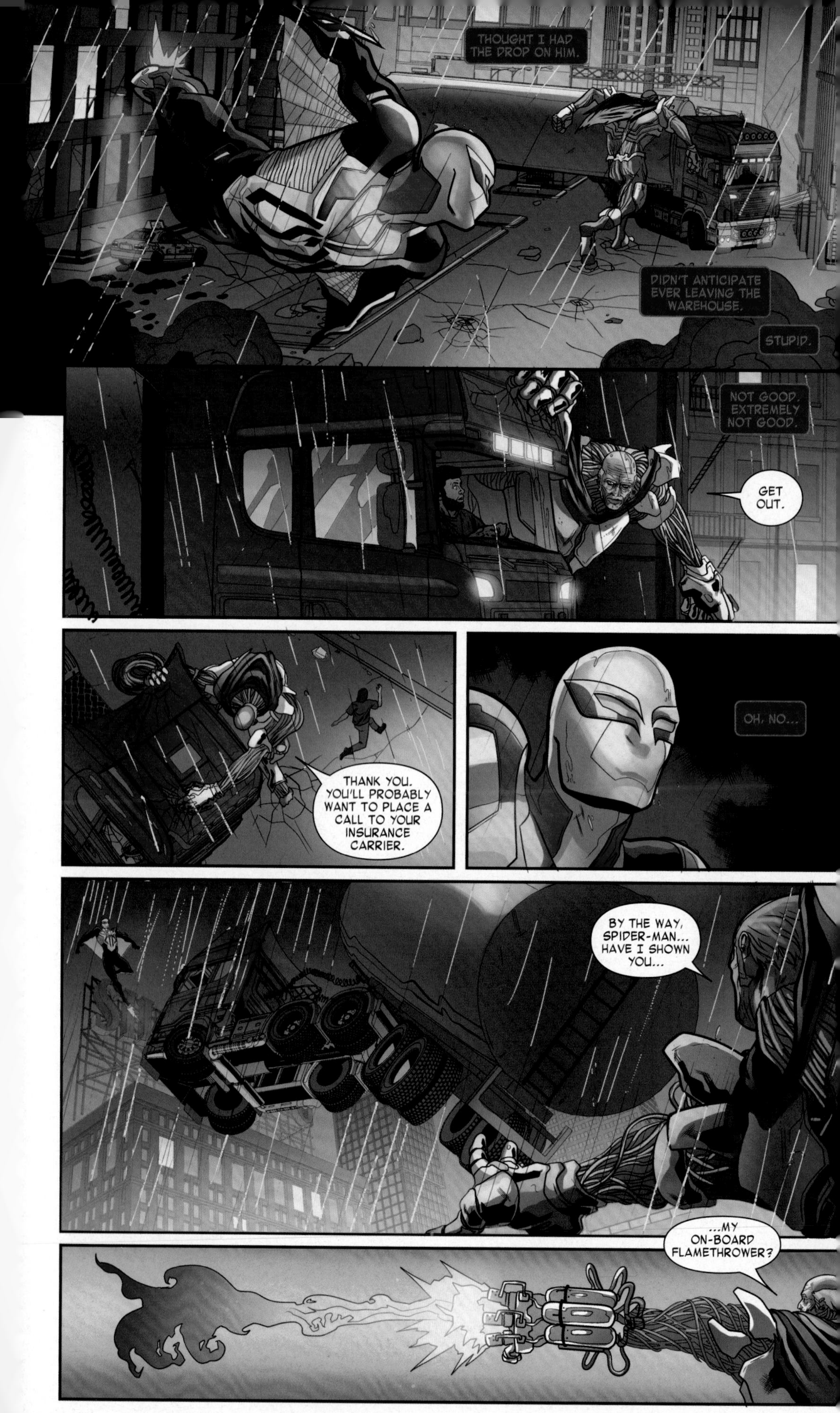
THOUGHT I HAD THE DROP ON HIM.
DIDN'T ANTICIPATE EVER LEAVING THE WAREHOUSE.
STUPID.
NOT GOOD. EXTREMELY NOT GOOD.
GET OUT.
THANK YOU. YOU'LL PROBABLY WANT TO PLACE A CALL TO YOUR INSURANCE CARRIER.
OH, NO...
BY THE WAY, SPIDER-MAN... HAVE I SHOWN YOU...
...MY ON-BOARD FLAMETHROWER?

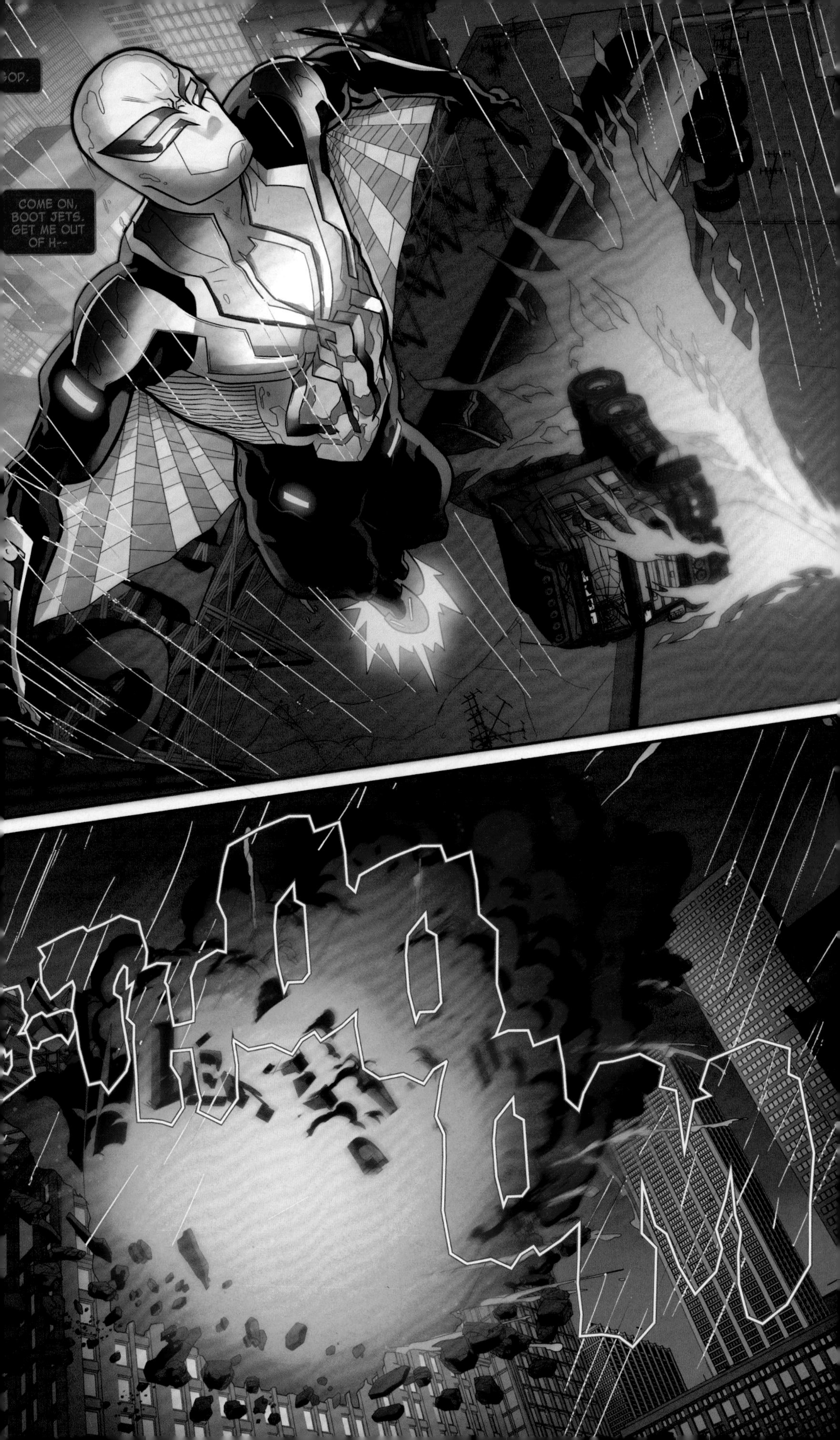

GOD.
COME ON, BOOT JETS. GET ME OUT OF H--

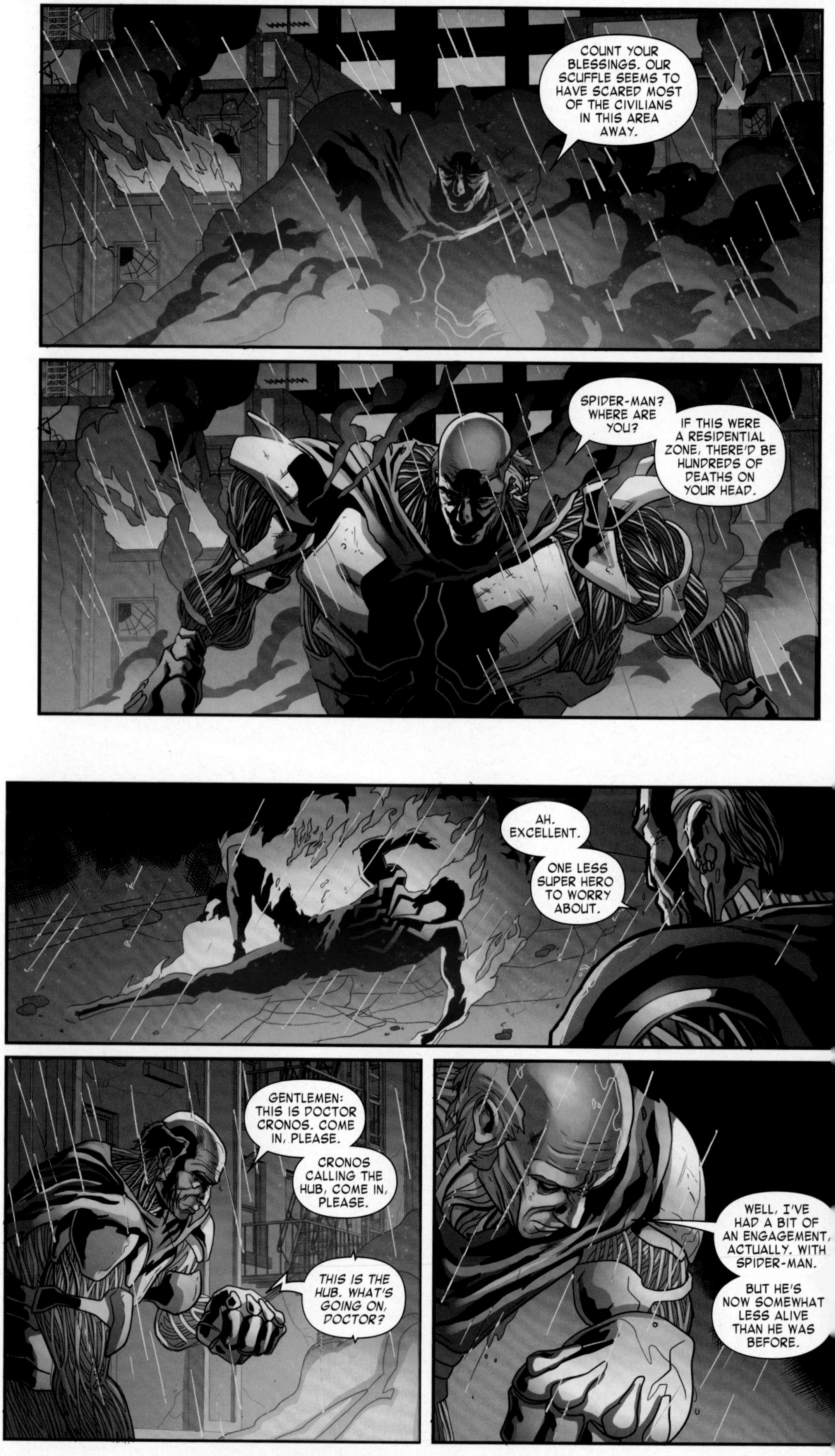
COUNT YOUR BLESSINGS. OUR SCUFFLE SEEMS TO HAVE SCARED MOST OF THE CIVILIANS IN THIS AREA AWAY.
SPIDER-MAN? WHERE ARE YOU?
IF THIS WERE A RESIDENTIAL ZONE, THERE'D BE HUNDREDS OF DEATHS ON YOUR HEAD.
AH. EXCELLENT.
ONE LESS SUPER HERO TO WORRY ABOUT.
GENTLEMEN: THIS IS DOCTOR CRONOS. COME IN, PLEASE.
CRONOS CALLING THE HUB, COME IN, PLEASE.
THIS IS THE HUB. WHAT'S GOING ON, DOCTOR?
WELL, I'VE HAD A BIT OF AN ENGAGEMENT, ACTUALLY. WITH SPIDER-MAN.
BUT HE'S NOW SOMEWHAT LESS ALIVE THAN HE WAS BEFORE.

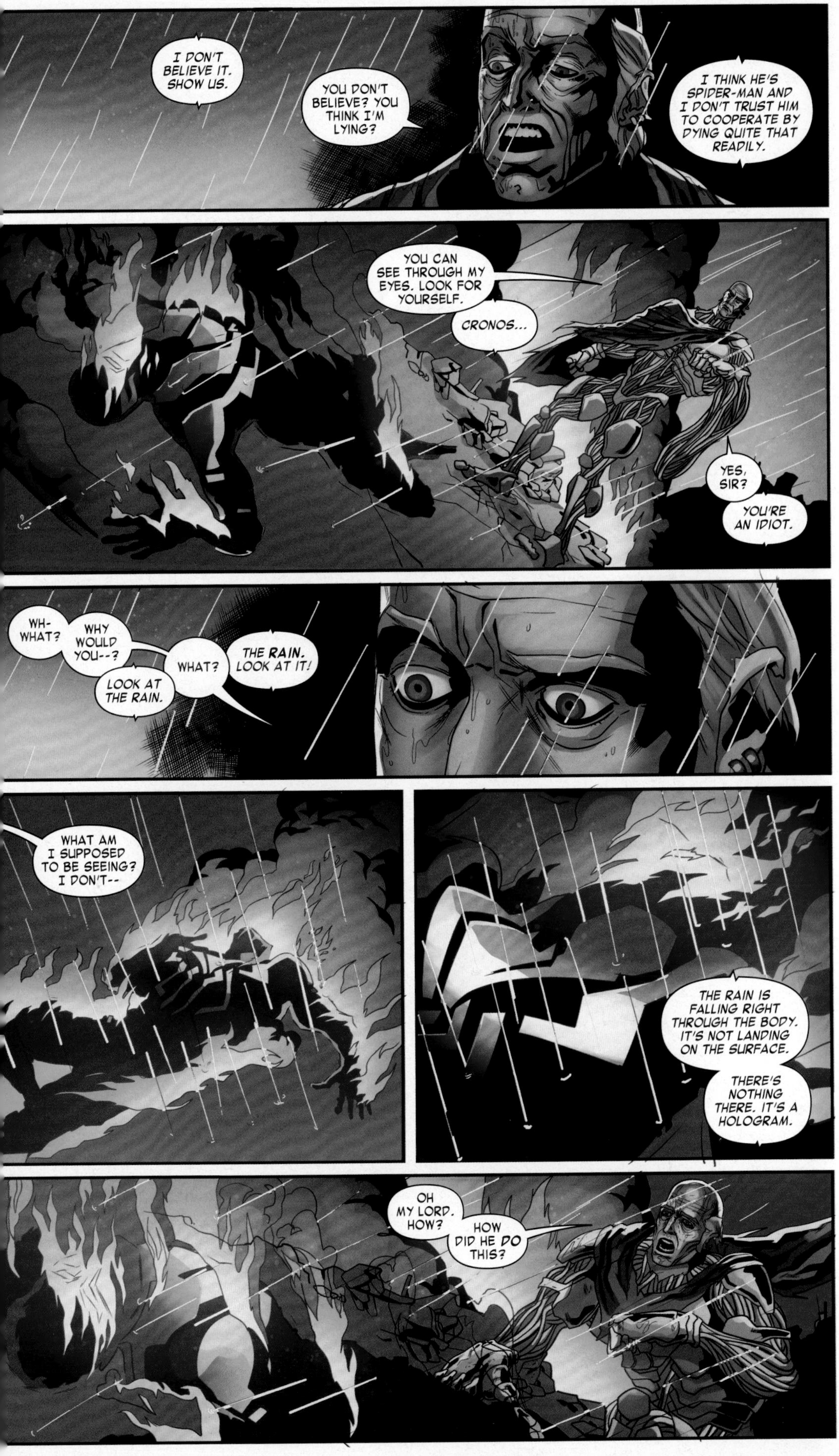
I DON'T BELIEVE IT. SHOW US.
YOU DON'T BELIEVE? YOU THINK I'M LYING?
I THINK HE'S SPIDER-MAN AND I DON'T TRUST HIM TO COOPERATE BY DYING QUITE THAT READILY.
YOU CAN SEE THROUGH MY EYES. LOOK FOR YOURSELF.
CRONOS...
YES, SIR?
YOU'RE AN IDIOT.
WH-WHAT?
WHY WOULD YOU--?
LOOK AT THE RAIN.
WHAT?
THE RAIN. LOOK AT IT!
WHAT AM I SUPPOSED TO BE SEEING? I DON'T--
THE RAIN IS FALLING RIGHT THROUGH THE BODY. IT'S NOT LANDING ON THE SURFACE.
THERE'S NOTHING THERE. IT'S A HOLOGRAM.
OH MY LORD. HOW?
HOW DID HE DO THIS?

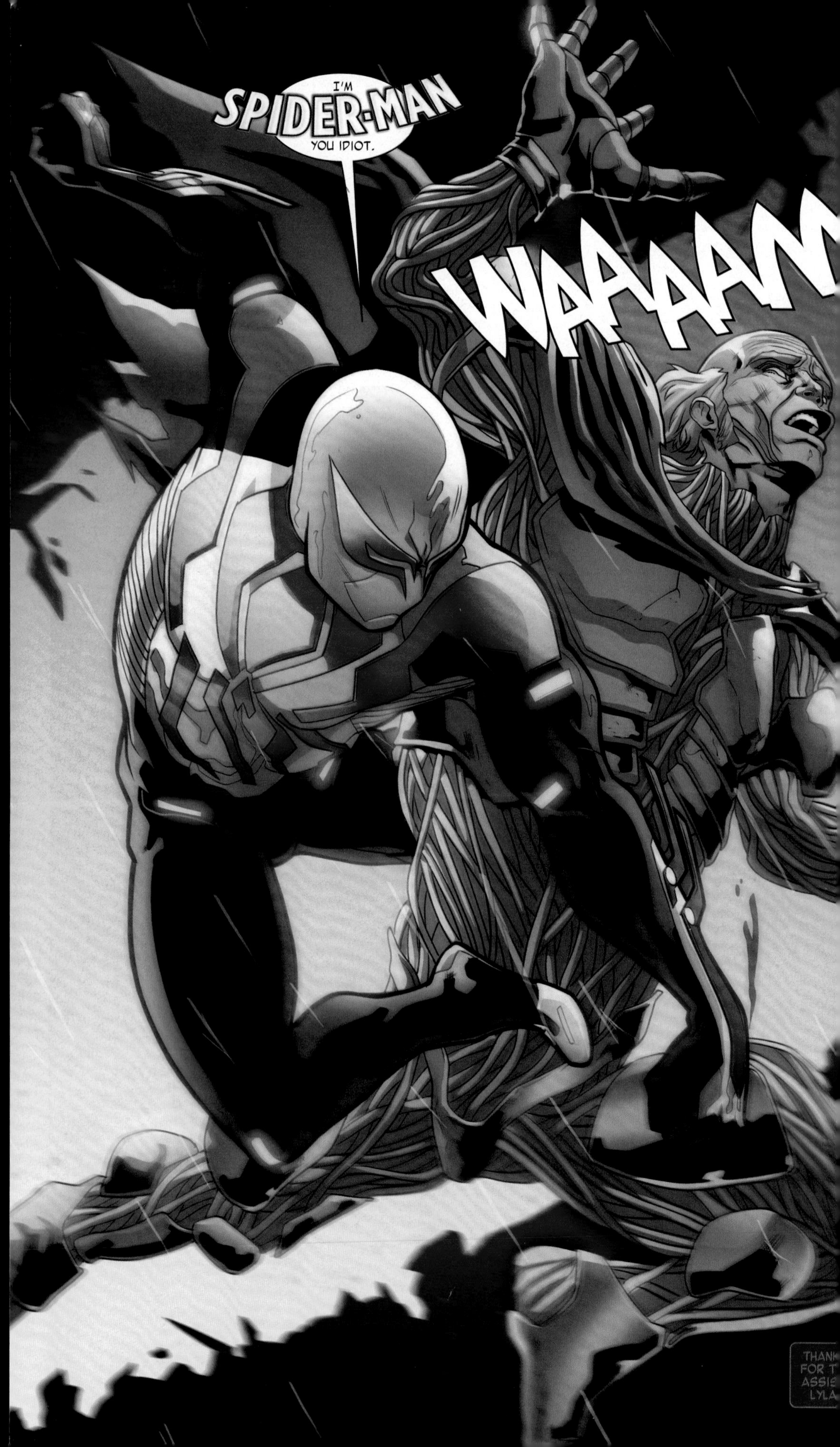
I'M SPIDER-MAN YOU IDIOT.
WAAAAM
THAN
FOR T
ASSIS
LYLA

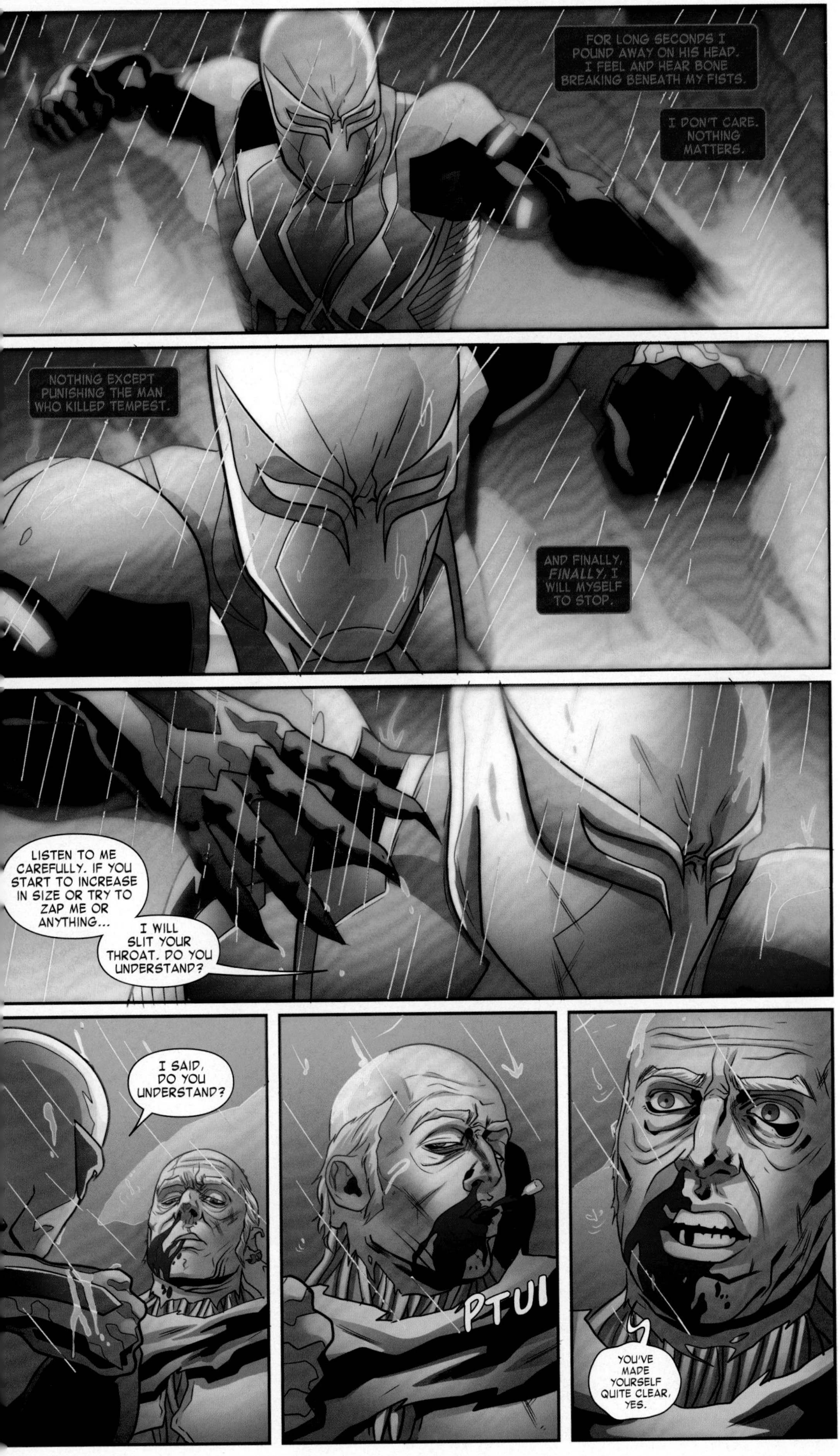
FOR LONG SECONDS I POUND AWAY ON HIS HEAD. I FEEL AND HEAR BONE BREAKING BENEATH MY FISTS.
I DON'T CARE. NOTHING MATTERS.
NOTHING EXCEPT PUNISHING THE MAN WHO KILLED TEMPEST.
AND FINALLY, *FINALLY*, I WILL MYSELF TO STOP.
LISTEN TO ME CAREFULLY. IF YOU START TO INCREASE IN SIZE OR TRY TO ZAP ME OR ANYTHING...
I WILL SLIT YOUR THROAT. DO YOU UNDERSTAND?
I SAID, DO YOU UNDERSTAND?
PTUI
YOU'VE MADE YOURSELF QUITE CLEAR, YES.

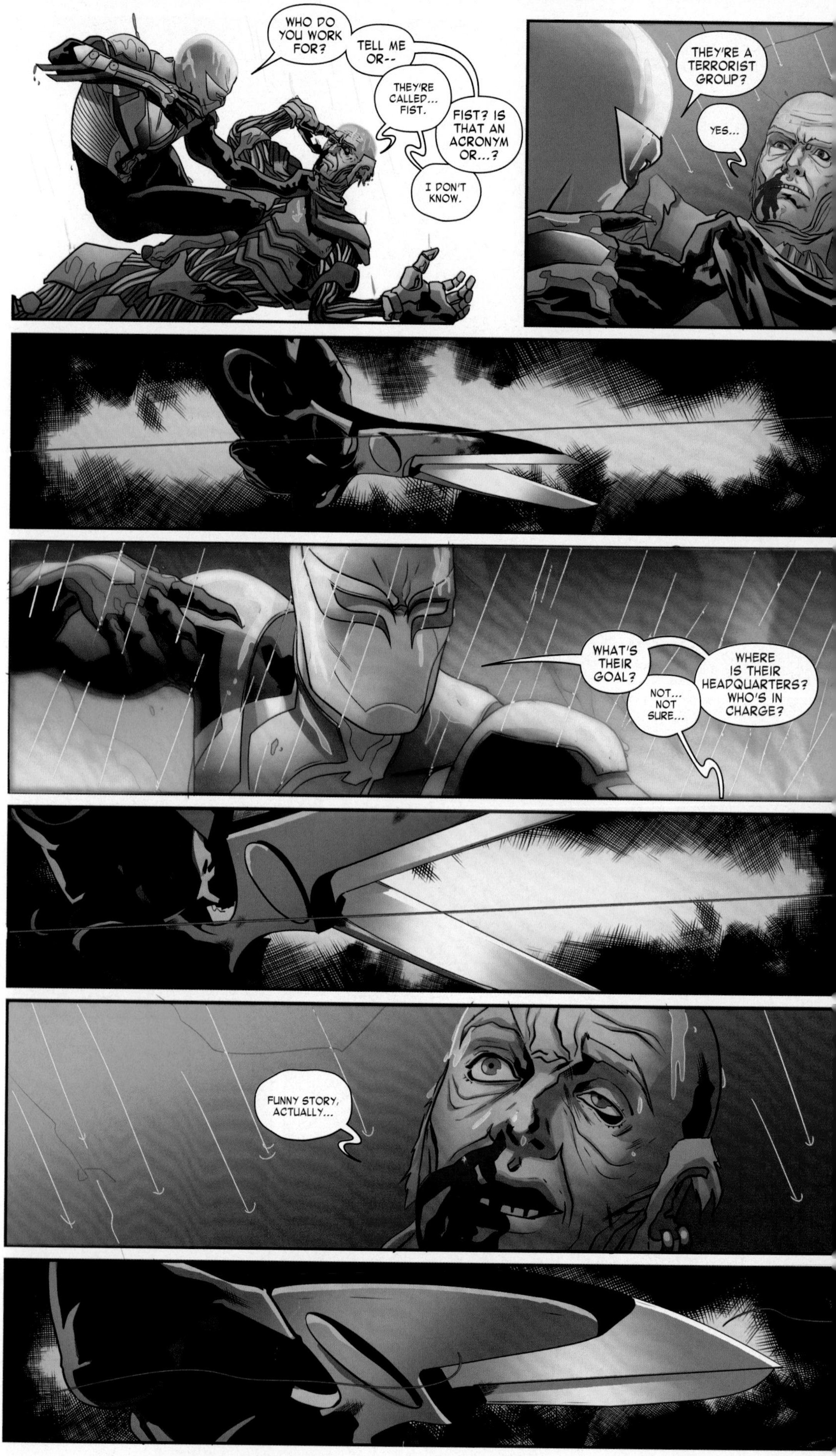
WHO DO YOU WORK FOR?
TELL ME OR--
THEY'RE CALLED... FIST.
FIST? IS THAT AN ACRONYM OR...?
I DON'T KNOW.
THEY'RE A TERRORIST GROUP?
YES...
WHAT'S THEIR GOAL?
NOT... NOT SURE...
WHERE IS THEIR HEADQUARTERS? WHO'S IN CHARGE?
FUNNY STORY, ACTUALLY...

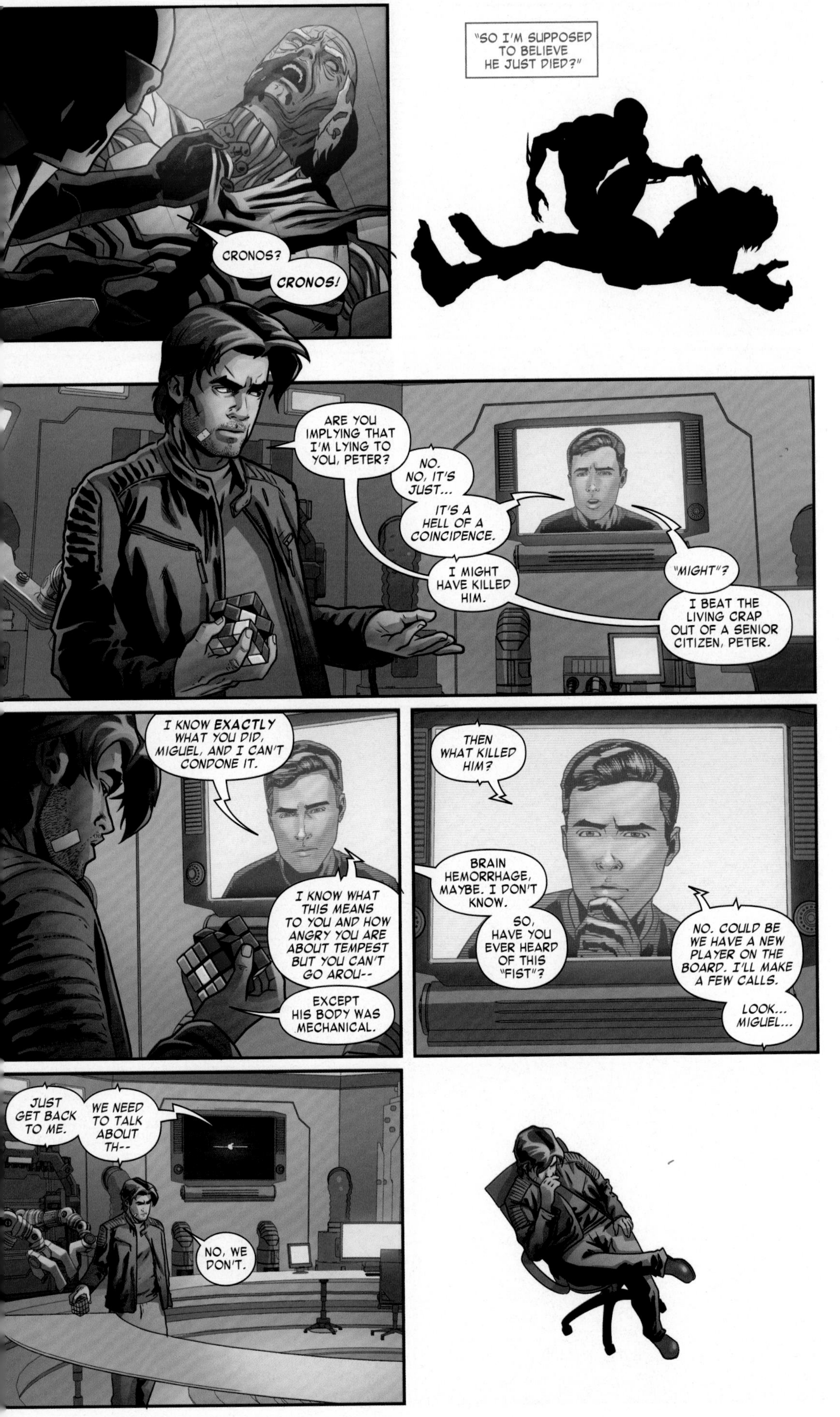
"SO I'M SUPPOSED TO BELIEVE HE JUST DIED?"
CRONOS?
CRONOS!
ARE YOU IMPLYING THAT I'M LYING TO YOU, PETER?
NO. NO, IT'S JUST...
IT'S A HELL OF A COINCIDENCE.
I MIGHT HAVE KILLED HIM.
"MIGHT"?
I BEAT THE LIVING CRAP OUT OF A SENIOR CITIZEN, PETER.
I KNOW EXACTLY WHAT YOU DID, MIGUEL, AND I CAN'T CONDONE IT.
I KNOW WHAT THIS MEANS TO YOU AND HOW ANGRY YOU ARE ABOUT TEMPEST BUT YOU CAN'T GO AROU--
EXCEPT HIS BODY WAS MECHANICAL.
THEN WHAT KILLED HIM?
BRAIN HEMORRHAGE, MAYBE. I DON'T KNOW.
SO, HAVE YOU EVER HEARD OF THIS "FIST"?
NO. COULD BE WE HAVE A NEW PLAYER ON THE BOARD. I'LL MAKE A FEW CALLS.
LOOK... MIGUEL...
JUST GET BACK TO ME.
WE NEED TO TALK ABOUT TH--
NO, WE DON'T.

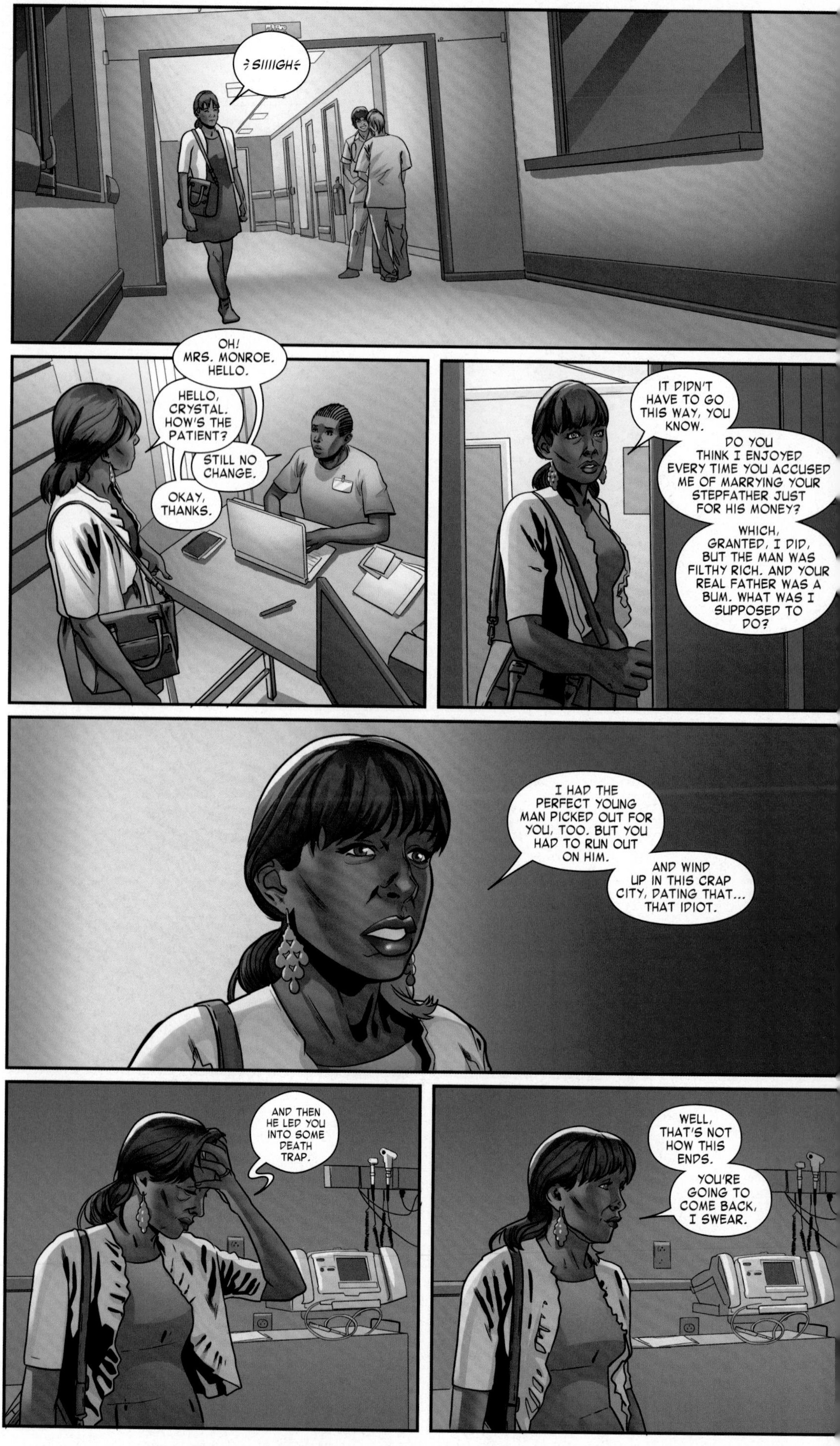
SIIIGH
OH! MRS. MONROE. HELLO.
HELLO, CRYSTAL. HOW'S THE PATIENT?
STILL NO CHANGE.
OKAY, THANKS.
IT DIDN'T HAVE TO GO THIS WAY, YOU KNOW.
DO YOU THINK I ENJOYED EVERY TIME YOU ACCUSED ME OF MARRYING YOUR STEPFATHER JUST FOR HIS MONEY?
WHICH, GRANTED, I DID, BUT THE MAN WAS FILTHY RICH. AND YOUR REAL FATHER WAS A BUM. WHAT WAS I SUPPOSED TO DO?
I HAD THE PERFECT YOUNG MAN PICKED OUT FOR YOU, TOO. BUT YOU HAD TO RUN OUT ON HIM.
AND WIND UP IN THIS CRAP CITY, DATING THAT... THAT IDIOT.
AND THEN HE LED YOU INTO SOME DEATH TRAP.
WELL, THAT'S NOT HOW THIS ENDS.
YOU'RE GOING TO COME BACK, I SWEAR.

AND WHEN YOU DO, THINGS ARE GOING TO FINALLY WORK OUT THE WAY THAT I WANT THEM TO.

AND IT WILL BE A COLD DAY IN HELL BEFORE MIGUEL O'HARA EVER SEES YOU AGAIN.

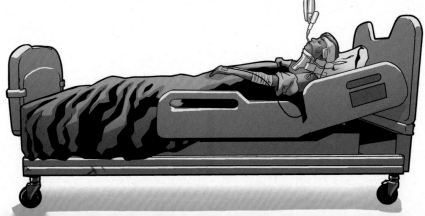

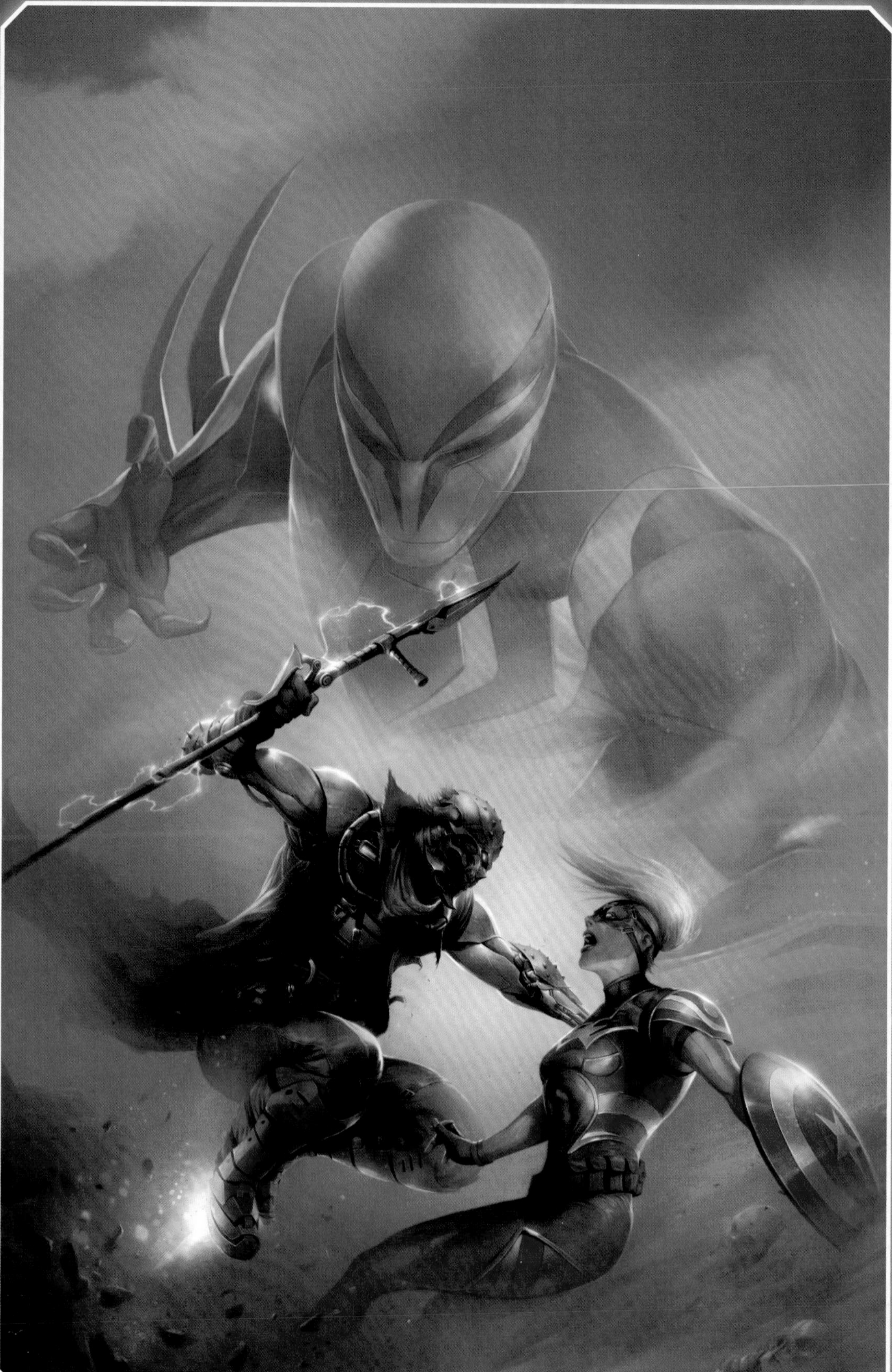

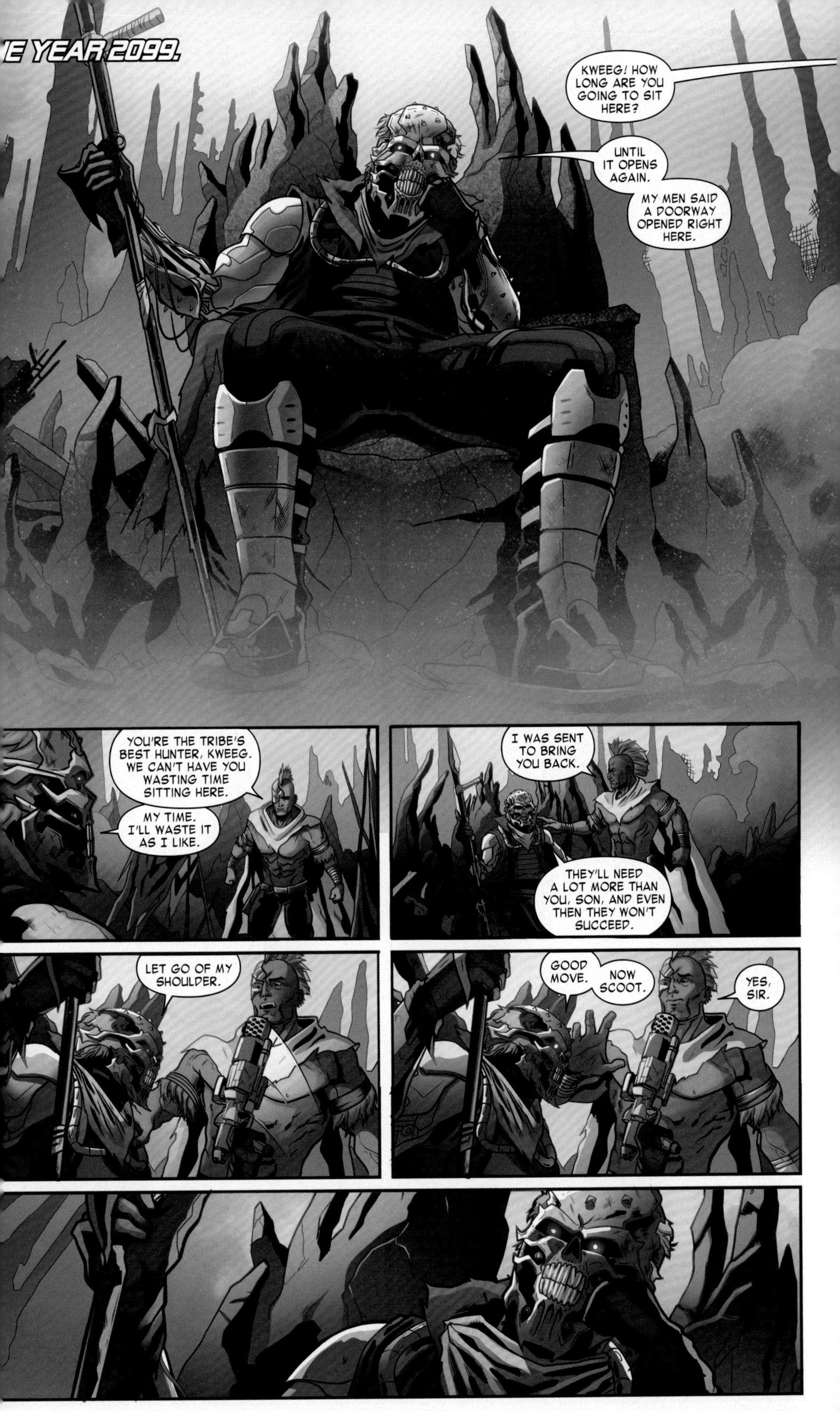
E YEAR 2099.
KWEEG! HOW LONG ARE YOU GOING TO SIT HERE?
UNTIL IT OPENS AGAIN.
MY MEN SAID A DOORWAY OPENED RIGHT HERE.
YOU'RE THE TRIBE'S BEST HUNTER, KWEEG. WE CAN'T HAVE YOU WASTING TIME SITTING HERE.
MY TIME. I'LL WASTE IT AS I LIKE.
I WAS SENT TO BRING YOU BACK.
THEY'LL NEED A LOT MORE THAN YOU, SON, AND EVEN THEN THEY WON'T SUCCEED.
LET GO OF MY SHOULDER.
GOOD MOVE.
NOW SCOOT.
YES, SIR.

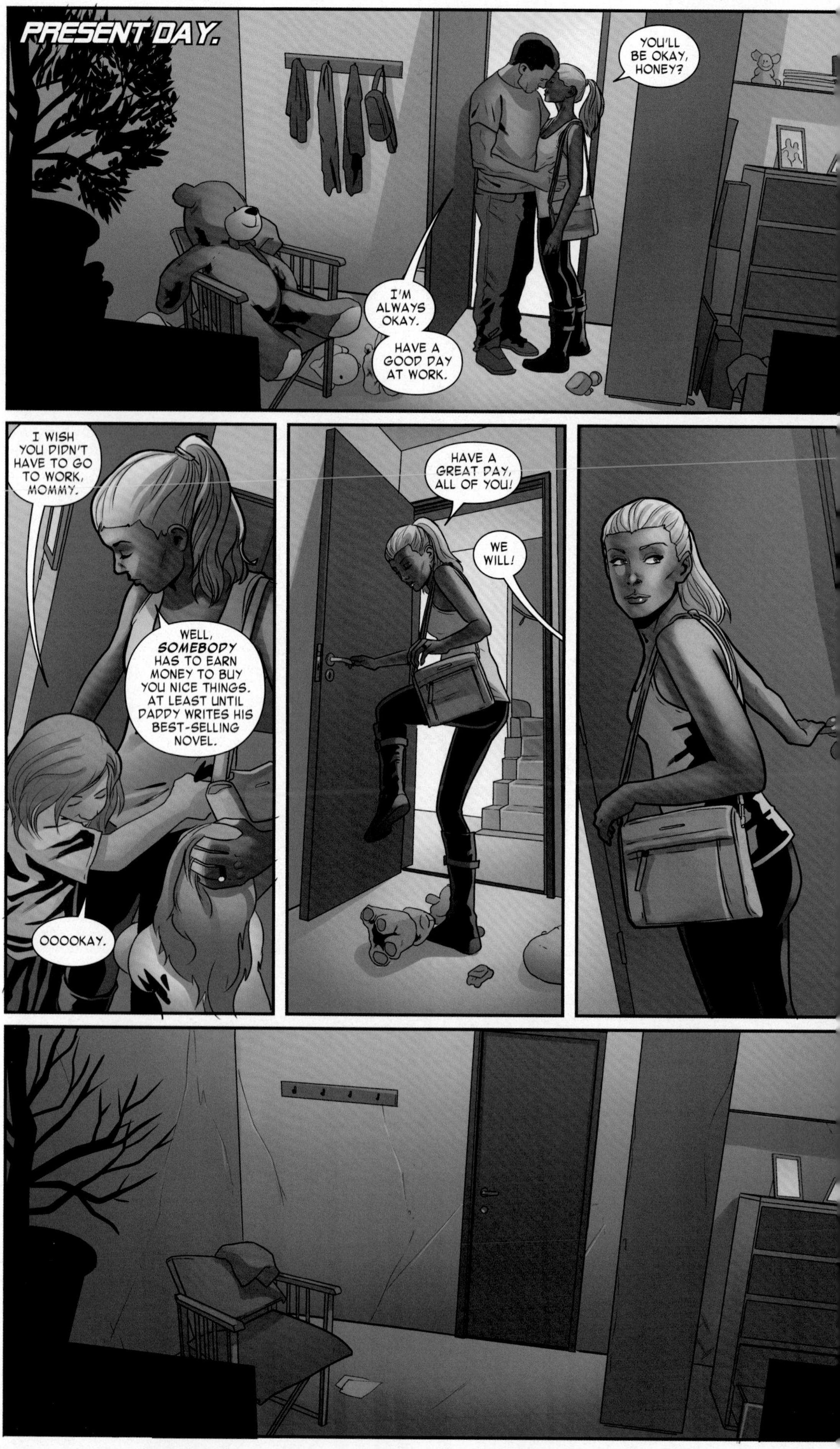
PRESENT DAY.
YOU'LL BE OKAY, HONEY?
I'M ALWAYS OKAY.
HAVE A GOOD DAY AT WORK.
I WISH YOU DIDN'T HAVE TO GO TO WORK, MOMMY.
WELL, SOMEBODY HAS TO EARN MONEY TO BUY YOU NICE THINGS. AT LEAST UNTIL DADDY WRITES HIS BEST-SELLING NOVEL.
OOOOKAY.
HAVE A GREAT DAY, ALL OF YOU!
WE WILL!

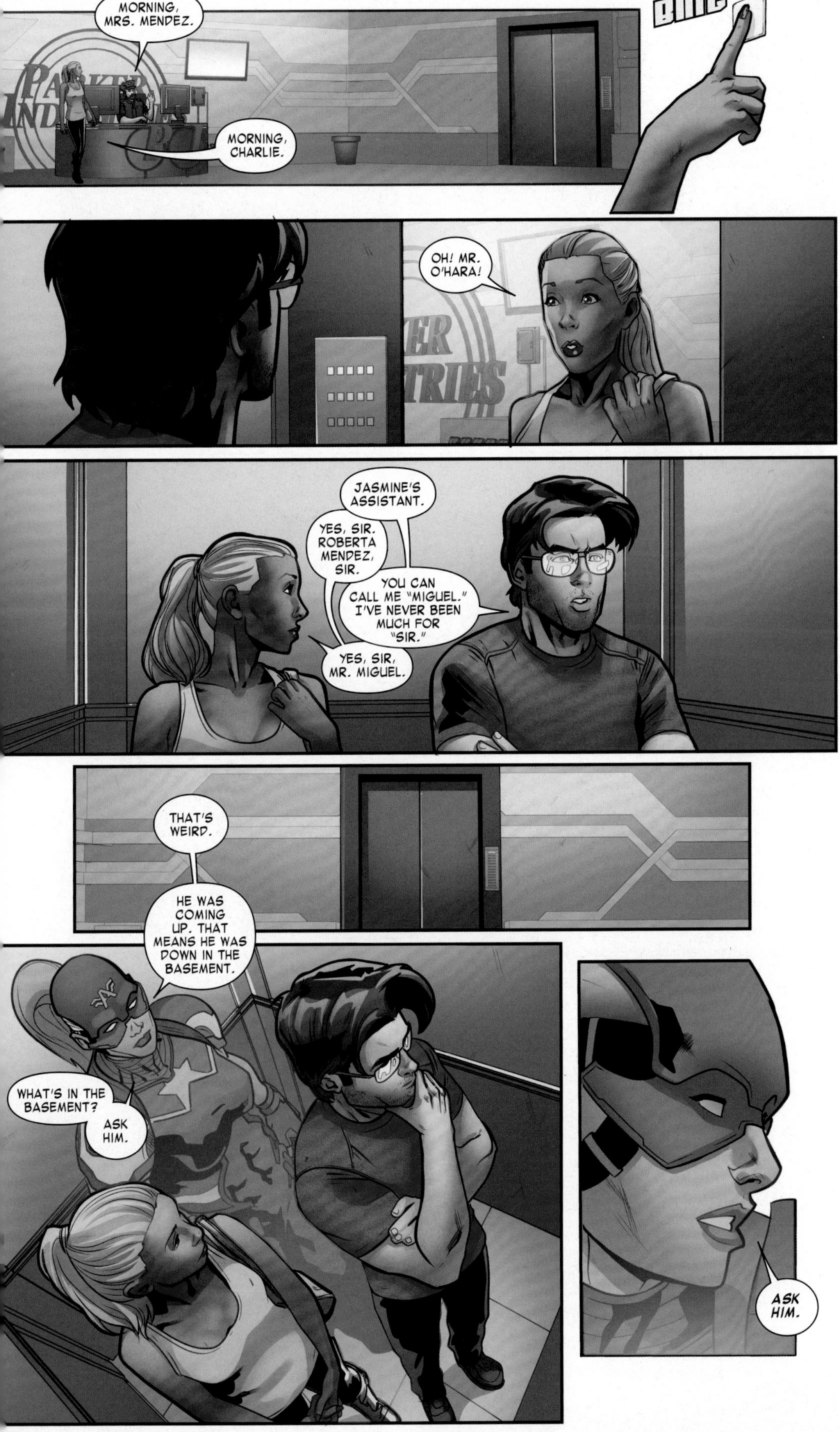
MORNING, MRS. MENDEZ.
MORNING, CHARLIE.
BING
OH! MR. O'HARA!
JASMINE'S ASSISTANT.
YES, SIR. ROBERTA MENDEZ, SIR.
YOU CAN CALL ME "MIGUEL." I'VE NEVER BEEN MUCH FOR "SIR."
YES, SIR, MR. MIGUEL.
THAT'S WEIRD.
HE WAS COMING UP. THAT MEANS HE WAS DOWN IN THE BASEMENT.
WHAT'S IN THE BASEMENT?
ASK HIM.
ASK HIM.

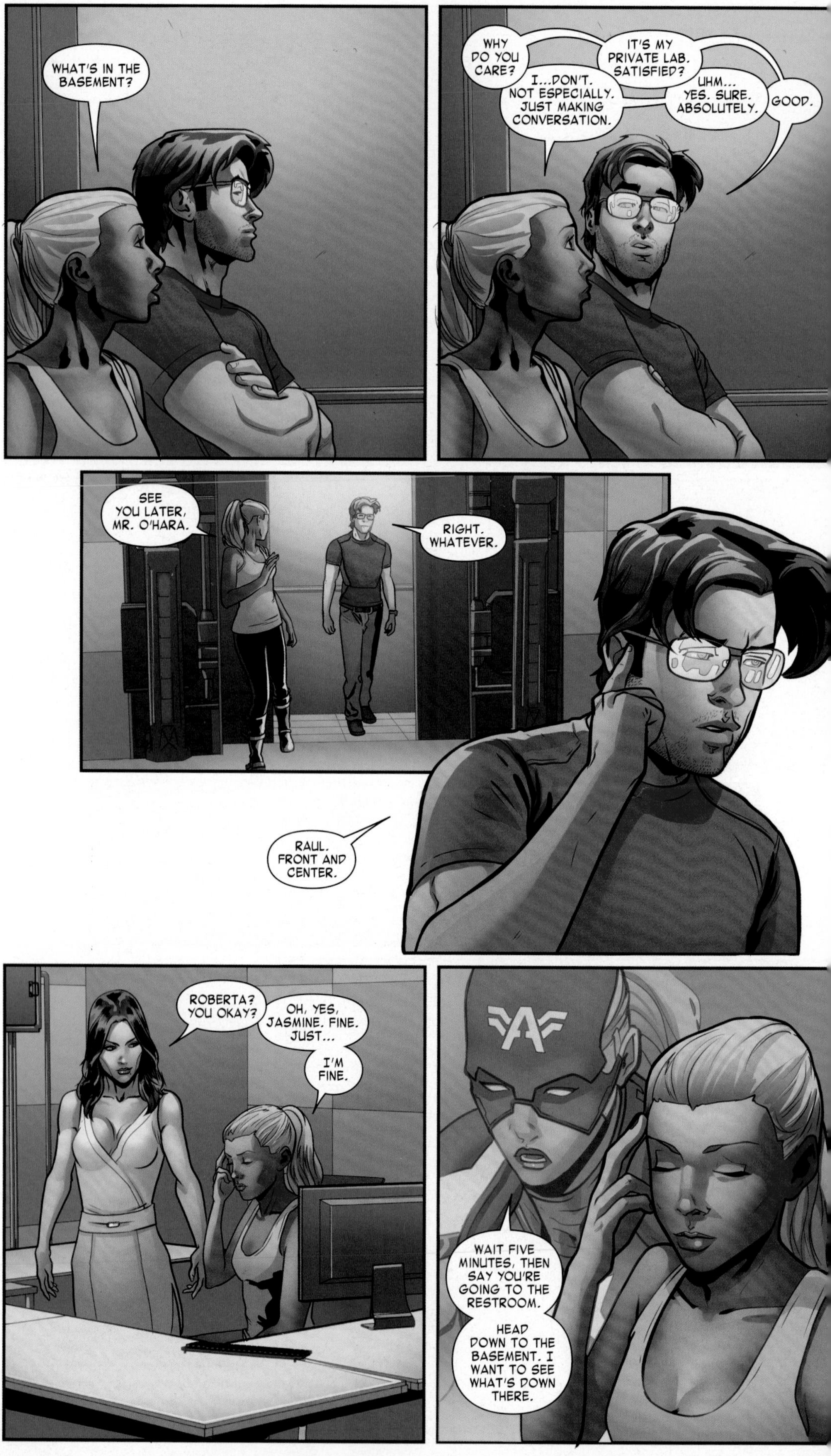
WHAT'S IN THE BASEMENT?
WHY DO YOU CARE?
I...DON'T. NOT ESPECIALLY. JUST MAKING CONVERSATION.
IT'S MY PRIVATE LAB. SATISFIED?
UHM... YES. SURE. ABSOLUTELY.
GOOD.
SEE YOU LATER, MR. O'HARA.
RIGHT. WHATEVER.
RAUL. FRONT AND CENTER.
ROBERTA? YOU OKAY?
OH, YES, JASMINE. FINE. JUST...
I'M FINE.
WAIT FIVE MINUTES, THEN SAY YOU'RE GOING TO THE RESTROOM.
HEAD DOWN TO THE BASEMENT. I WANT TO SEE WHAT'S DOWN THERE.

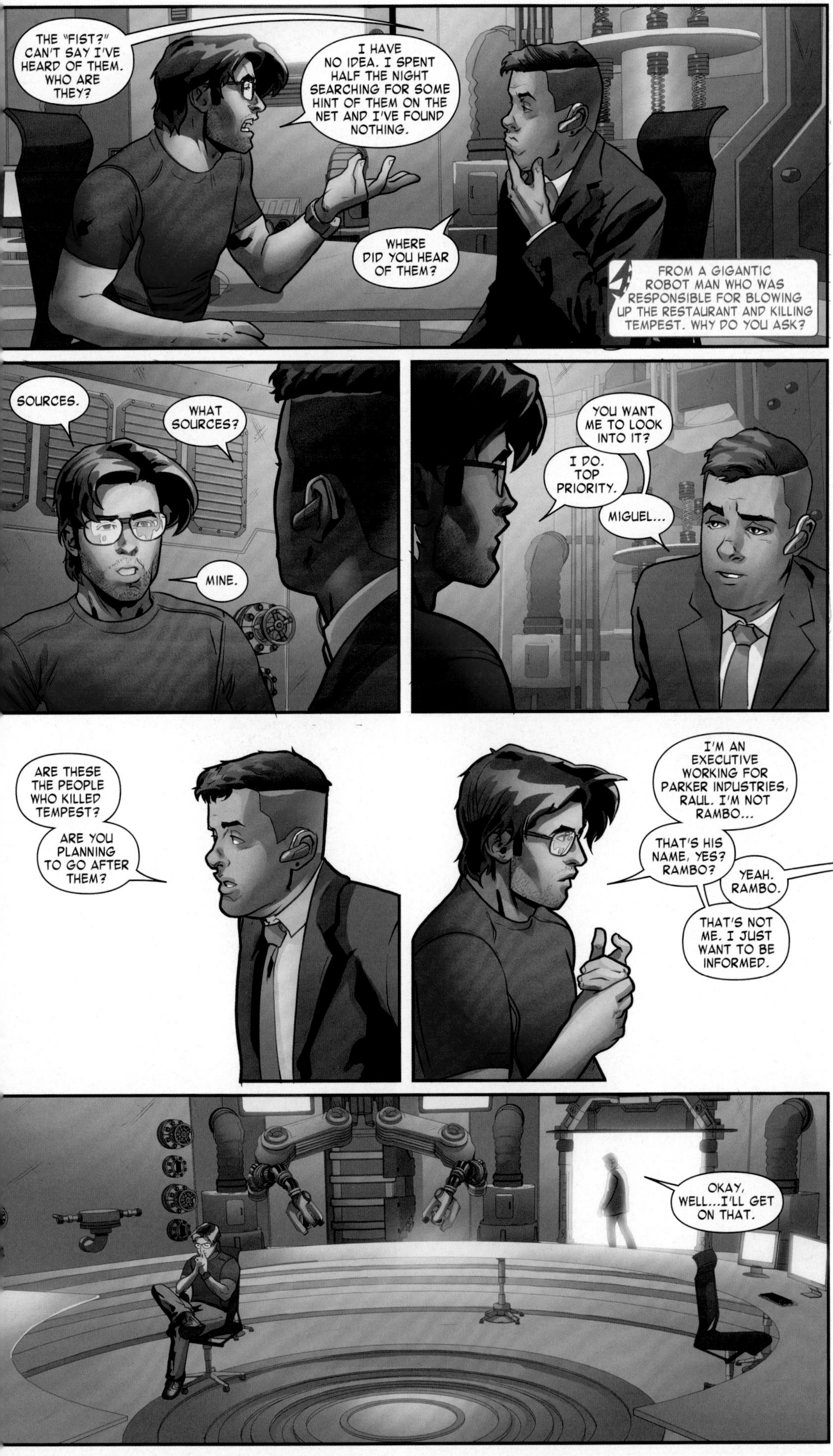
THE "FIST?" CAN'T SAY I'VE HEARD OF THEM. WHO ARE THEY?
I HAVE NO IDEA. I SPENT HALF THE NIGHT SEARCHING FOR SOME HINT OF THEM ON THE NET AND I'VE FOUND NOTHING.
WHERE DID YOU HEAR OF THEM?
FROM A GIGANTIC ROBOT MAN WHO WAS RESPONSIBLE FOR BLOWING UP THE RESTAURANT AND KILLING TEMPEST. WHY DO YOU ASK?
SOURCES.
WHAT SOURCES?
MINE.
YOU WANT ME TO LOOK INTO IT?
I DO. TOP PRIORITY.
MIGUEL...
ARE THESE THE PEOPLE WHO KILLED TEMPEST?
ARE YOU PLANNING TO GO AFTER THEM?
I'M AN EXECUTIVE WORKING FOR PARKER INDUSTRIES, RAUL. I'M NOT RAMBO...
THAT'S HIS NAME, YES? RAMBO?
YEAH. RAMBO.
THAT'S NOT ME. I JUST WANT TO BE INFORMED.
OKAY, WELL...I'LL GET ON THAT.

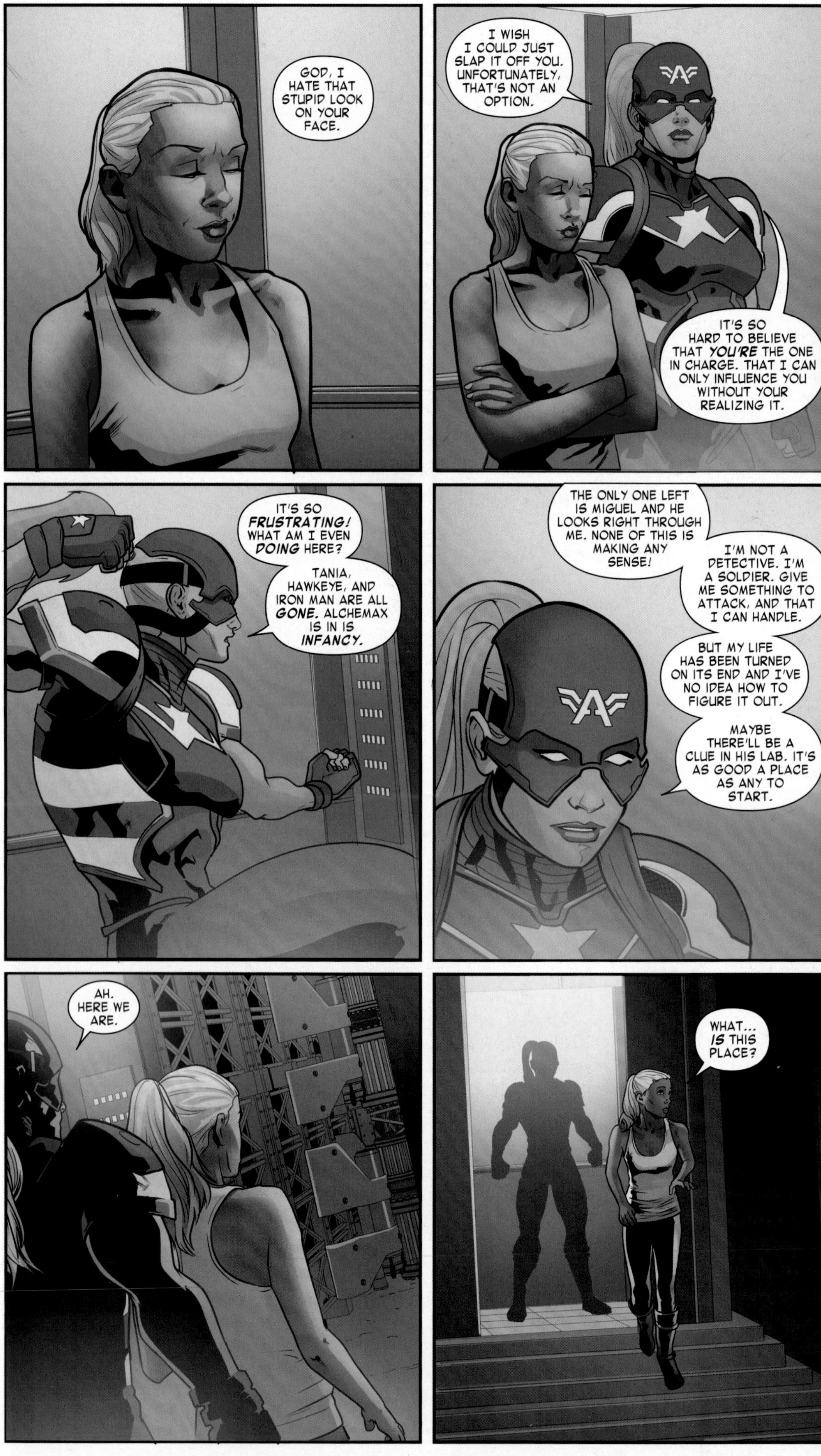
GOD, I HATE THAT STUPID LOOK ON YOUR FACE.
I WISH I COULD JUST SLAP IT OFF YOU. UNFORTUNATELY, THAT'S NOT AN OPTION.
IT'S SO HARD TO BELIEVE THAT YOU'RE THE ONE IN CHARGE. THAT I CAN ONLY INFLUENCE YOU WITHOUT YOUR REALIZING IT.
IT'S SO FRUSTRATING! WHAT AM I EVEN DOING HERE?
TANIA, HAWKEYE, AND IRON MAN ARE ALL GONE. ALCHEMAX IS IN IS INFANCY.
THE ONLY ONE LEFT IS MIGUEL AND HE LOOKS RIGHT THROUGH ME. NONE OF THIS IS MAKING ANY SENSE!
I'M NOT A DETECTIVE. I'M A SOLDIER. GIVE ME SOMETHING TO ATTACK, AND THAT I CAN HANDLE.
BUT MY LIFE HAS BEEN TURNED ON ITS END AND I'VE NO IDEA HOW TO FIGURE IT OUT.
MAYBE THERE'LL BE A CLUE IN HIS LAB. IT'S AS GOOD A PLACE AS ANY TO START.
AH. HERE WE ARE.
WHAT... IS THIS PLACE?

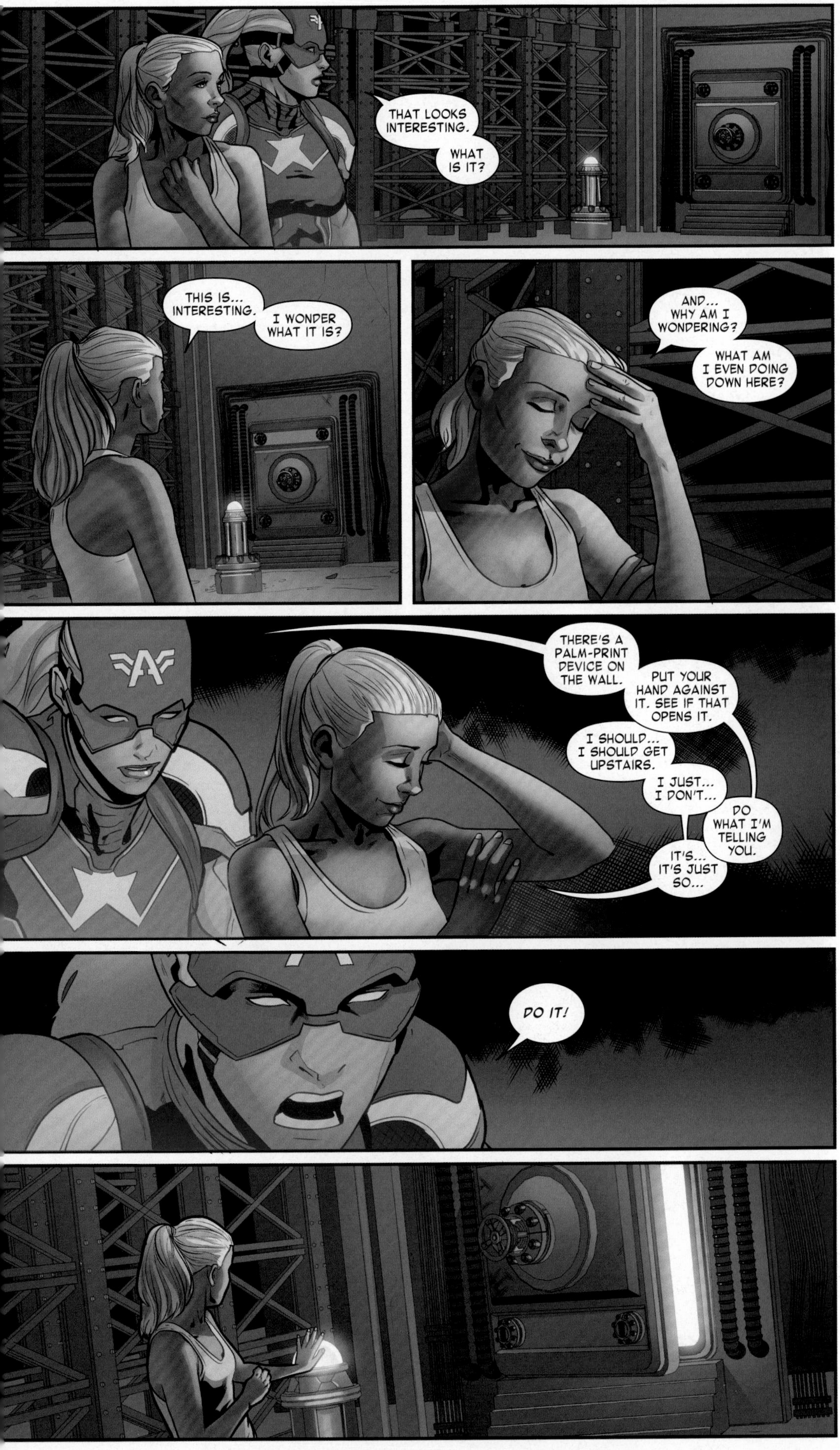
THAT LOOKS INTERESTING.
WHAT IS IT?
THIS IS... INTERESTING.
I WONDER WHAT IT IS?
AND... WHY AM I WONDERING?
WHAT AM I EVEN DOING DOWN HERE?
THERE'S A PALM-PRINT DEVICE ON THE WALL.
PUT YOUR HAND AGAINST IT. SEE IF THAT OPENS IT.
I SHOULD... I SHOULD GET UPSTAIRS.
I JUST... I DON'T...
DO WHAT I'M TELLING YOU.
IT'S... IT'S JUST SO...
DO IT!

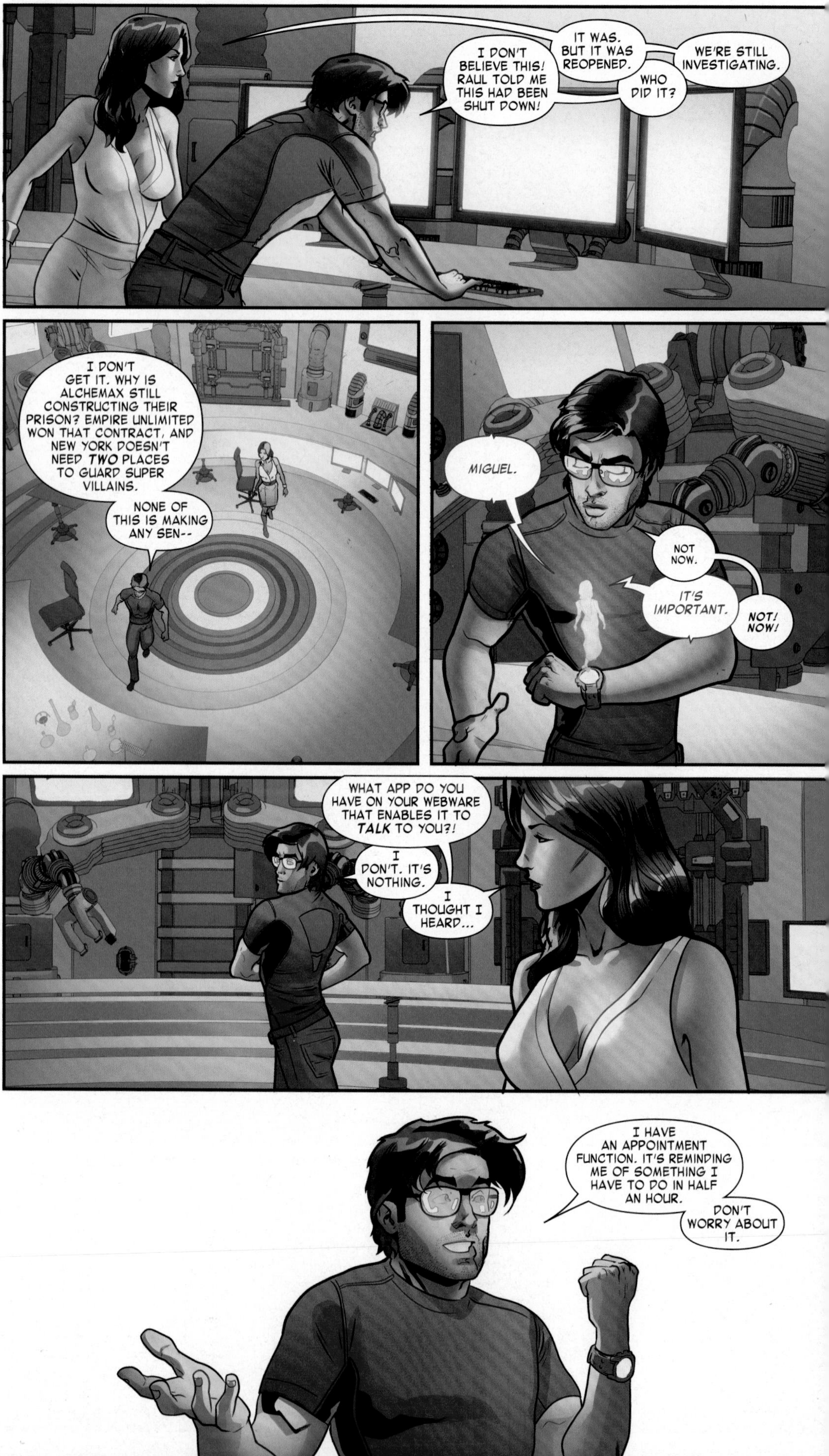
I DON'T BELIEVE THIS! RAUL TOLD ME THIS HAD BEEN SHUT DOWN!
IT WAS. BUT IT WAS REOPENED.
WHO DID IT?
WE'RE STILL INVESTIGATING.
I DON'T GET IT. WHY IS ALCHEMAX STILL CONSTRUCTING THEIR PRISON? EMPIRE UNLIMITED WON THAT CONTRACT, AND NEW YORK DOESN'T NEED *TWO* PLACES TO GUARD SUPER VILLAINS.
NONE OF THIS IS MAKING ANY SEN--
MIGUEL.
NOT NOW.
IT'S IMPORTANT.
NOT! NOW!
WHAT APP DO YOU HAVE ON YOUR WEBWARE THAT ENABLES IT TO *TALK* TO YOU?!
I DON'T. IT'S NOTHING.
I THOUGHT I HEARD...
I HAVE AN APPOINTMENT FUNCTION. IT'S REMINDING ME OF SOMETHING I HAVE TO DO IN HALF AN HOUR.
DON'T WORRY ABOUT IT.

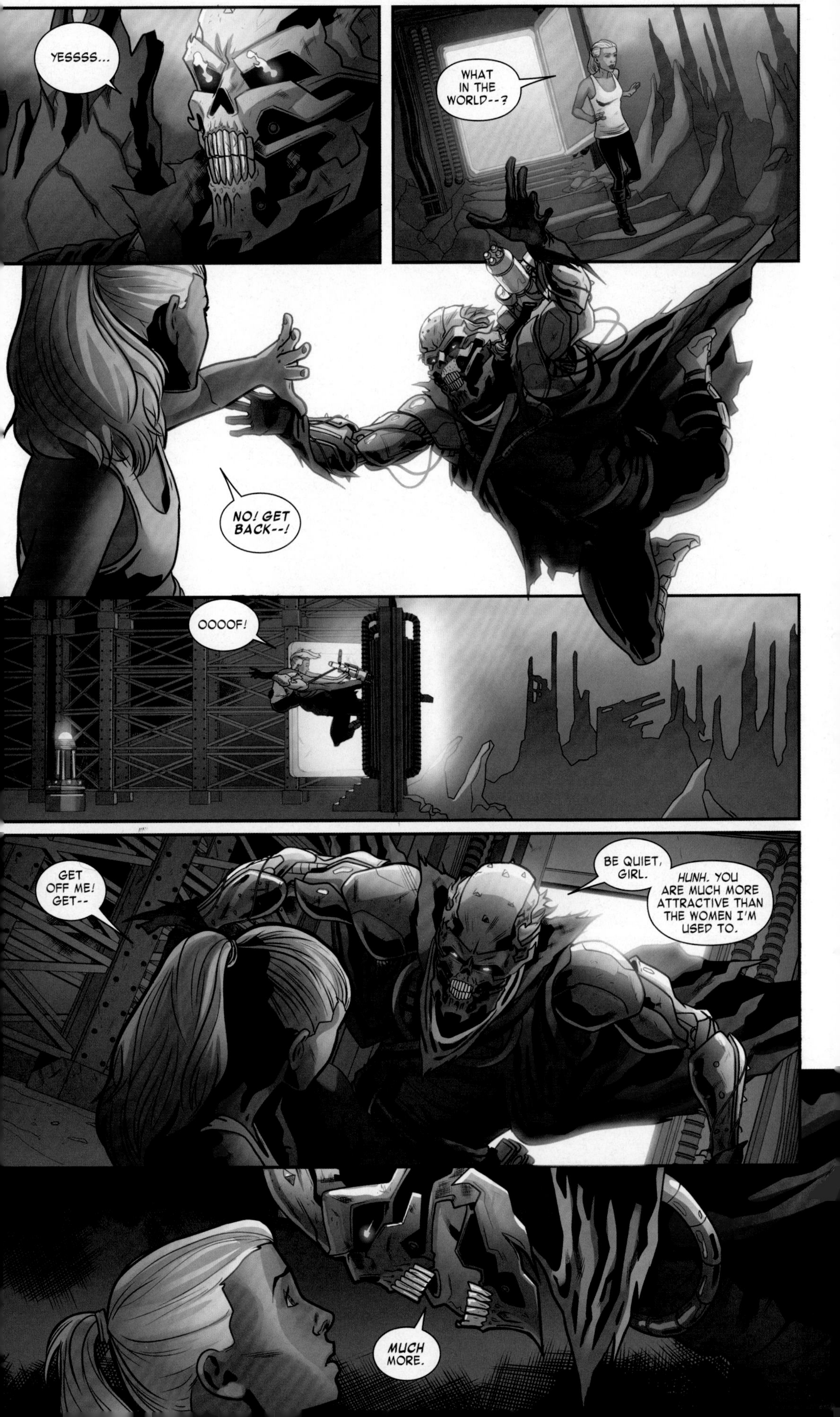
YESSSS...
WHAT IN THE WORLD--?
NO! GET BACK--!
OOOOF!
GET OFF ME! GET--
BE QUIET, GIRL.
HUNH. YOU ARE MUCH MORE ATTRACTIVE THAN THE WOMEN I'M USED TO.
MUCH MORE.

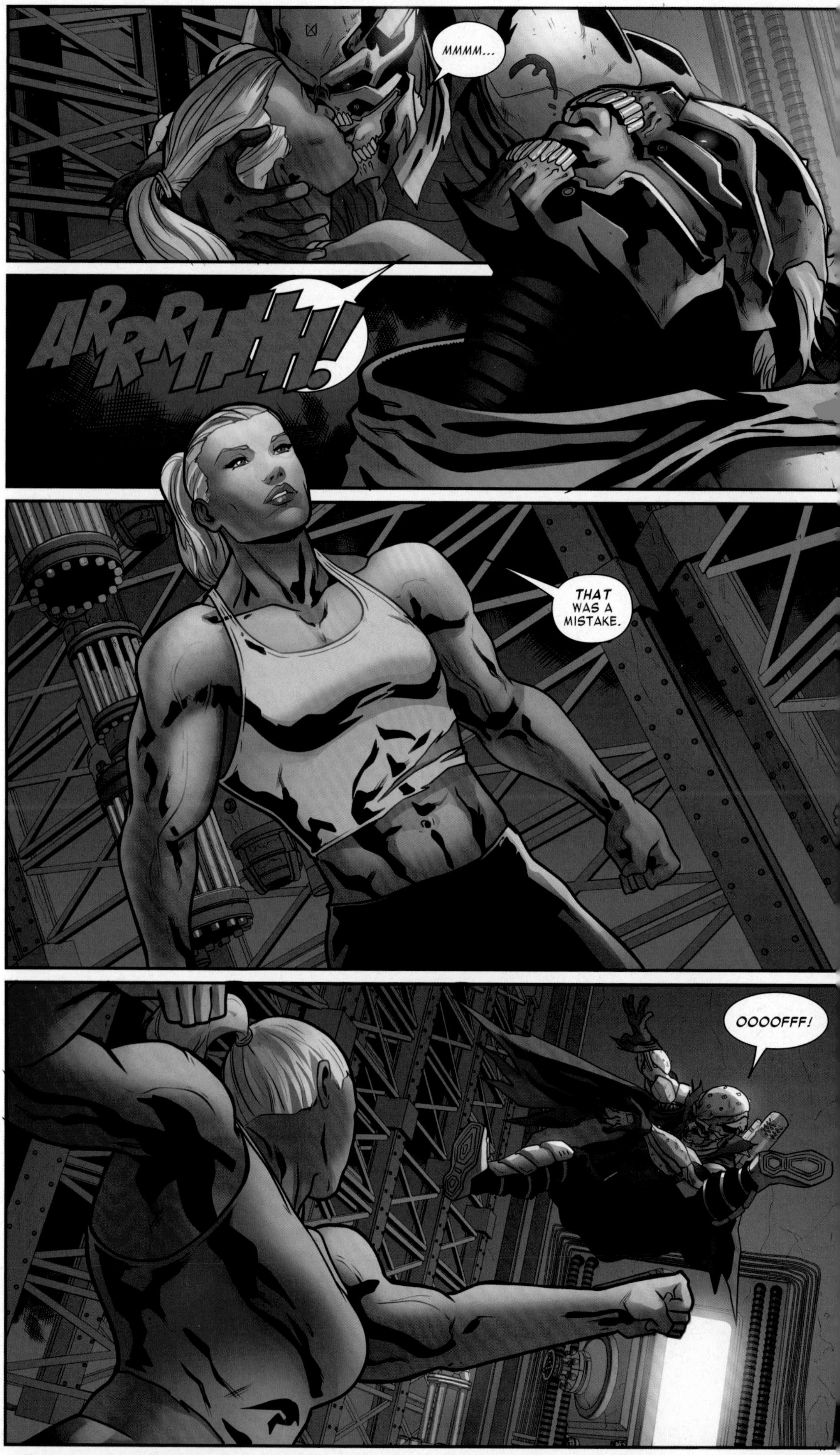
MMMM...
ARRRHHH!
THAT WAS A MISTAKE.
OOOOFFF!

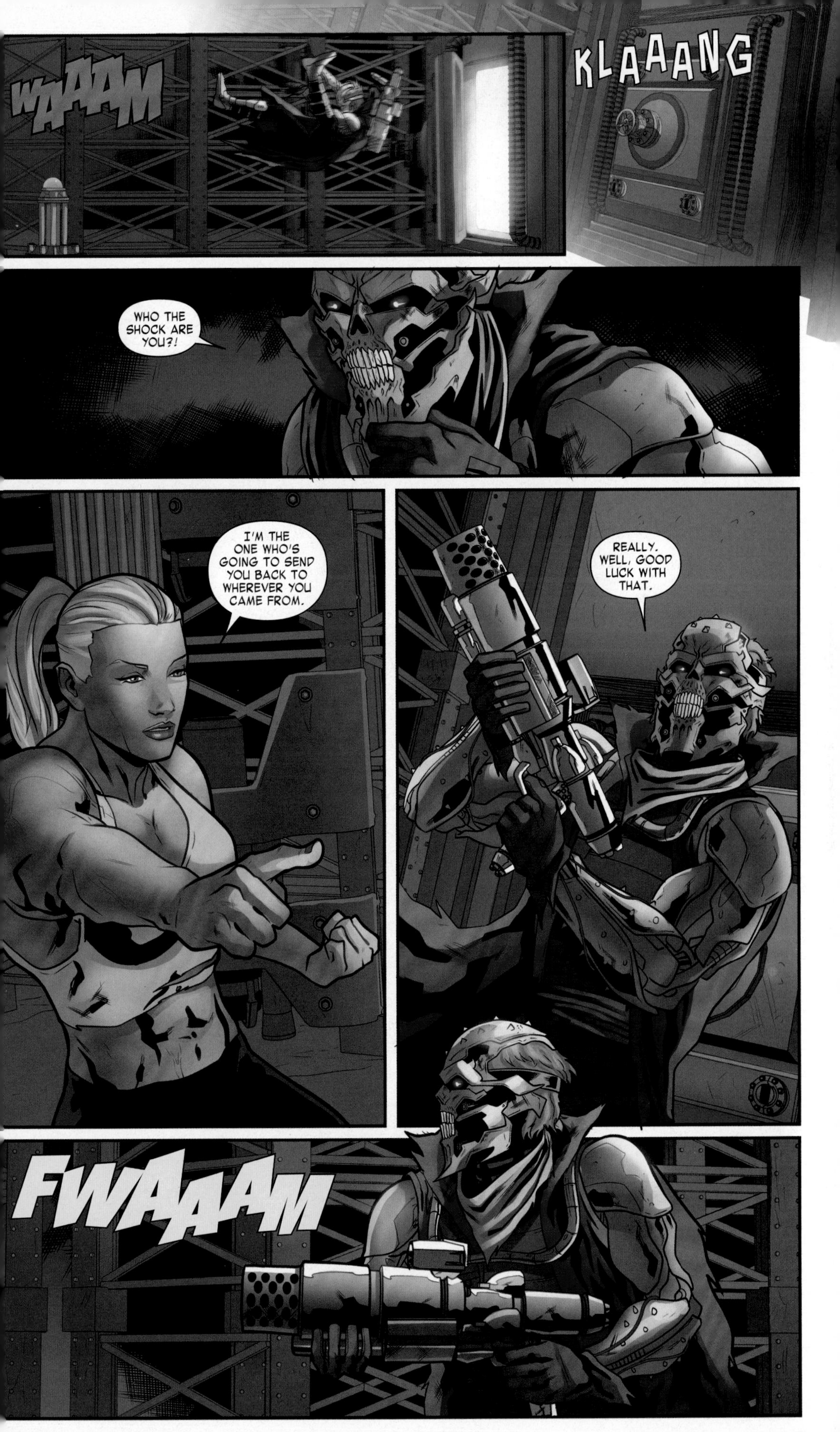
WAAAM
KLAAANG
WHO THE SHOCK ARE YOU?!
I'M THE ONE WHO'S GOING TO SEND YOU BACK TO WHEREVER YOU CAME FROM.
REALLY. WELL, GOOD LUCK WITH THAT.
FWAAAAM

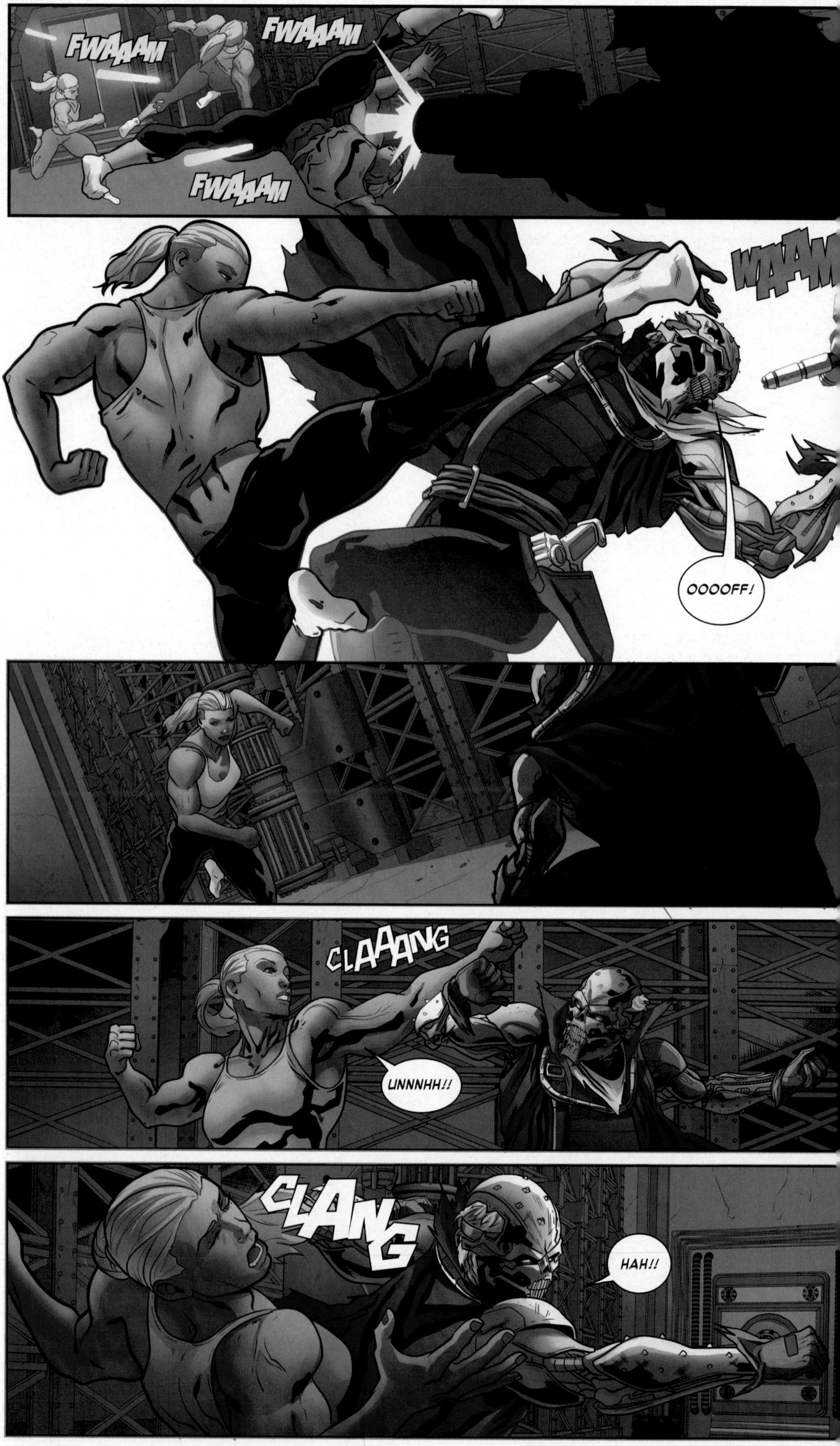

FWAAAM
FWAAAM
FWAAAM
WAAM
OOOOFF!
CLAAANG
UNNNHH!!
CLANG
HAH!!

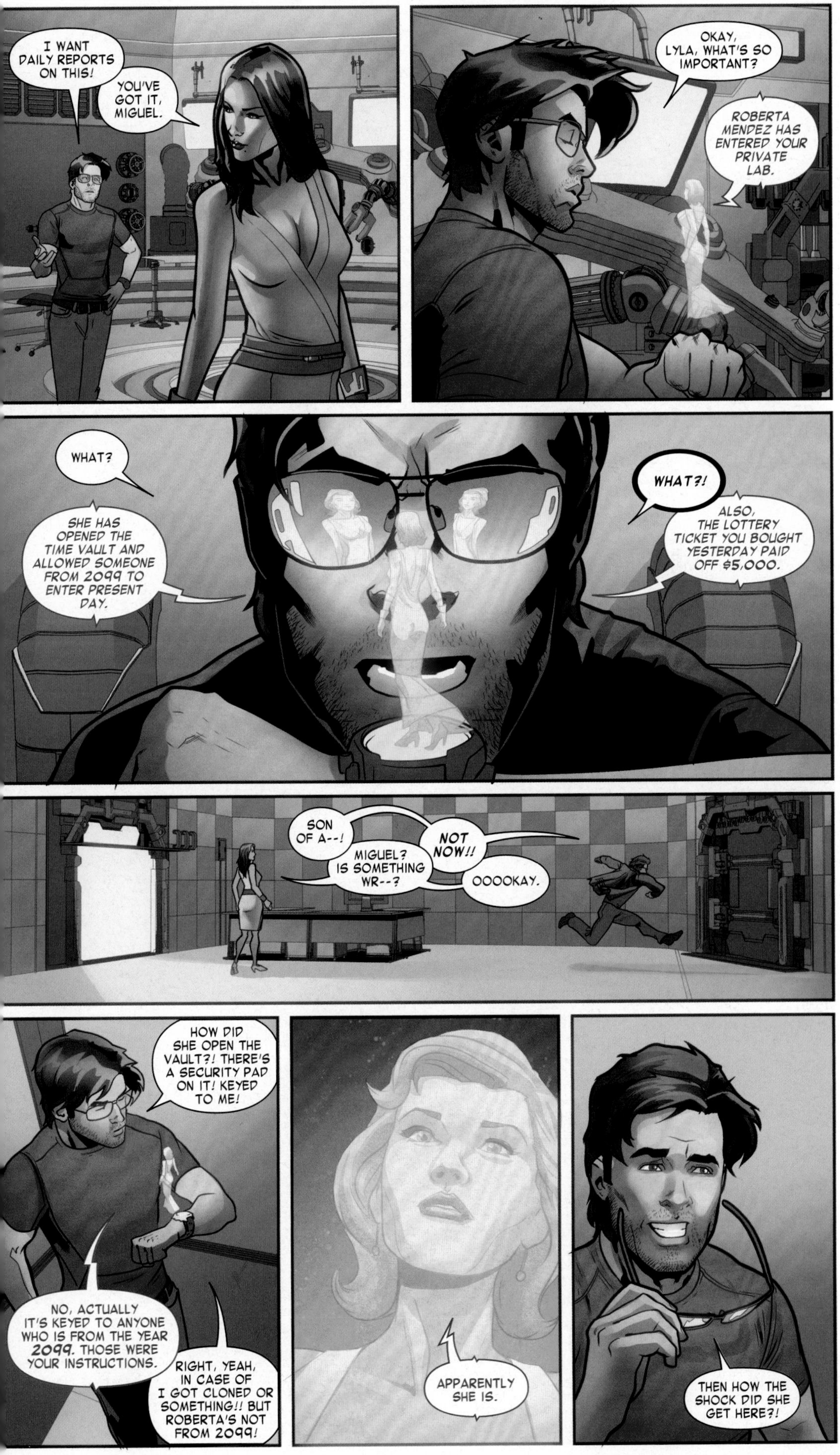
I WANT DAILY REPORTS ON THIS!
YOU'VE GOT IT, MIGUEL.
OKAY, LYLA, WHAT'S SO IMPORTANT?
ROBERTA MENDEZ HAS ENTERED YOUR PRIVATE LAB.
WHAT?
SHE HAS OPENED THE TIME VAULT AND ALLOWED SOMEONE FROM 2099 TO ENTER PRESENT DAY.
WHAT?!
ALSO, THE LOTTERY TICKET YOU BOUGHT YESTERDAY PAID OFF $5,000.
SON OF A--!
MIGUEL? IS SOMETHING WR--?
NOT NOW!!
OOOOKAY.
HOW DID SHE OPEN THE VAULT?! THERE'S A SECURITY PAD ON IT! KEYED TO ME!
NO, ACTUALLY IT'S KEYED TO ANYONE WHO IS FROM THE YEAR 2099. THOSE WERE YOUR INSTRUCTIONS.
RIGHT, YEAH, IN CASE OF I GOT CLONED OR SOMETHING!! BUT ROBERTA'S NOT FROM 2099!
APPARENTLY SHE IS.
THEN HOW THE SHOCK DID SHE GET HERE?!

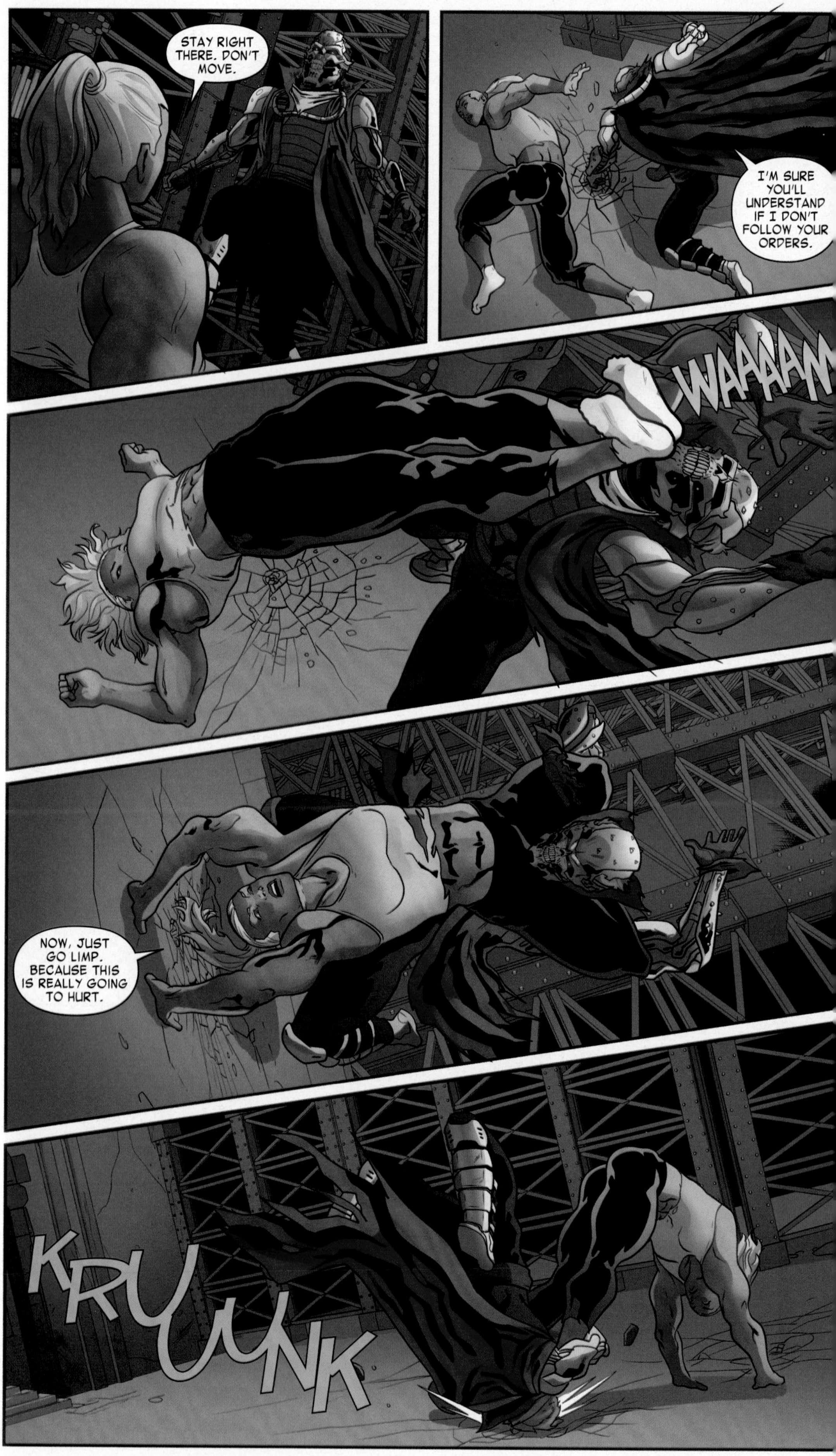

STAY RIGHT THERE. DON'T MOVE.
I'M SURE YOU'LL UNDERSTAND IF I DON'T FOLLOW YOUR ORDERS.
WAAAAM
NOW, JUST GO LIMP. BECAUSE THIS IS REALLY GOING TO HURT.
KRUUNK

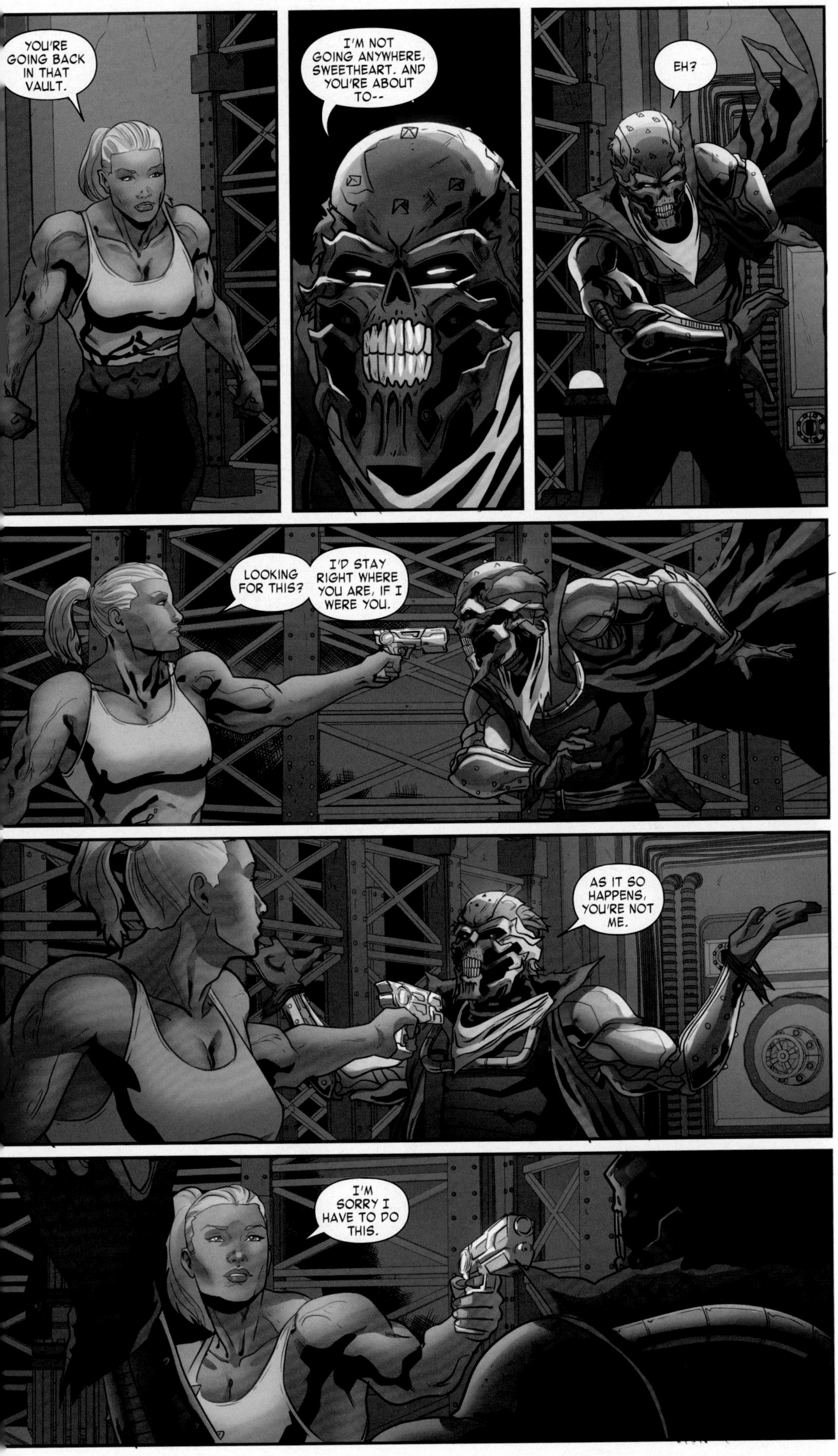
YOU'RE GOING BACK IN THAT VAULT.
I'M NOT GOING ANYWHERE, SWEETHEART. AND YOU'RE ABOUT TO--
EH?
LOOKING FOR THIS?
I'D STAY RIGHT WHERE YOU ARE, IF I WERE YOU.
AS IT SO HAPPENS, YOU'RE NOT ME.
I'M SORRY I HAVE TO DO THIS.

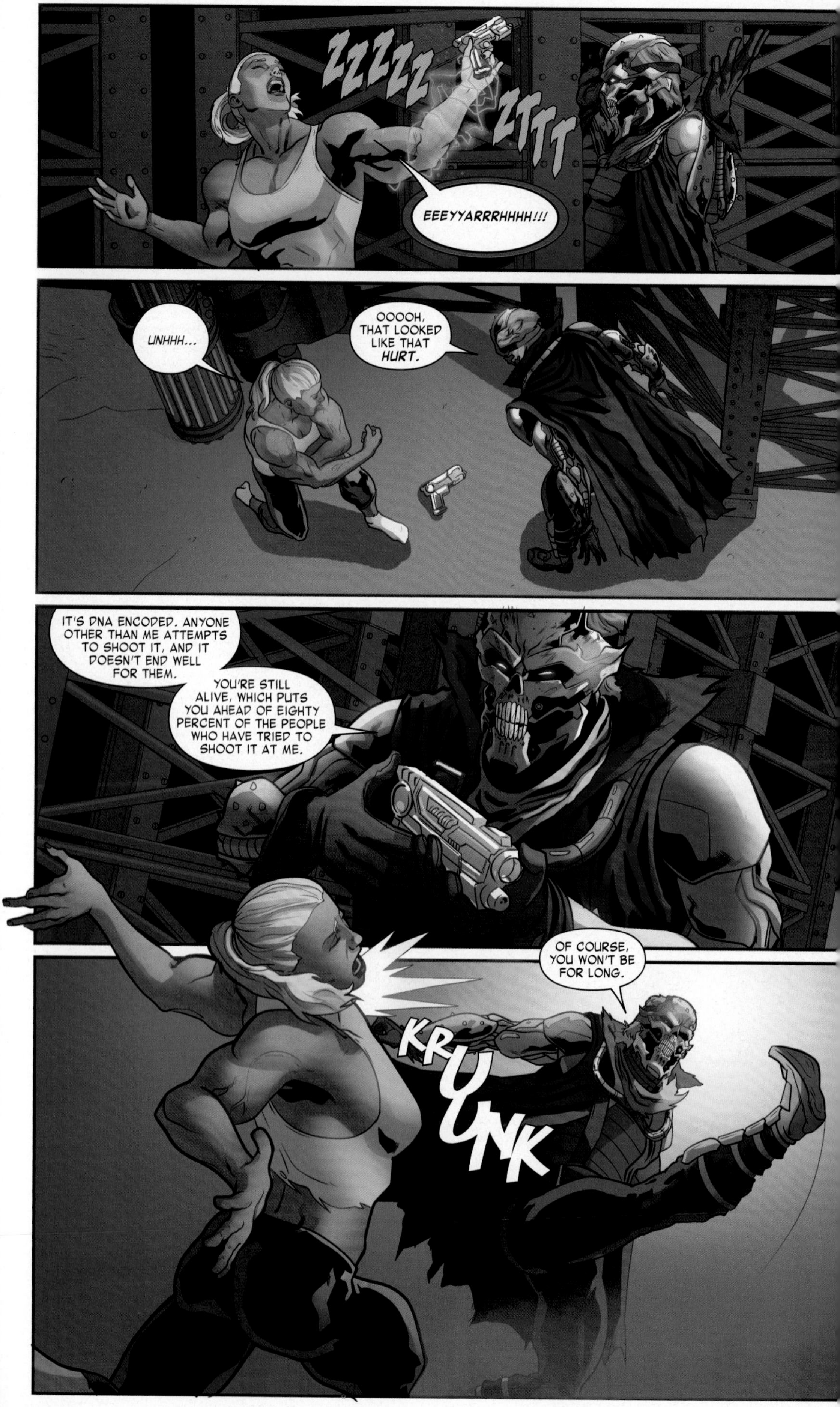
ZZZZZ ZTTTT
EEEYYARRRHHHH!!!
UNHHH...
OOOOH, THAT LOOKED LIKE THAT HURT.
IT'S DNA ENCODED. ANYONE OTHER THAN ME ATTEMPTS TO SHOOT IT, AND IT DOESN'T END WELL FOR THEM.
YOU'RE STILL ALIVE, WHICH PUTS YOU AHEAD OF EIGHTY PERCENT OF THE PEOPLE WHO HAVE TRIED TO SHOOT IT AT ME.
OF COURSE, YOU WON'T BE FOR LONG.
KRUUNK

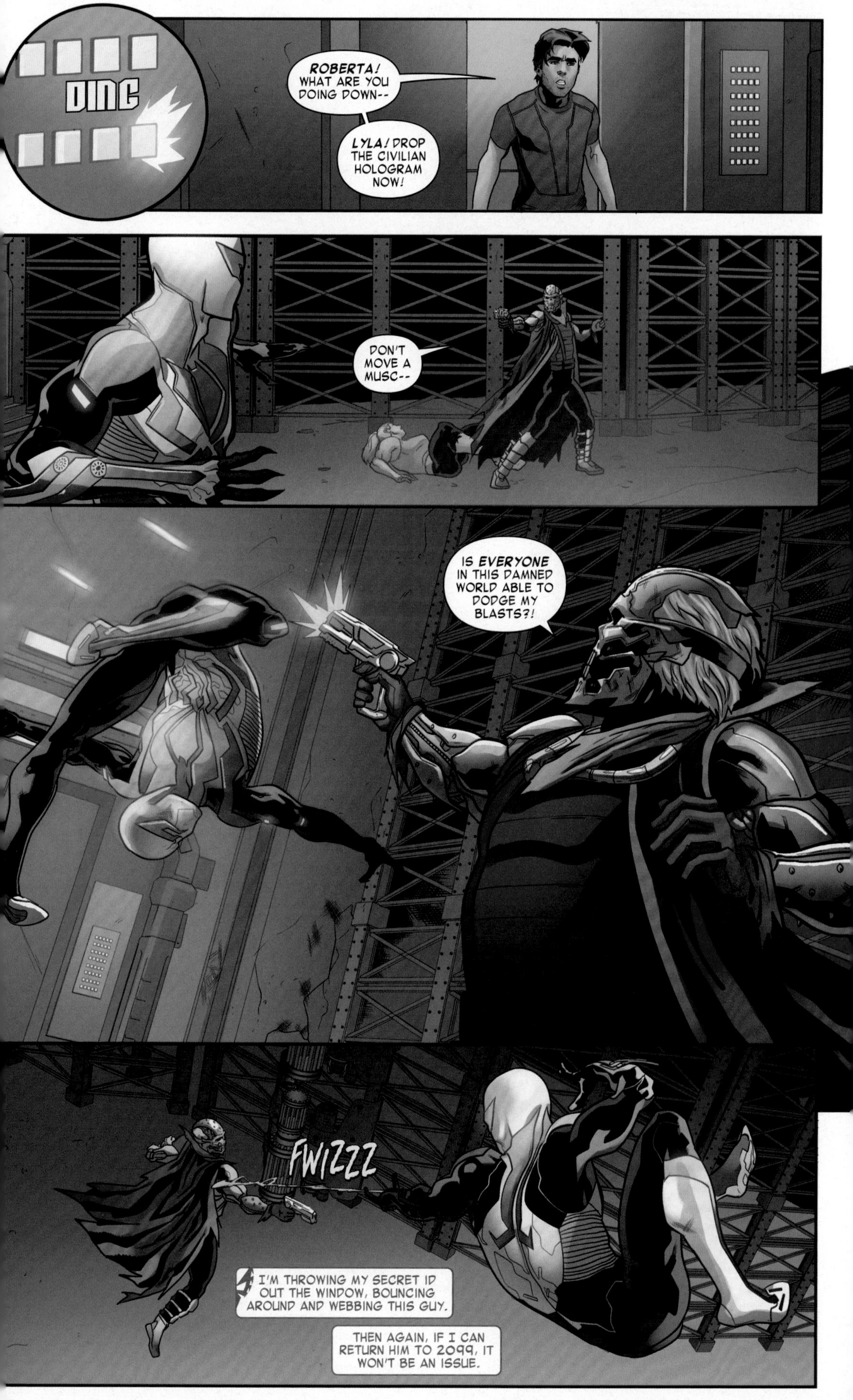
DING
ROBERTA! WHAT ARE YOU DOING DOWN--
LYLA! DROP THE CIVILIAN HOLOGRAM NOW!
DON'T MOVE A MUSC--
IS EVERYONE IN THIS DAMNED WORLD ABLE TO DODGE MY BLASTS?!
FWIZZZ
I'M THROWING MY SECRET ID OUT THE WINDOW, BOUNCING AROUND AND WEBBING THIS GUY.
THEN AGAIN, IF I CAN RETURN HIM TO 2099, IT WON'T BE AN ISSUE.

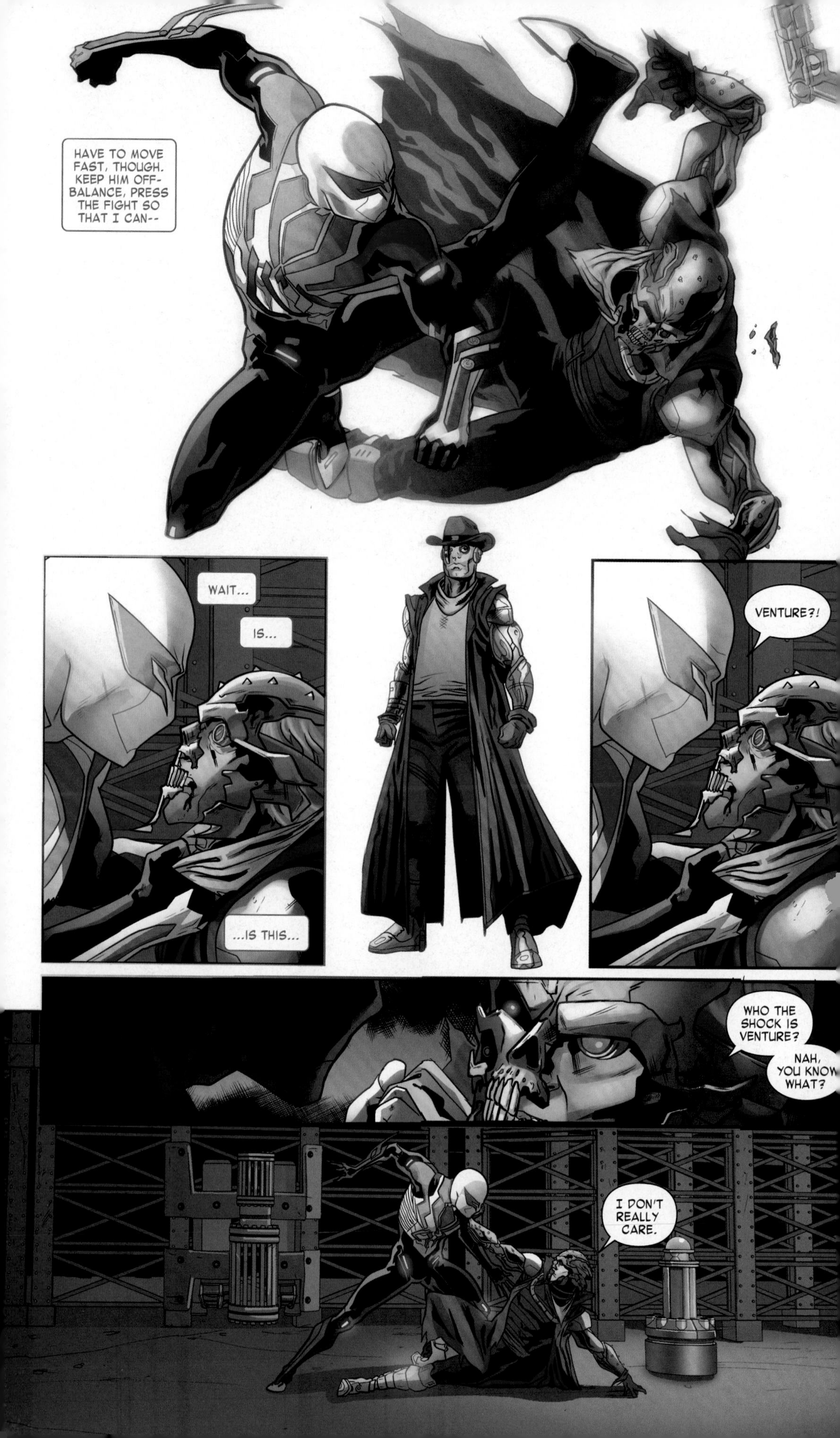
HAVE TO MOVE FAST, THOUGH. KEEP HIM OFF-BALANCE, PRESS THE FIGHT SO THAT I CAN--
WAIT...
IS...
...IS THIS...
VENTURE?!
WHO THE SHOCK IS VENTURE?
NAH, YOU KNOW WHAT?
I DON'T REALLY CARE.

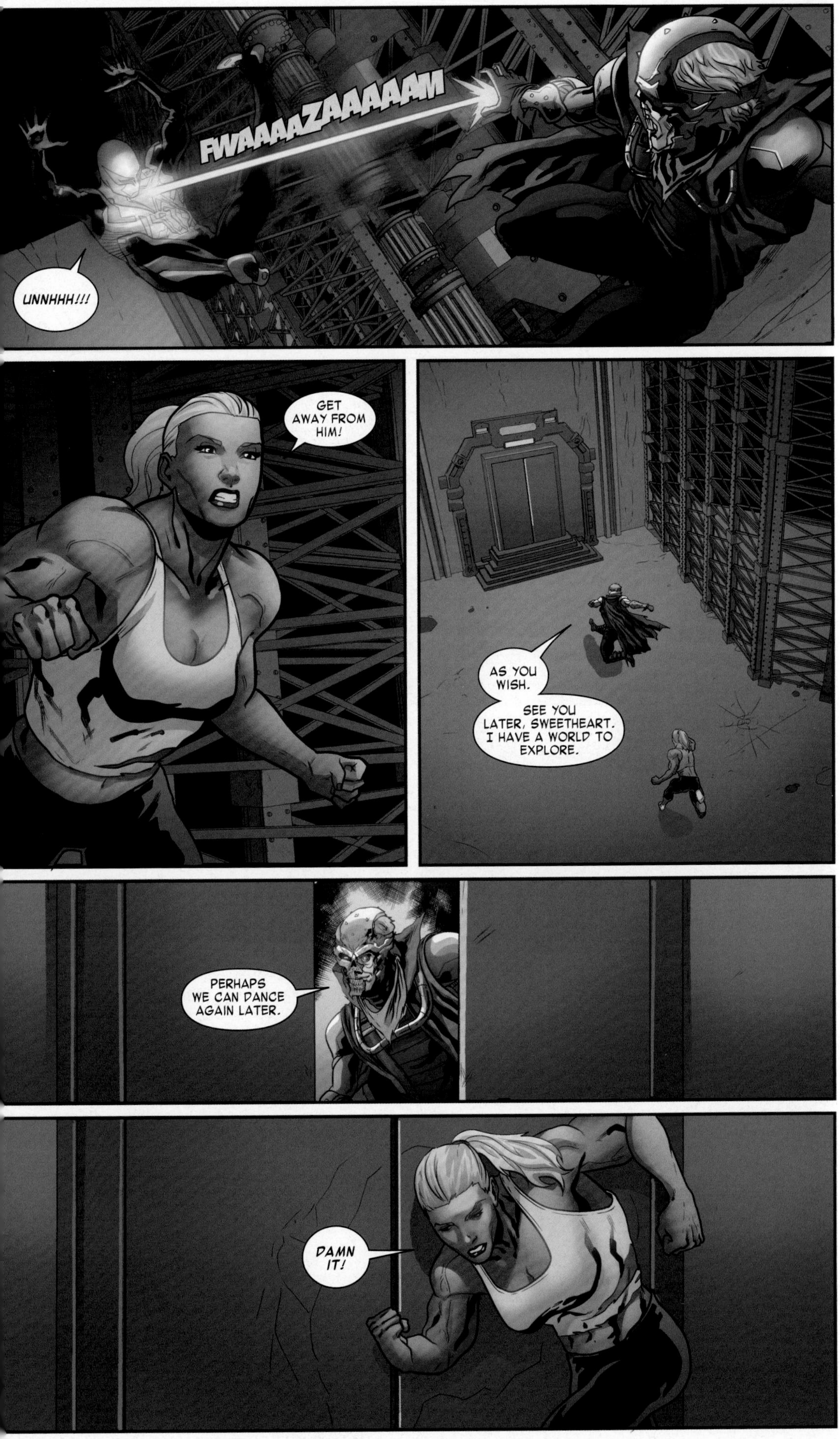
FWAAAAZAAAAAM
UNNHHH!!!
GET AWAY FROM HIM!
AS YOU WISH.
SEE YOU LATER, SWEETHEART. I HAVE A WORLD TO EXPLORE.
PERHAPS WE CAN DANCE AGAIN LATER.
DAMN IT!

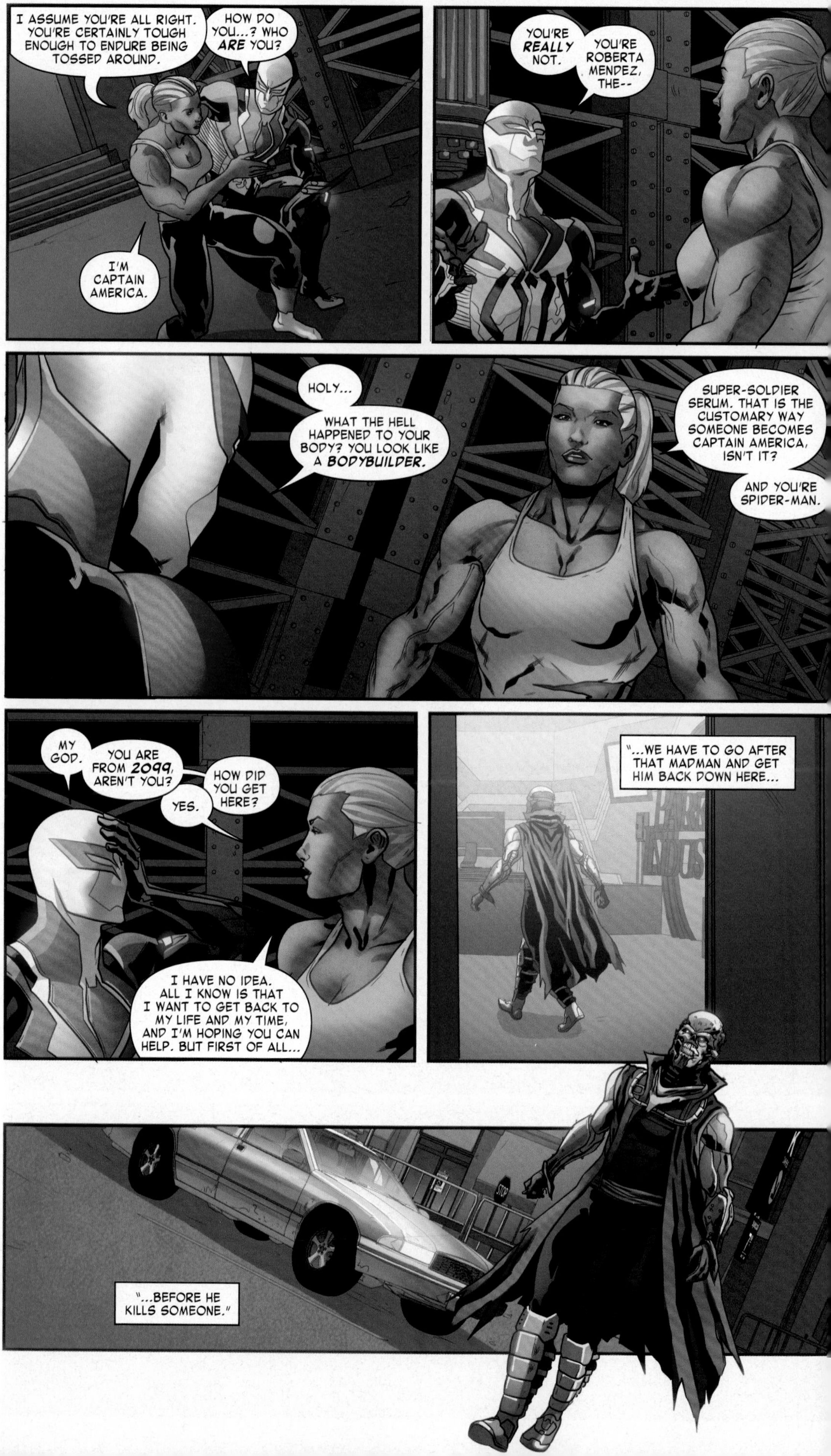
I ASSUME YOU'RE ALL RIGHT. YOU'RE CERTAINLY TOUGH ENOUGH TO ENDURE BEING TOSSED AROUND.
HOW DO YOU...? WHO ARE YOU?
I'M CAPTAIN AMERICA.
YOU'RE REALLY NOT.
YOU'RE ROBERTA MENDEZ, THE--
HOLY...
WHAT THE HELL HAPPENED TO YOUR BODY? YOU LOOK LIKE A BODYBUILDER.
SUPER-SOLDIER SERUM. THAT IS THE CUSTOMARY WAY SOMEONE BECOMES CAPTAIN AMERICA, ISN'T IT?
AND YOU'RE SPIDER-MAN.
MY GOD.
YOU ARE FROM 2099, AREN'T YOU?
YES.
HOW DID YOU GET HERE?
I HAVE NO IDEA. ALL I KNOW IS THAT I WANT TO GET BACK TO MY LIFE AND MY TIME, AND I'M HOPING YOU CAN HELP. BUT FIRST OF ALL...
"...WE HAVE TO GO AFTER THAT MADMAN AND GET HIM BACK DOWN HERE...
"...BEFORE HE KILLS SOMEONE."

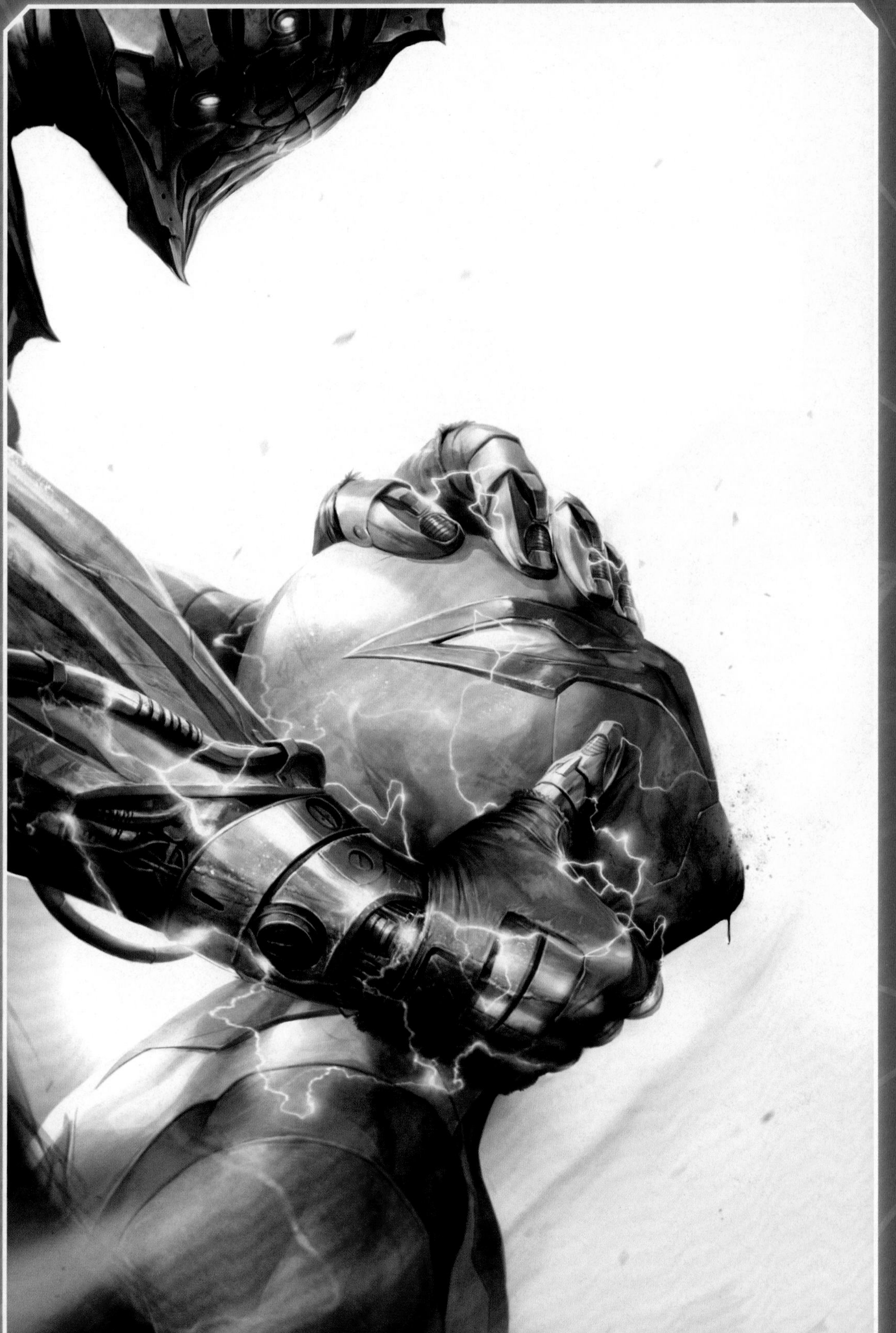

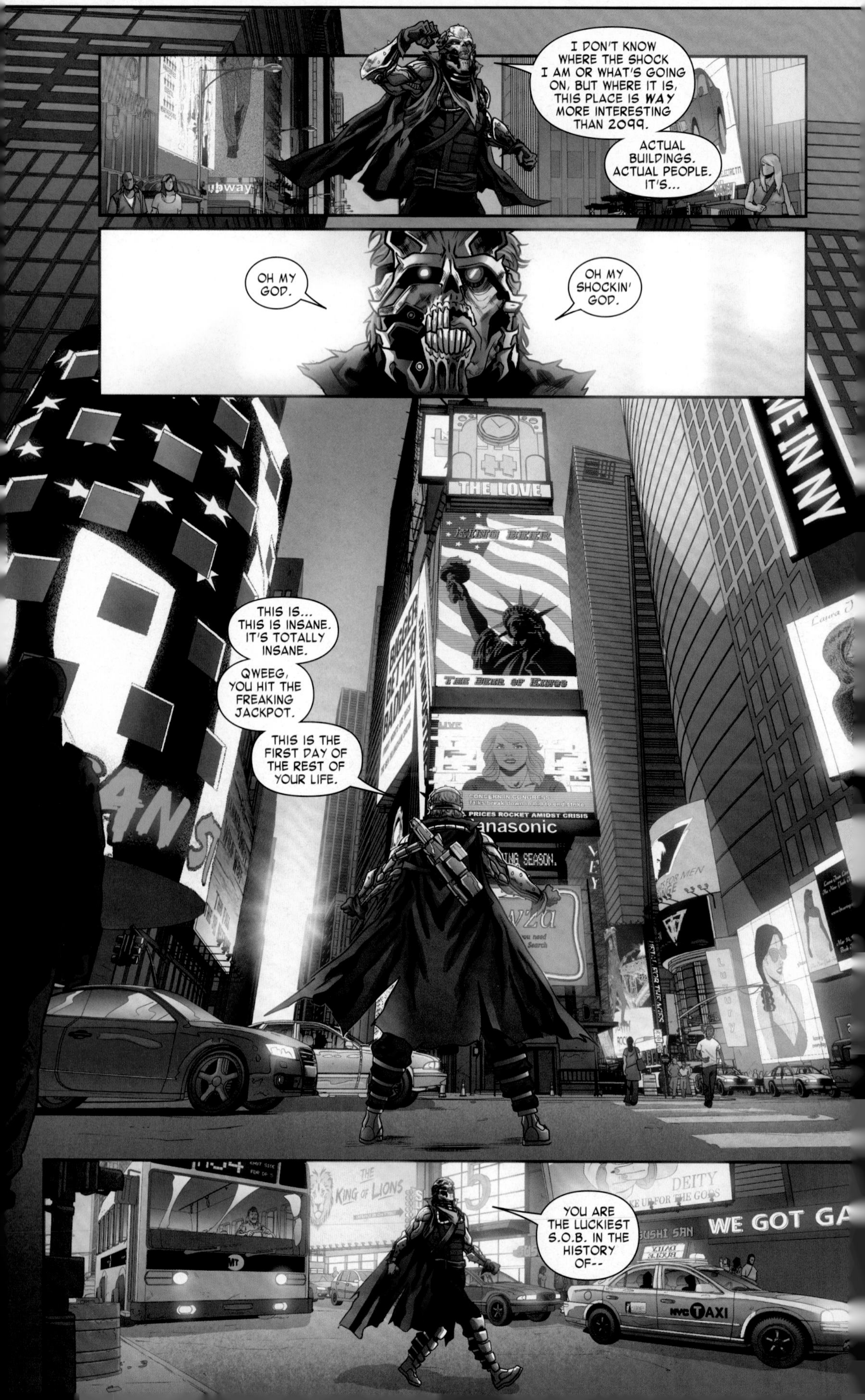
I DON'T KNOW WHERE THE SHOCK I AM OR WHAT'S GOING ON, BUT WHERE IT IS, THIS PLACE IS WAY MORE INTERESTING THAN 2099.
ACTUAL BUILDINGS. ACTUAL PEOPLE. IT'S...
OH MY GOD.
OH MY SHOCKIN' GOD.
THE LOVE
KING BEER
THE BEER OF KINGS
THIS IS... THIS IS INSANE. IT'S TOTALLY INSANE.
QWEEG, YOU HIT THE FREAKING JACKPOT.
THIS IS THE FIRST DAY OF THE REST OF YOUR LIFE.
CONCERN IN CONGRESS
PRICES ROCKET AMIDST CRISIS
Panasonic
YOU ARE THE LUCKIEST S.O.B. IN THE HISTORY OF--
THE KING of LIONS
DEITY
WE GOT GA
SUSHI SAN
NYC TAXI

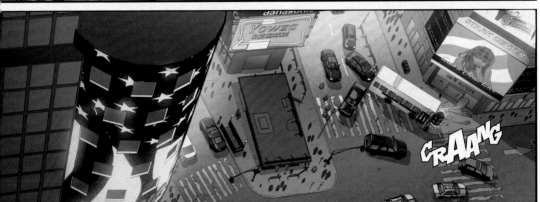

CRAANG

HOLY CRAP! HE RAN RIGHT IN FRONT OF ME!

WHAT AN IDIOT!

IS HE OKAY?! TELL ME HE'S OKAY!

WHAT'S WITH HIS ARM?

IT'S SOME KIND OF PROSTHETIC.

THINK HE WAS A SOLDIER?

MAYBE. THAT WOULD EXPLAIN--

LOOK AT THE SIZE OF THAT GUN.

AND HE'S GOT ANOTHER ONE STRAPPED ON HIS BACK!

MAYBE HE'S A COP!

OR FROM TEXAS.

YEAH, 9-1-1? WE GOT AN ACCIDENT VICTIM IN TIMES SQUARE.

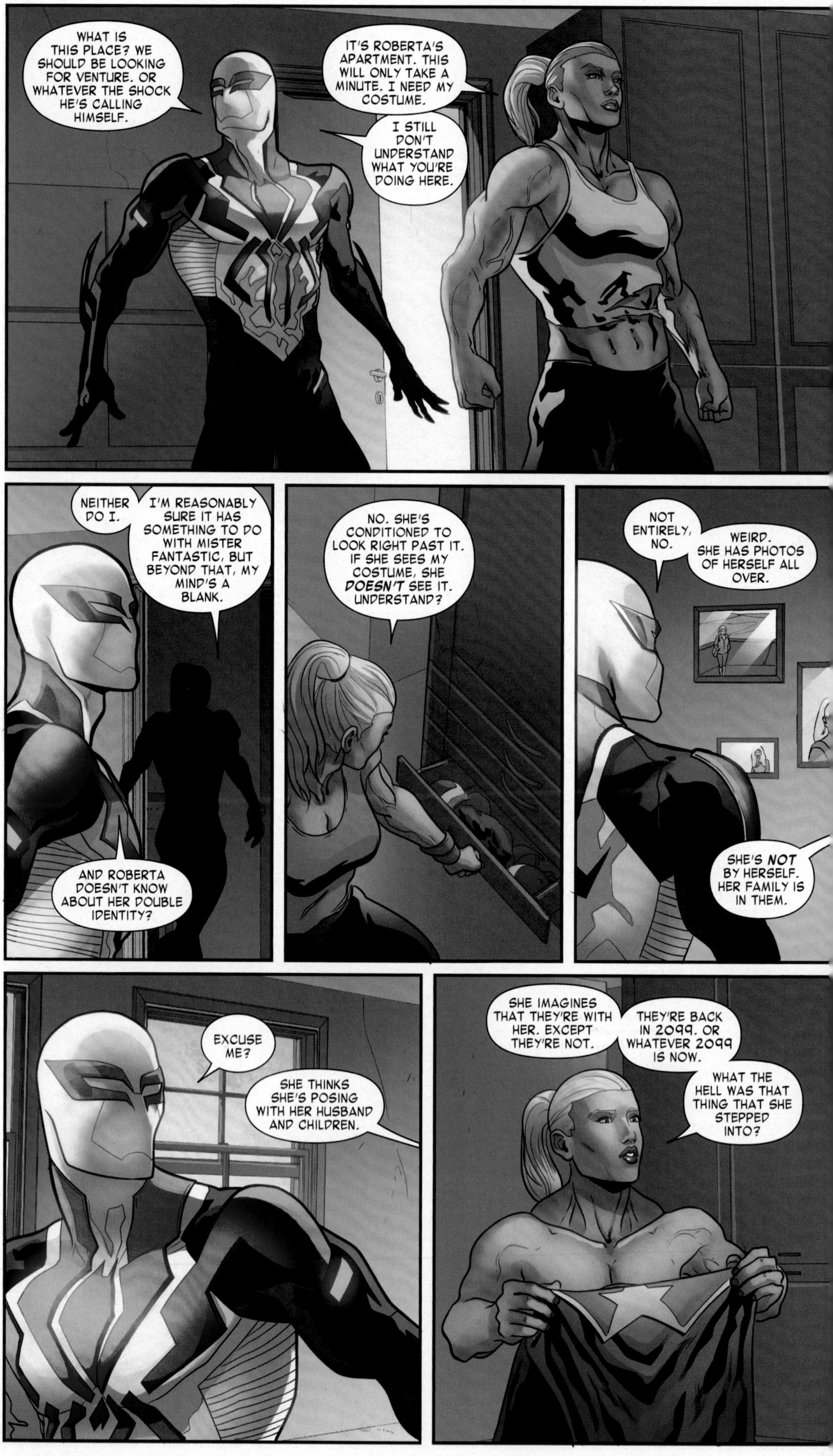
WHAT IS THIS PLACE? WE SHOULD BE LOOKING FOR VENTURE. OR WHATEVER THE SHOCK HE'S CALLING HIMSELF.
IT'S ROBERTA'S APARTMENT. THIS WILL ONLY TAKE A MINUTE. I NEED MY COSTUME.
I STILL DON'T UNDERSTAND WHAT YOU'RE DOING HERE.
NEITHER DO I.
I'M REASONABLY SURE IT HAS SOMETHING TO DO WITH MISTER FANTASTIC, BUT BEYOND THAT, MY MIND'S A BLANK.
AND ROBERTA DOESN'T KNOW ABOUT HER DOUBLE IDENTITY?
NO. SHE'S CONDITIONED TO LOOK RIGHT PAST IT. IF SHE SEES MY COSTUME, SHE *DOESN'T* SEE IT. UNDERSTAND?
NOT ENTIRELY, NO.
WEIRD. SHE HAS PHOTOS OF HERSELF ALL OVER.
SHE'S **NOT** BY HERSELF. HER FAMILY IS IN THEM.
EXCUSE ME?
SHE THINKS SHE'S POSING WITH HER HUSBAND AND CHILDREN.
SHE IMAGINES THAT THEY'RE WITH HER. EXCEPT THEY'RE NOT.
THEY'RE BACK IN 2099. OR WHATEVER 2099 IS NOW.
WHAT THE HELL WAS THAT THING THAT SHE STEPPED INTO?

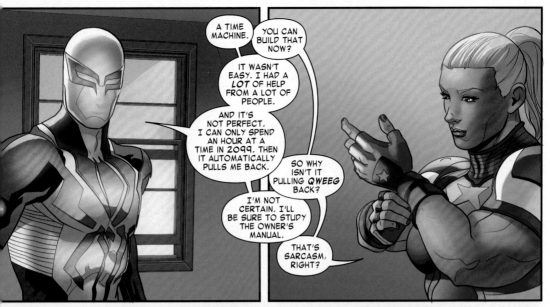

A TIME MACHINE.

YOU CAN BUILD THAT NOW?

IT WASN'T EASY. I HAD A *LOT* OF HELP FROM A LOT OF PEOPLE.

AND IT'S NOT PERFECT. I CAN ONLY SPEND AN HOUR AT A TIME IN 2099. THEN IT AUTOMATICALLY PULLS ME BACK.

SO WHY ISN'T IT PULLING *QWEEG* BACK?

I'M NOT CERTAIN. I'LL BE SURE TO STUDY THE OWNER'S MANUAL.

THAT'S SARCASM, RIGHT?

I'VE BEEN KNOWN TO INDULGE, YES. SO WHO *ARE* YOU?

YOU DON'T REMEMBER?

AM I SUPPOSED TO?

WE MET SEVERAL YEARS AGO. YOU WERE A SCIENTIST AT ALCHEMAX. I WAS A TEST SUBJECT.

YOU MADE A PASS AT ME, MIGUEL.

OH MY GOD. THAT WAS *YOU*?

THAT WAS ME. YOU SEEM LIKE MUCH LESS OF A BASTARD THAN YOU WERE.

WELL, THAT'S GOOD TO KNOW.

WAIT, YOU KNOW I'M MIGUEL O'HARA?

YES, I SAW YOUR FACE BEFORE YOU ACTIVATED YOUR COSTUME AT PARKER INDUSTRIES.

WHEN QWEEG FIRST CAME THROUGH THE TIME VAULT? THAT WAS ONLY FOR A *SECOND!* YOU RECOGNIZED ME THAT QUICKLY?

YOU'RE MEMORABLE.

NOT SURE IF THAT'S A COMPLIMENT OR NOT...

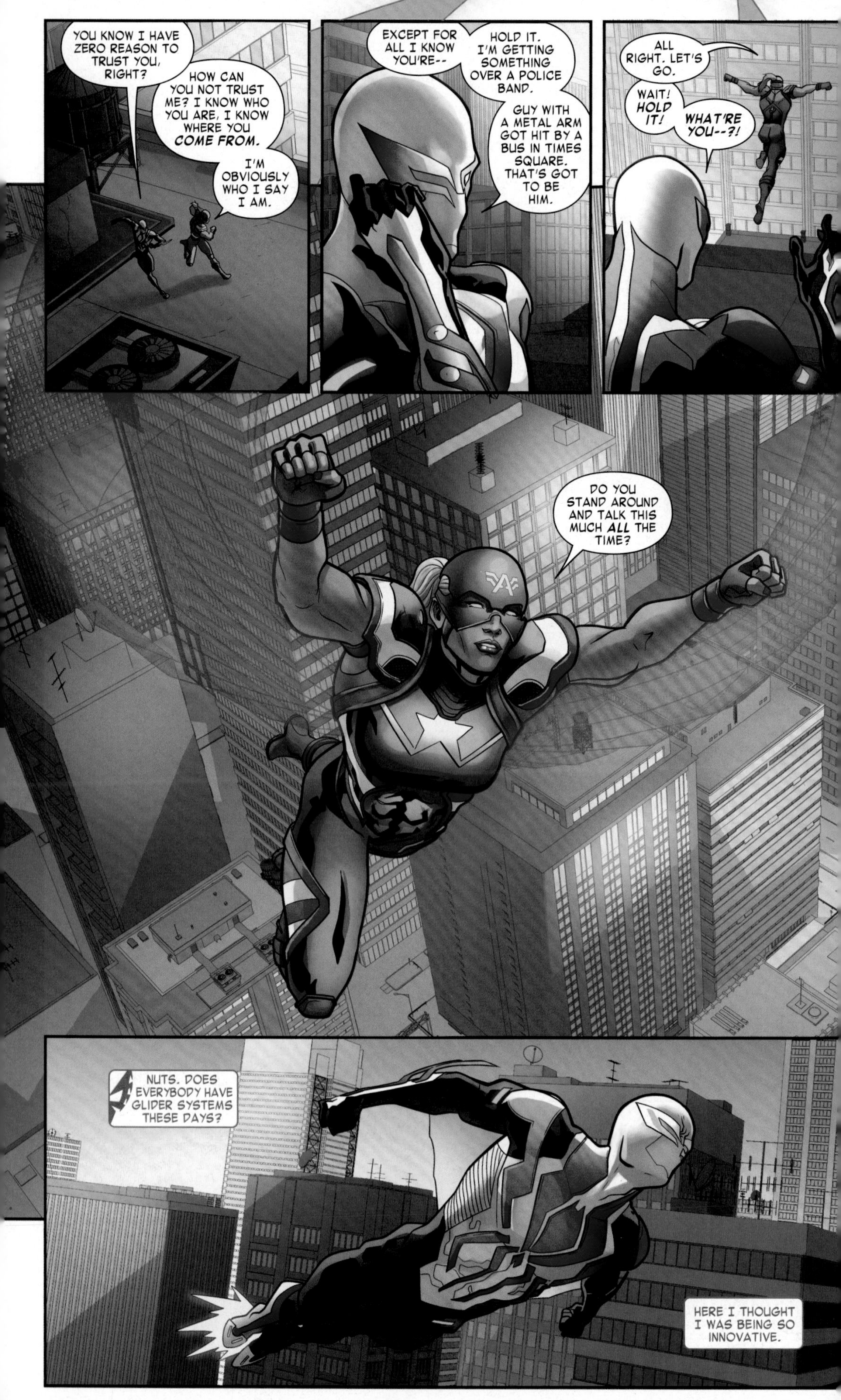
YOU KNOW I HAVE ZERO REASON TO TRUST YOU, RIGHT?
HOW CAN YOU NOT TRUST ME? I KNOW WHO YOU ARE, I KNOW WHERE YOU COME FROM.
I'M OBVIOUSLY WHO I SAY I AM.
EXCEPT FOR ALL I KNOW YOU'RE--
HOLD IT. I'M GETTING SOMETHING OVER A POLICE BAND.
GUY WITH A METAL ARM GOT HIT BY A BUS IN TIMES SQUARE. THAT'S GOT TO BE HIM.
ALL RIGHT. LET'S GO.
WAIT! HOLD IT!
WHAT'RE YOU--?!
DO YOU STAND AROUND AND TALK THIS MUCH ALL THE TIME?
NUTS. DOES EVERYBODY HAVE GLIDER SYSTEMS THESE DAYS?
HERE I THOUGHT I WAS BEING SO INNOVATIVE.

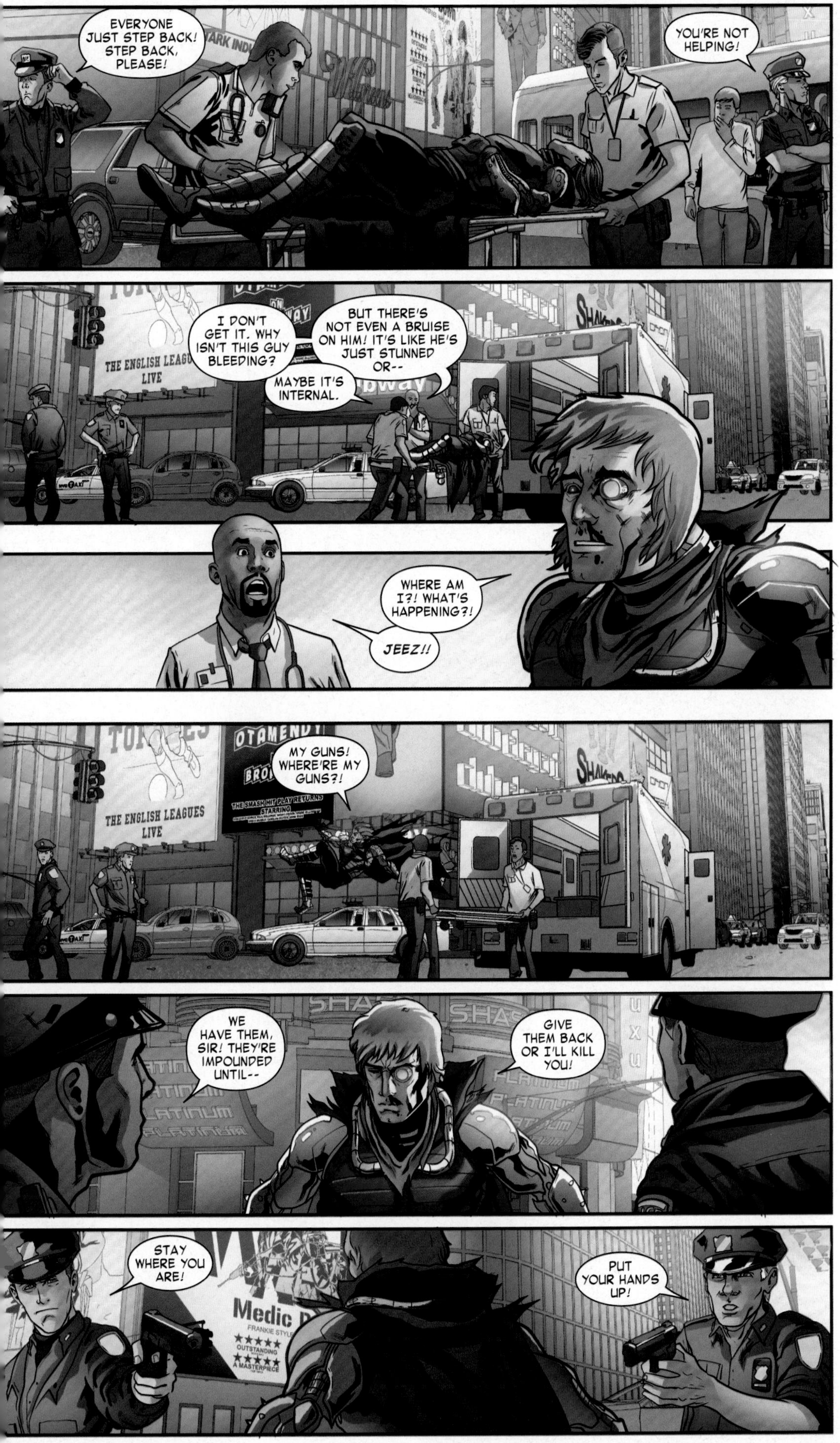
EVERYONE JUST STEP BACK! STEP BACK, PLEASE!
YOU'RE NOT HELPING!
THE ENGLISH LEAGUES LIVE
I DON'T GET IT. WHY ISN'T THIS GUY BLEEDING?
BUT THERE'S NOT EVEN A BRUISE ON HIM! IT'S LIKE HE'S JUST STUNNED OR--
MAYBE IT'S INTERNAL.
WHERE AM I?! WHAT'S HAPPENING?!
JEEZ!!
OTAMENDY
THE SMASH HIT PLAY RETURNS
STARRING
THE ENGLISH LEAGUES LIVE
MY GUNS! WHERE'RE MY GUNS?!
WE HAVE THEM, SIR! THEY'RE IMPOUNDED UNTIL--
GIVE THEM BACK OR I'LL KILL YOU!
STAY WHERE YOU ARE!
PUT YOUR HANDS UP!
Medic
OUTSTANDING
A MASTERPIECE

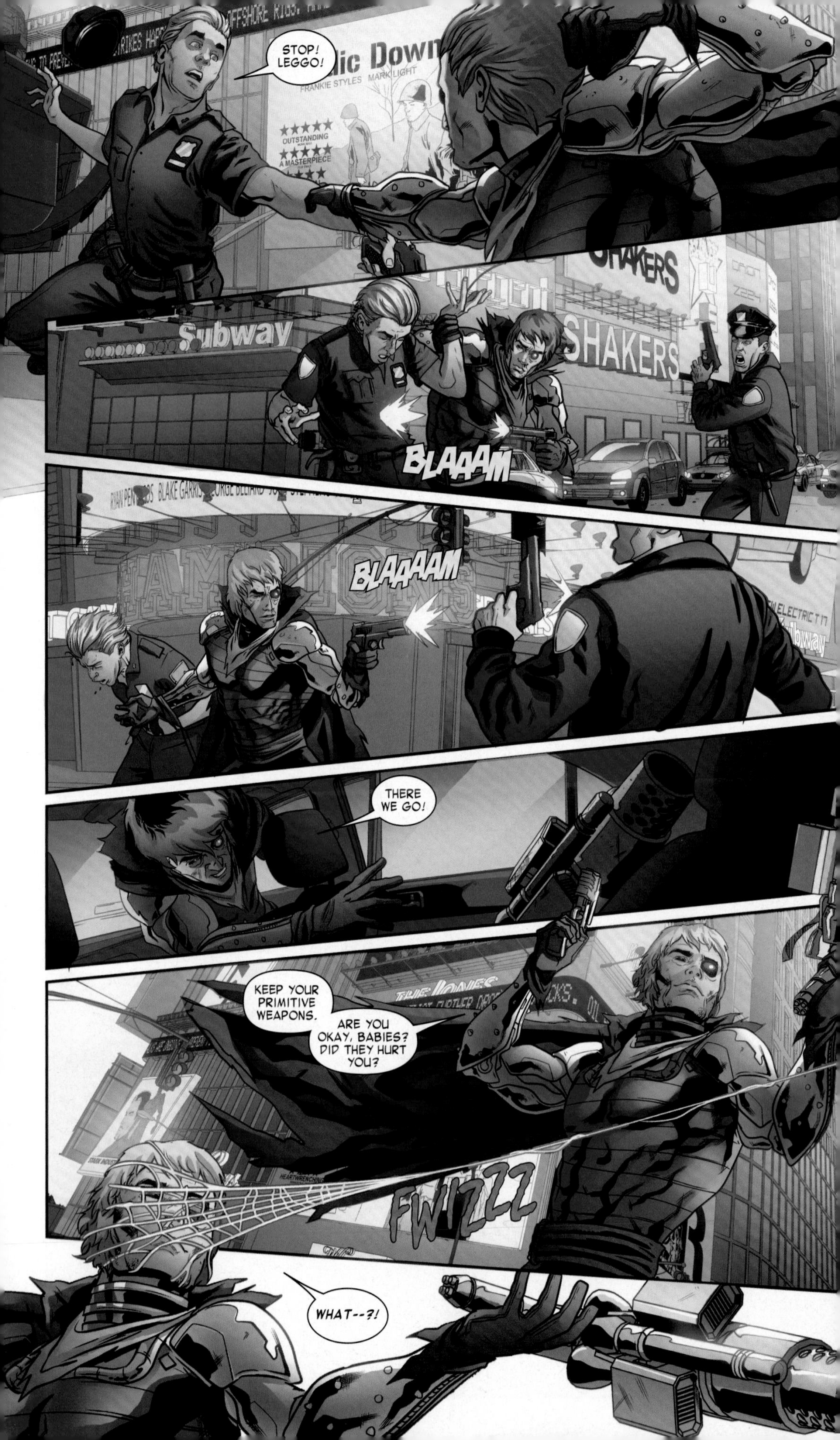
STOP! LEGGO!
BLAAAM
BLAAAAM
THERE WE GO!
KEEP YOUR PRIMITIVE WEAPONS.
ARE YOU OKAY, BABIES? DID THEY HURT YOU?
FWIZZZ
WHAT--?!

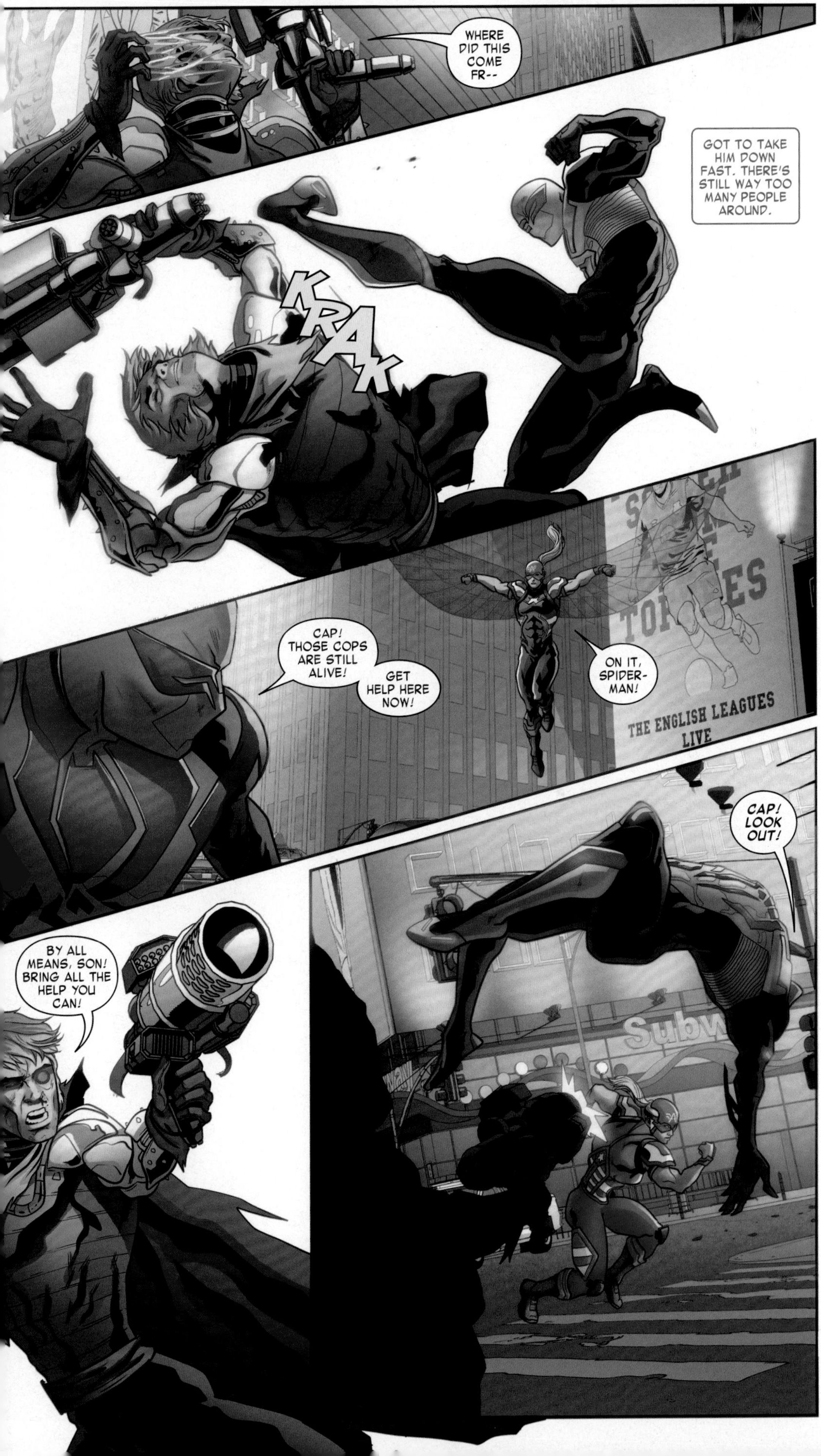
WHERE DID THIS COME FR--
GOT TO TAKE HIM DOWN FAST. THERE'S STILL WAY TOO MANY PEOPLE AROUND.
KRAK
CAP! THOSE COPS ARE STILL ALIVE!
GET HELP HERE NOW!
ON IT, SPIDER-MAN!
THE ENGLISH LEAGUES LIVE
CAP! LOOK OUT!
BY ALL MEANS, SON! BRING ALL THE HELP YOU CAN!

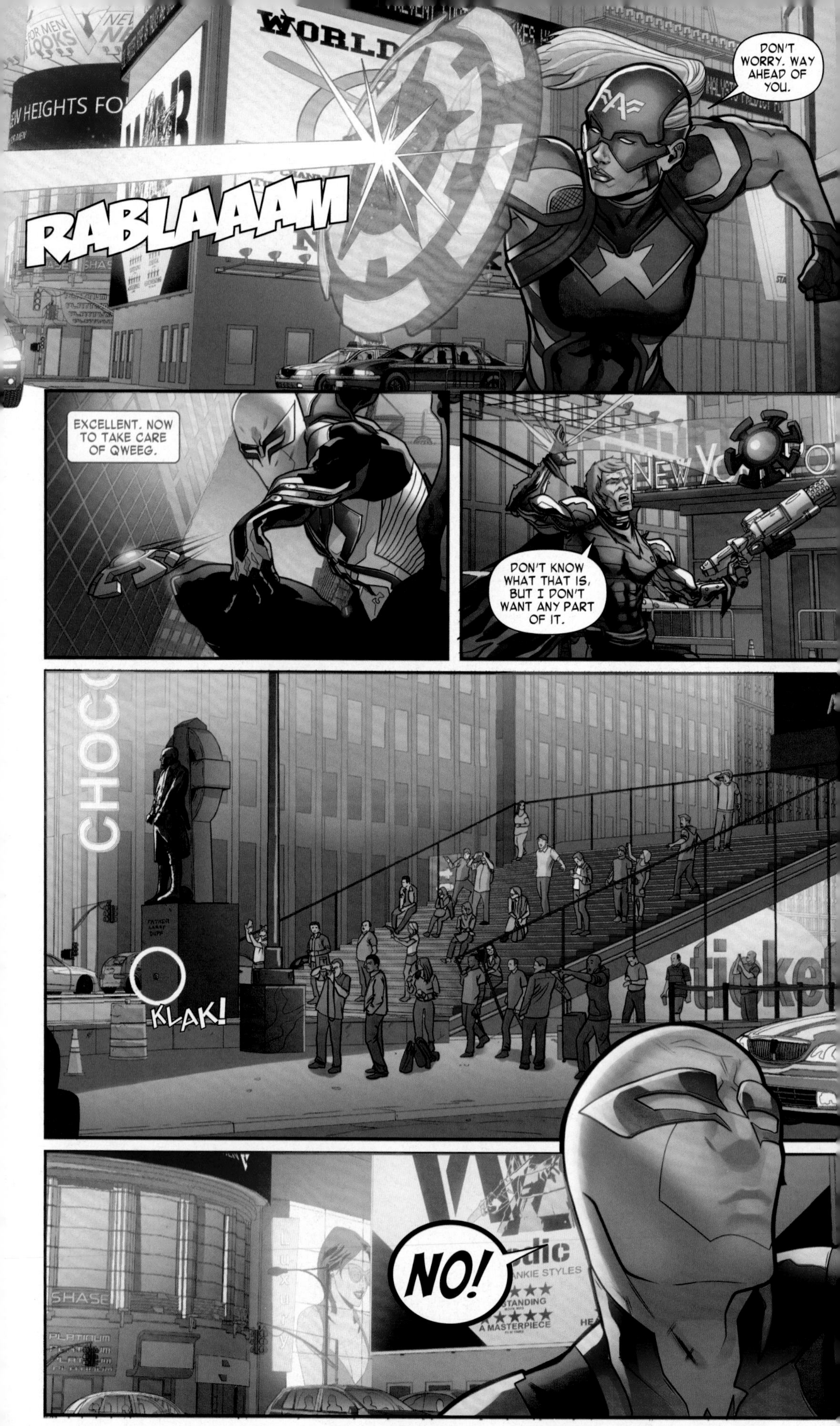
RABLAAAM
DON'T WORRY. WAY AHEAD OF YOU.
EXCELLENT. NOW TO TAKE CARE OF QWEEG.
DON'T KNOW WHAT THAT IS, BUT I DON'T WANT ANY PART OF IT.
KLAK!
NO!

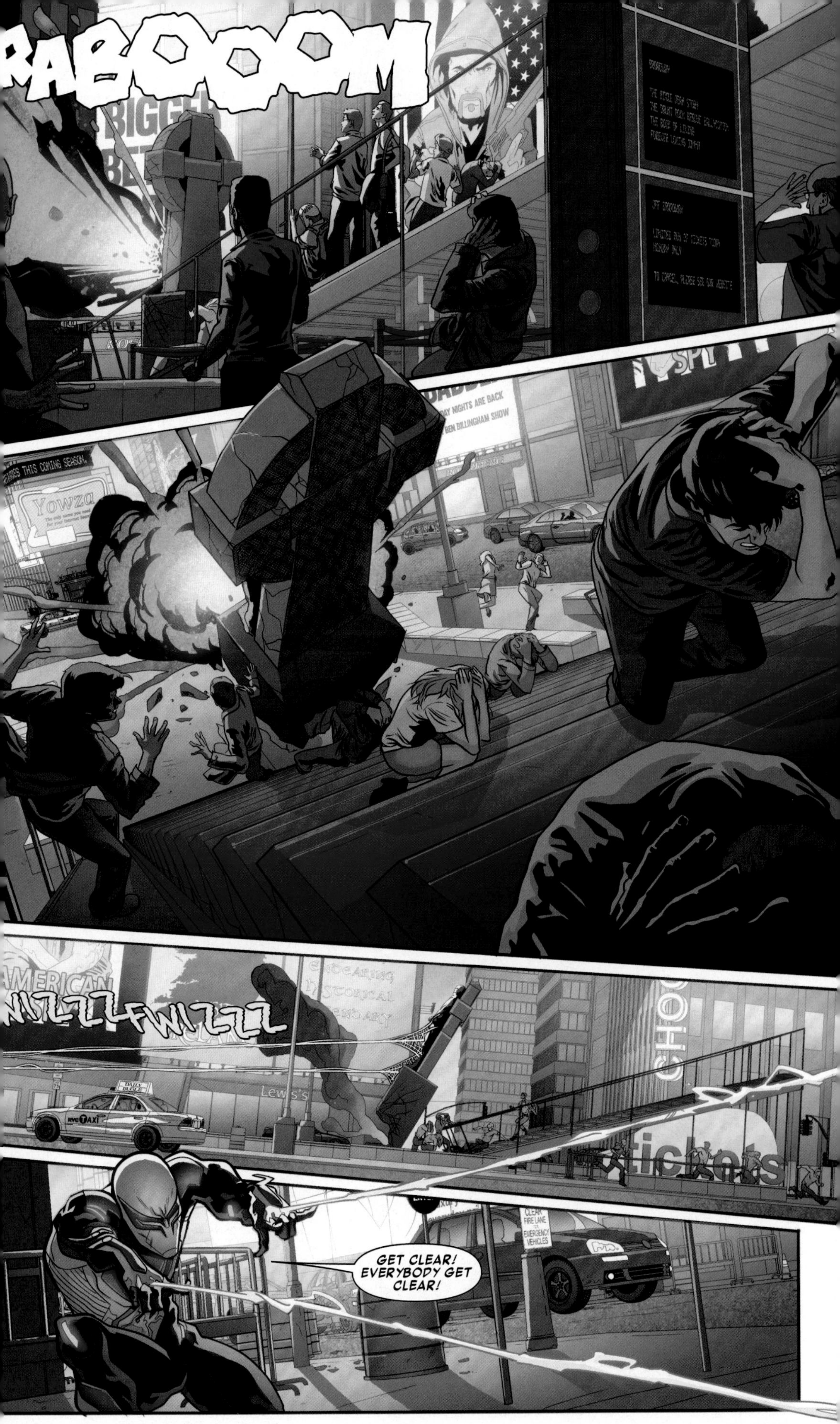
RABOOOM
FWIZZZ FWIZZZ
GET CLEAR! EVERYBODY GET CLEAR!

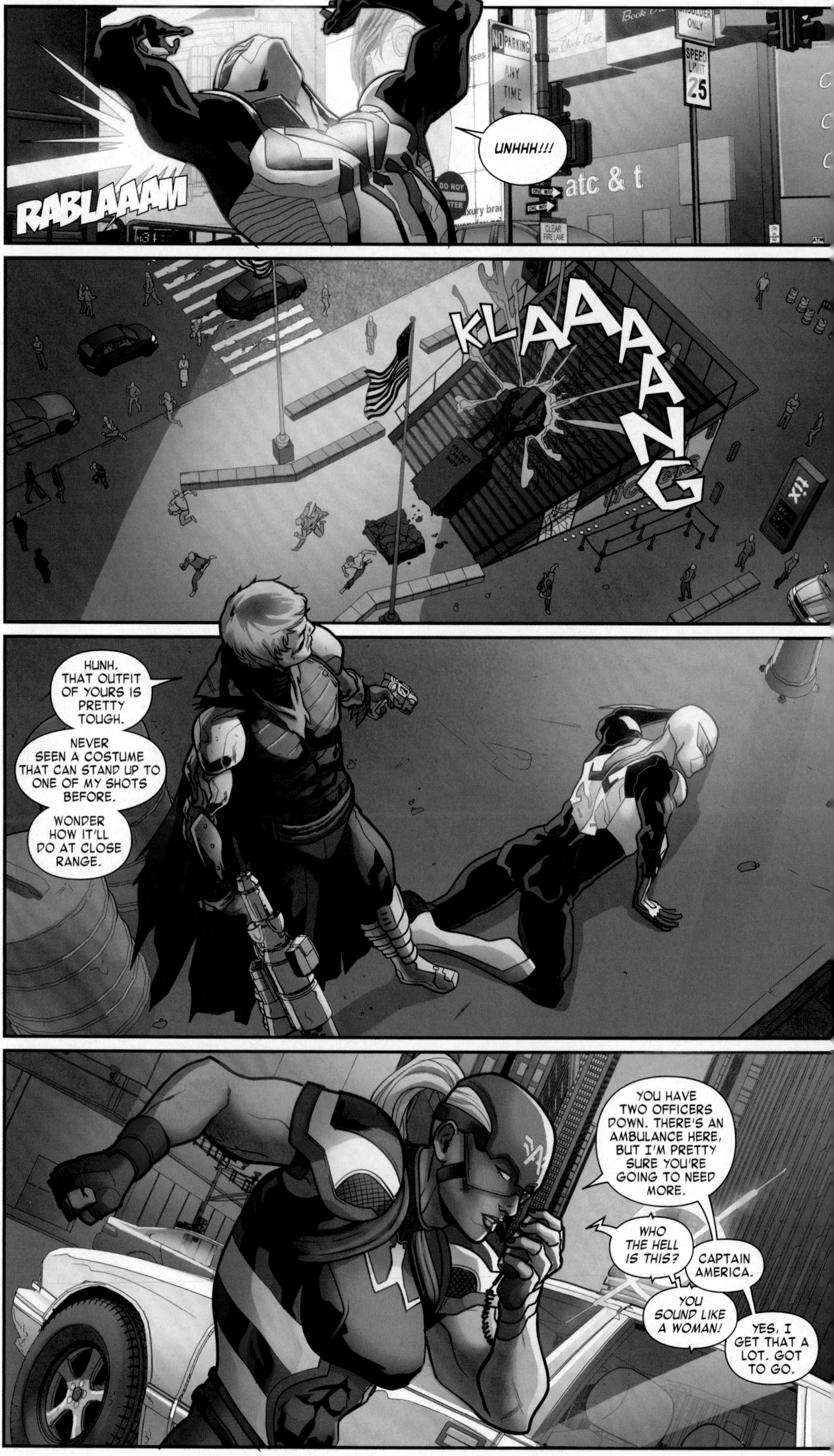
RABLAAAM
UNHHH!!!
NO PARKING ANY TIME
SPEED LIMIT 25
ONE WAY
CLEAR FIRE LANE
DO NOT ENTER
atc & t
KLAAAAAANG
HUNH. THAT OUTFIT OF YOURS IS PRETTY TOUGH.
NEVER SEEN A COSTUME THAT CAN STAND UP TO ONE OF MY SHOTS BEFORE.
WONDER HOW IT'LL DO AT CLOSE RANGE.
YOU HAVE TWO OFFICERS DOWN. THERE'S AN AMBULANCE HERE, BUT I'M PRETTY SURE YOU'RE GOING TO NEED MORE.
WHO THE HELL IS THIS?
CAPTAIN AMERICA.
YOU SOUND LIKE A WOMAN!
YES, I GET THAT A LOT. GOT TO GO.

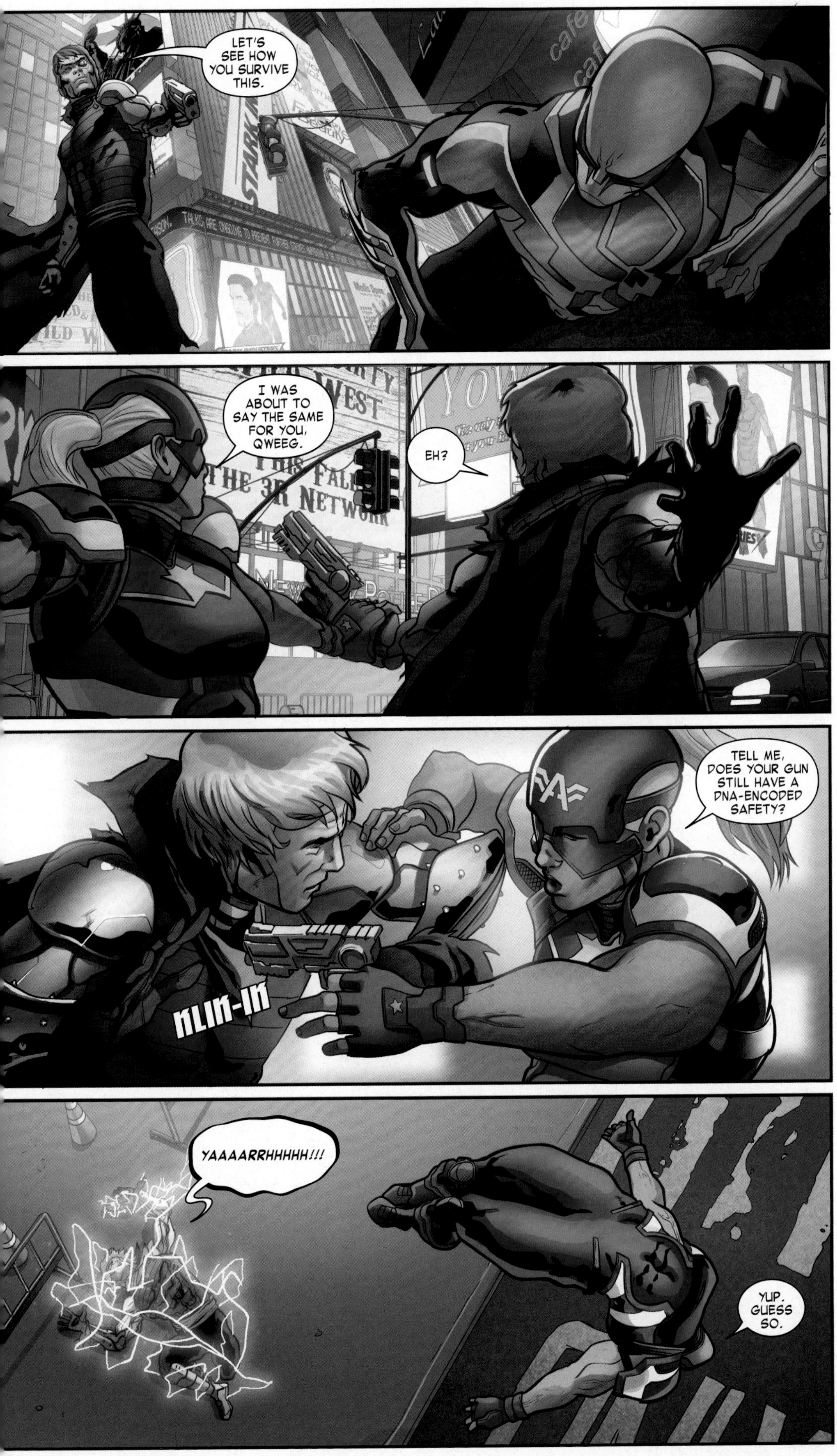
LET'S SEE HOW YOU SURVIVE THIS.
I WAS ABOUT TO SAY THE SAME FOR YOU, QWEEG.
EH?
TELL ME, DOES YOUR GUN STILL HAVE A DNA-ENCODED SAFETY?
KLIK-IK
YAAAARRHHHHH!!!
YUP. GUESS SO.

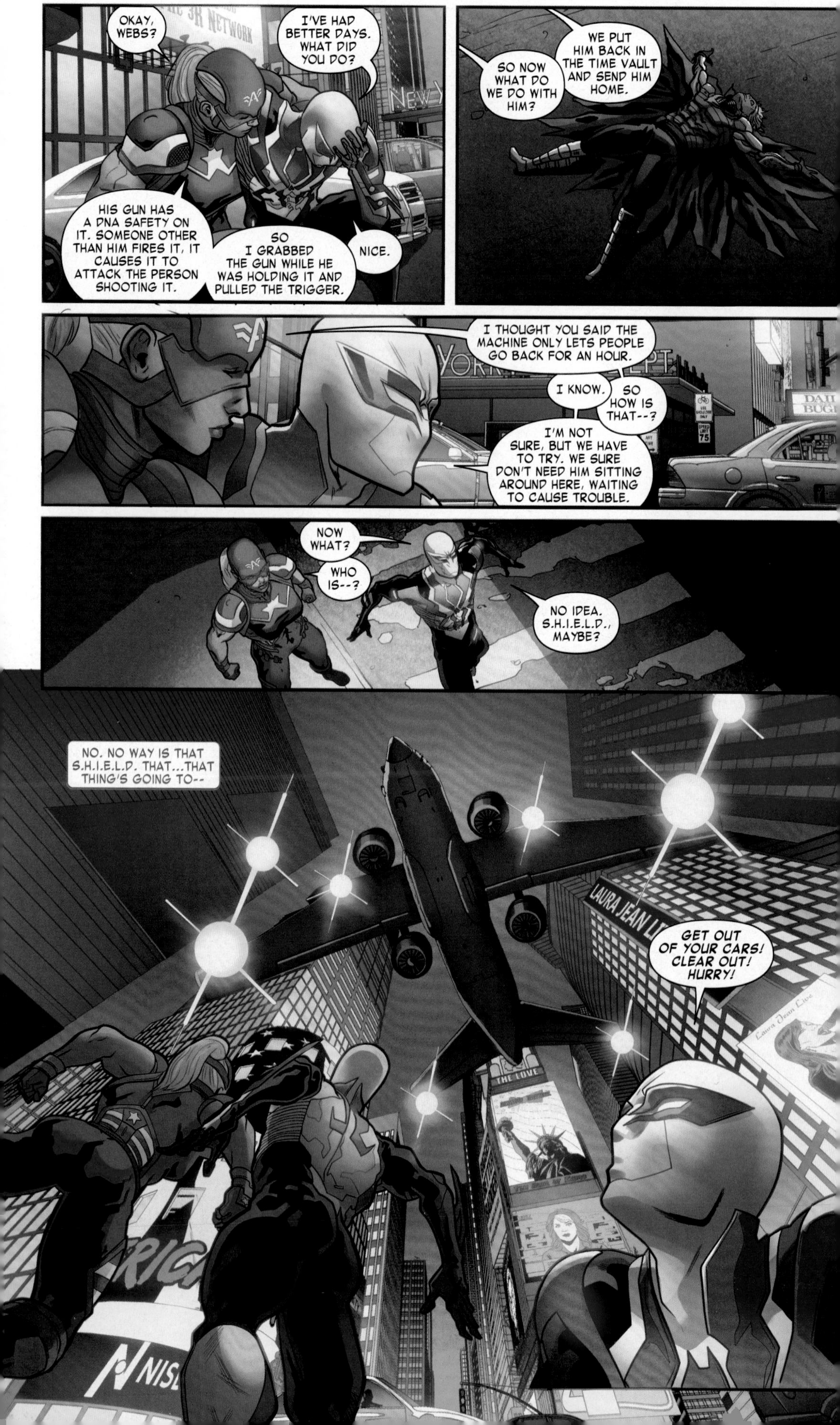
OKAY, WEBS?
I'VE HAD BETTER DAYS. WHAT DID YOU DO?
HIS GUN HAS A DNA SAFETY ON IT. SOMEONE OTHER THAN HIM FIRES IT, IT CAUSES IT TO ATTACK THE PERSON SHOOTING IT.
SO I GRABBED THE GUN WHILE HE WAS HOLDING IT AND PULLED THE TRIGGER.
NICE.
SO NOW WHAT DO WE DO WITH HIM?
WE PUT HIM BACK IN THE TIME VAULT AND SEND HIM HOME.
I THOUGHT YOU SAID THE MACHINE ONLY LETS PEOPLE GO BACK FOR AN HOUR.
I KNOW.
SO HOW IS THAT--?
I'M NOT SURE, BUT WE HAVE TO TRY. WE SURE DON'T NEED HIM SITTING AROUND HERE, WAITING TO CAUSE TROUBLE.
NOW WHAT?
WHO IS--?
NO IDEA. S.H.I.E.L.D., MAYBE?
NO. NO WAY IS THAT S.H.I.E.L.D. THAT...THAT THING'S GOING TO--
GET OUT OF YOUR CARS! CLEAR OUT! HURRY!

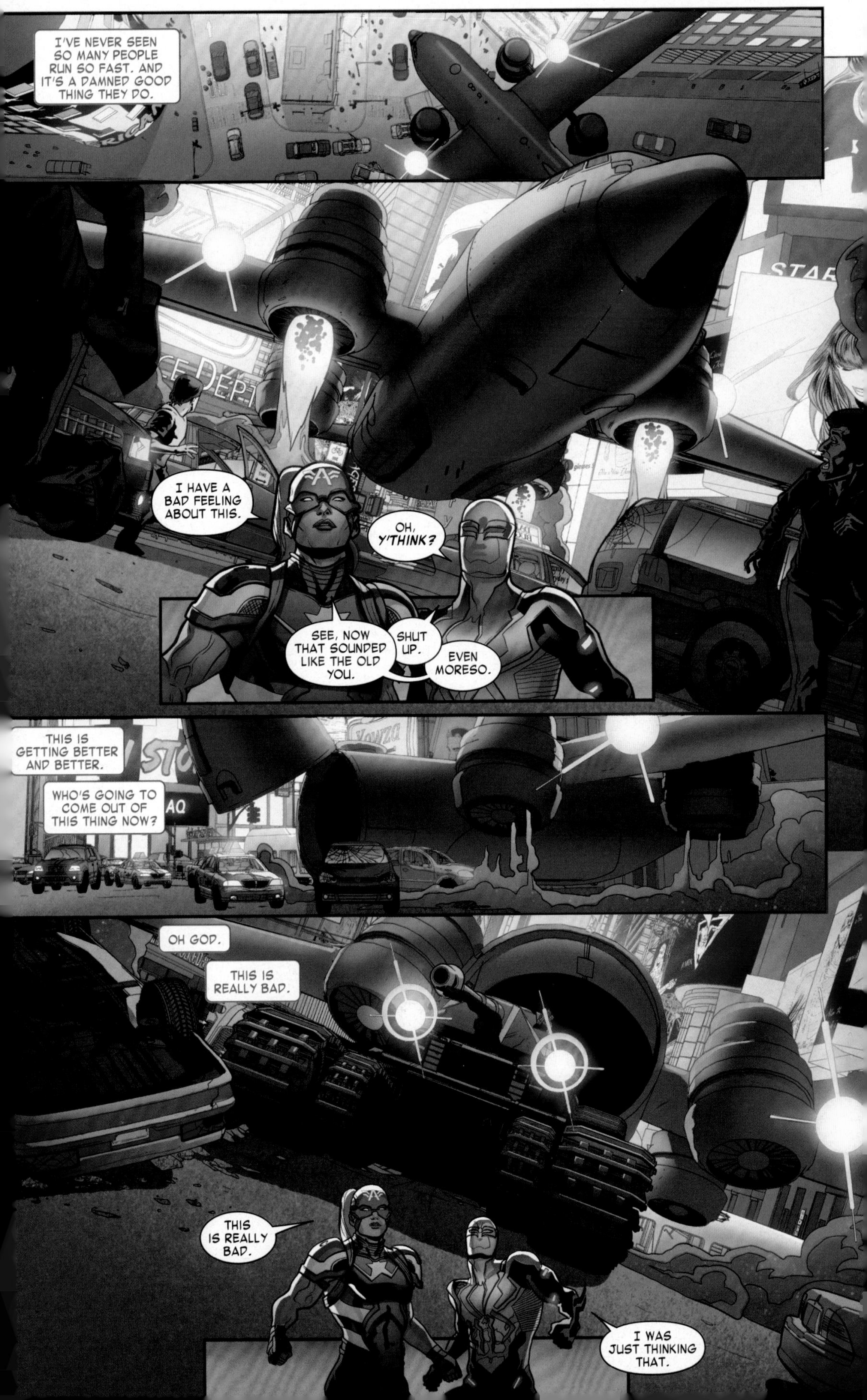
I'VE NEVER SEEN SO MANY PEOPLE RUN SO FAST. AND IT'S A DAMNED GOOD THING THEY DO.
I HAVE A BAD FEELING ABOUT THIS.
OH, Y'THINK?
SEE, NOW THAT SOUNDED LIKE THE OLD YOU.
SHUT UP.
EVEN MORESO.
THIS IS GETTING BETTER AND BETTER.
WHO'S GOING TO COME OUT OF THIS THING NOW?
OH GOD.
THIS IS REALLY BAD.
THIS IS REALLY BAD.
I WAS JUST THINKING THAT.

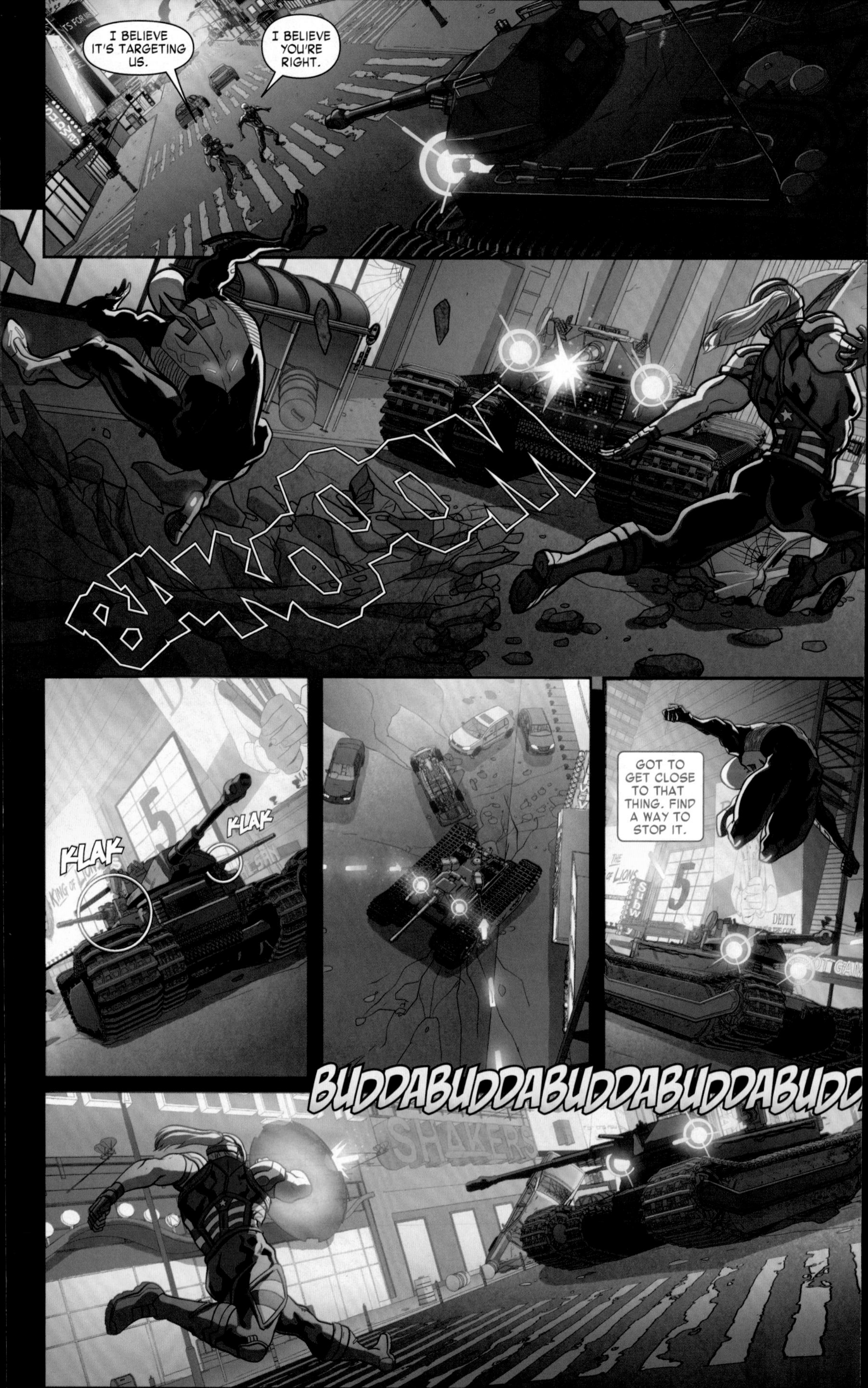
I BELIEVE IT'S TARGETING US.
I BELIEVE YOU'RE RIGHT.
BAKOOOM
KLAK
KLAK
GOT TO GET CLOSE TO THAT THING. FIND A WAY TO STOP IT.
BUDDABUDDABUDDABUDDABUDD

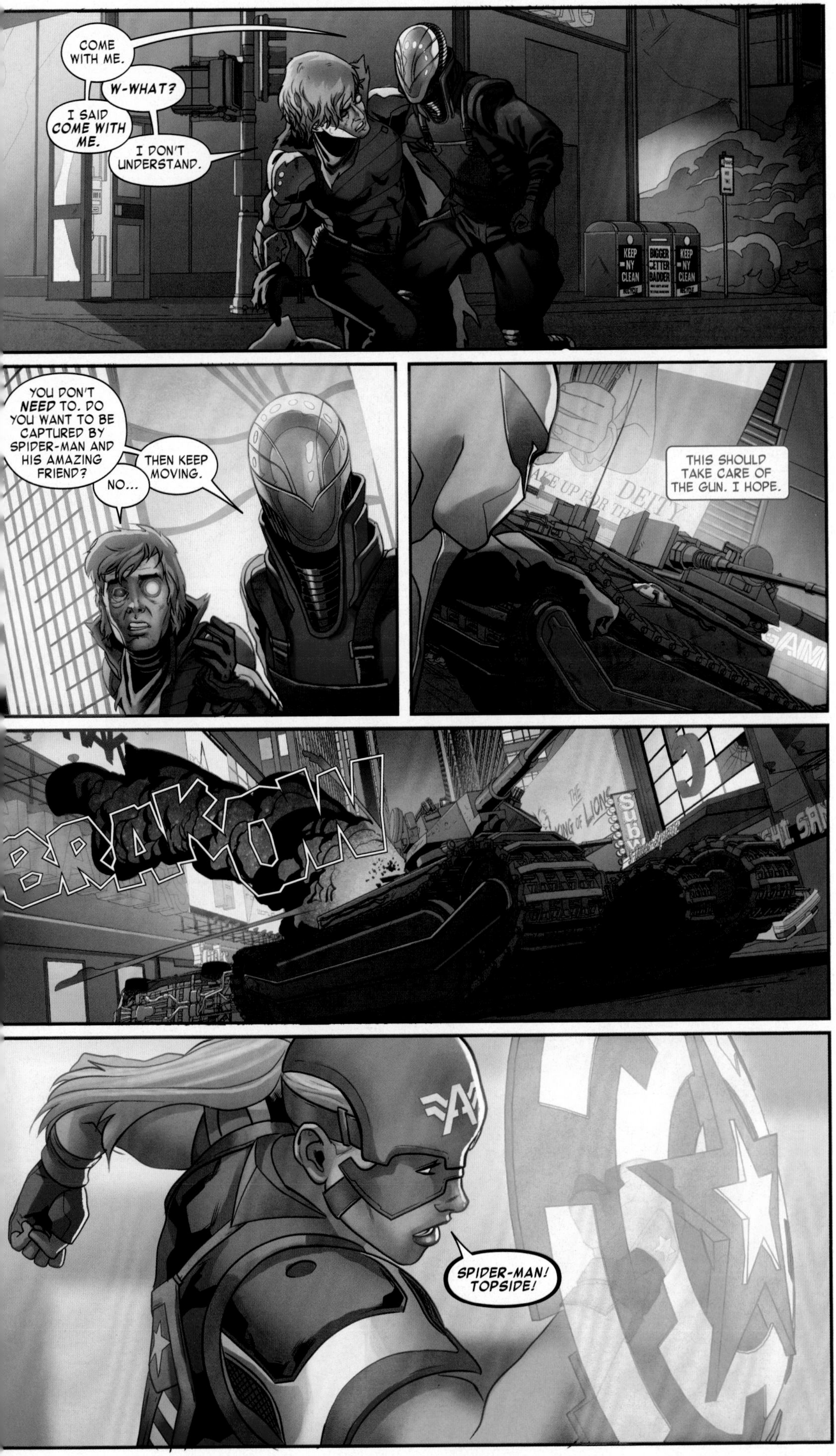
COME WITH ME.
W-WHAT?
I SAID COME WITH ME.
I DON'T UNDERSTAND.
KEEP NY CLEAN
BIGGER BETTER BADDER
KEEP NY CLEAN
YOU DON'T NEED TO. DO YOU WANT TO BE CAPTURED BY SPIDER-MAN AND HIS AMAZING FRIEND?
NO...
THEN KEEP MOVING.
THIS SHOULD TAKE CARE OF THE GUN. I HOPE.
DEITY
BRAKOW
THE KING OF LIONS
SPIDER-MAN! TOPSIDE!

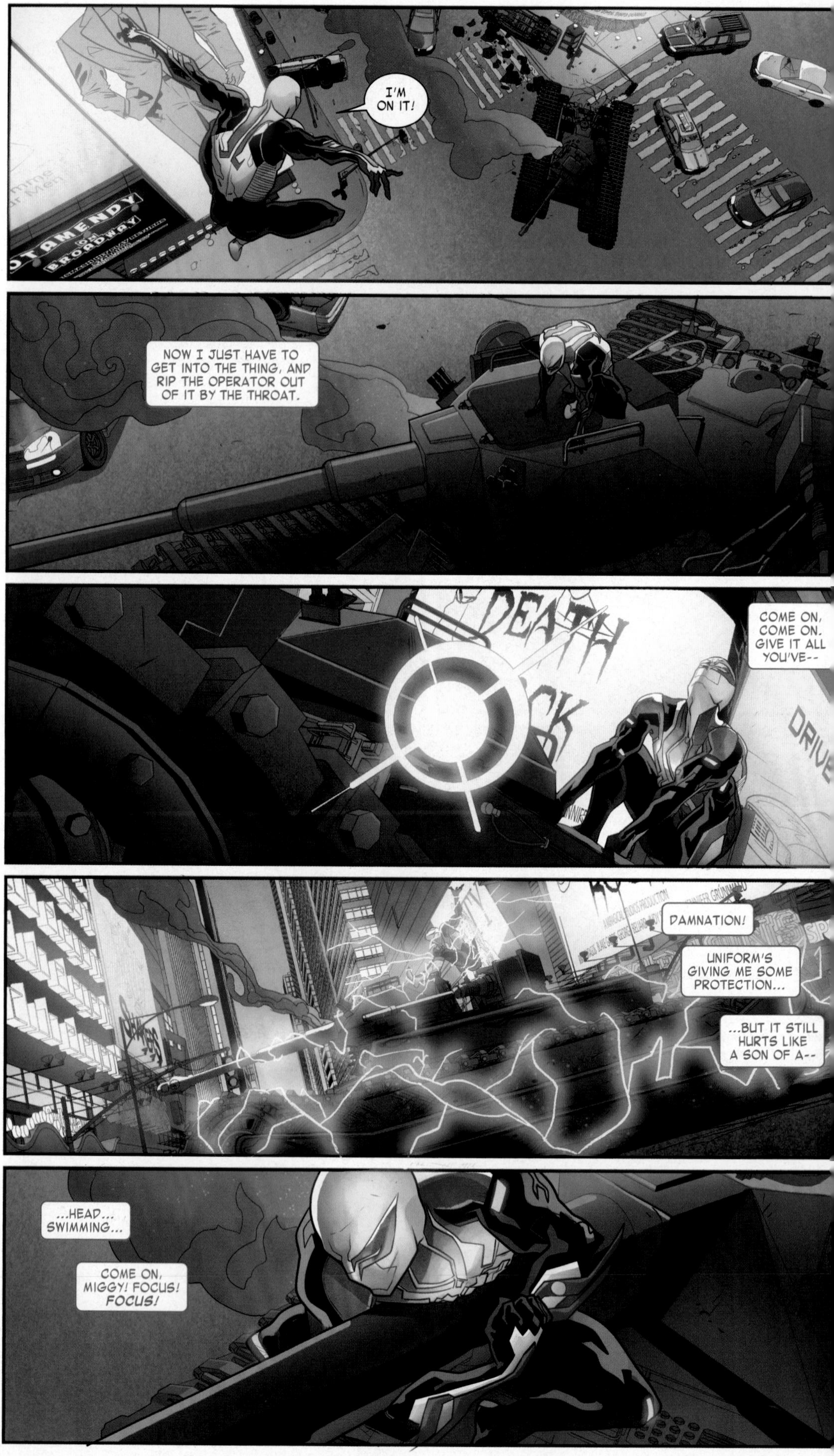
I'M ON IT!
TAMENDY
ON BROADWAY
NOW I JUST HAVE TO GET INTO THE THING, AND RIP THE OPERATOR OUT OF IT BY THE THROAT.
COME ON, COME ON. GIVE IT ALL YOU'VE--
DEATH
DRIVE
DAMNATION!
UNIFORM'S GIVING ME SOME PROTECTION...
...BUT IT STILL HURTS LIKE A SON OF A--
...HEAD... SWIMMING...
COME ON, MIGGY! FOCUS! FOCUS!

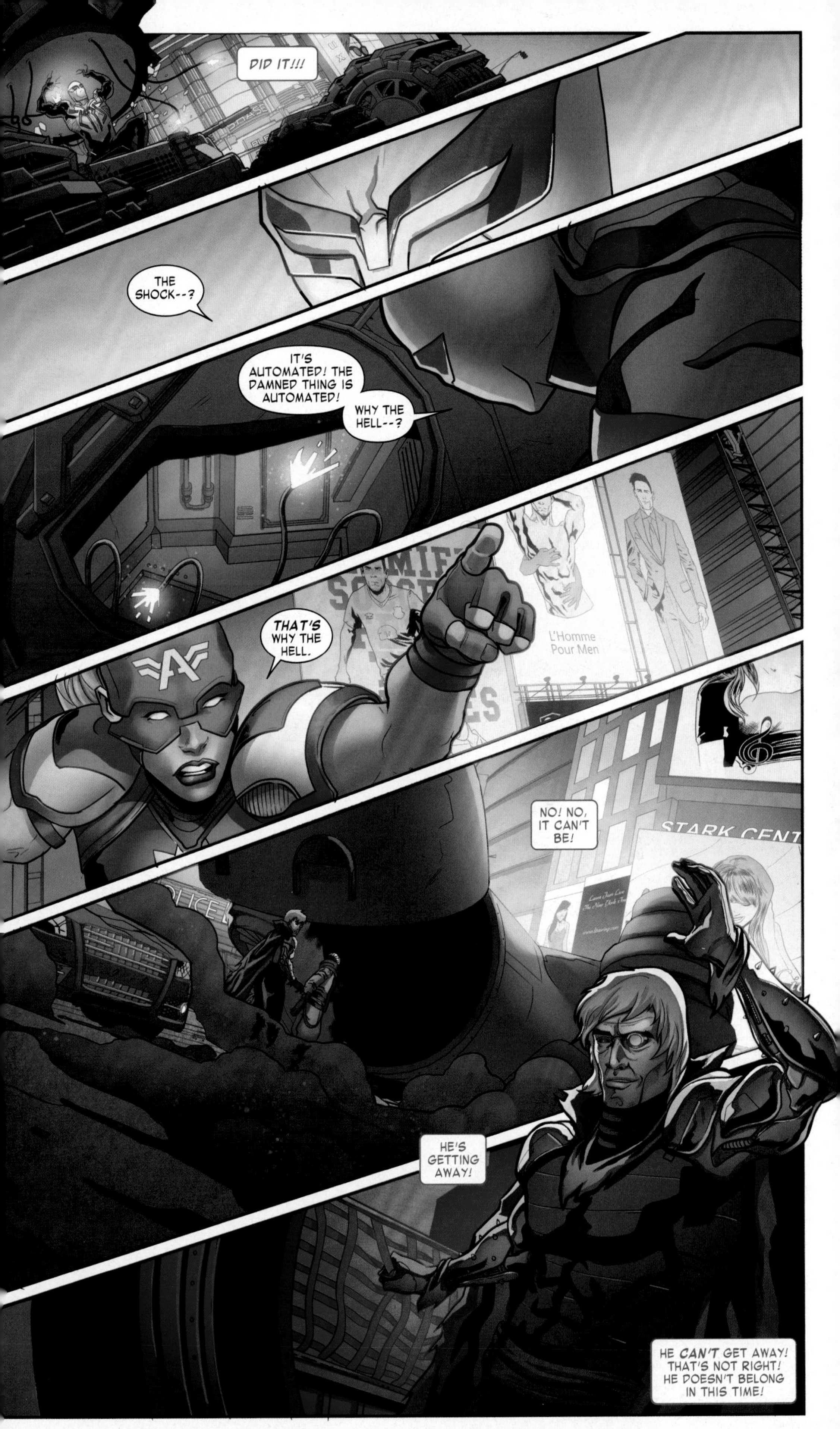
DID IT!!!
THE SHOCK--?
IT'S AUTOMATED! THE DAMNED THING IS AUTOMATED!
WHY THE HELL--?
THAT'S WHY THE HELL.
L'Homme Pour Men
STARK CENT
NO! NO, IT CAN'T BE!
HE'S GETTING AWAY!
HE CAN'T GET AWAY! THAT'S NOT RIGHT! HE DOESN'T BELONG IN THIS TIME!

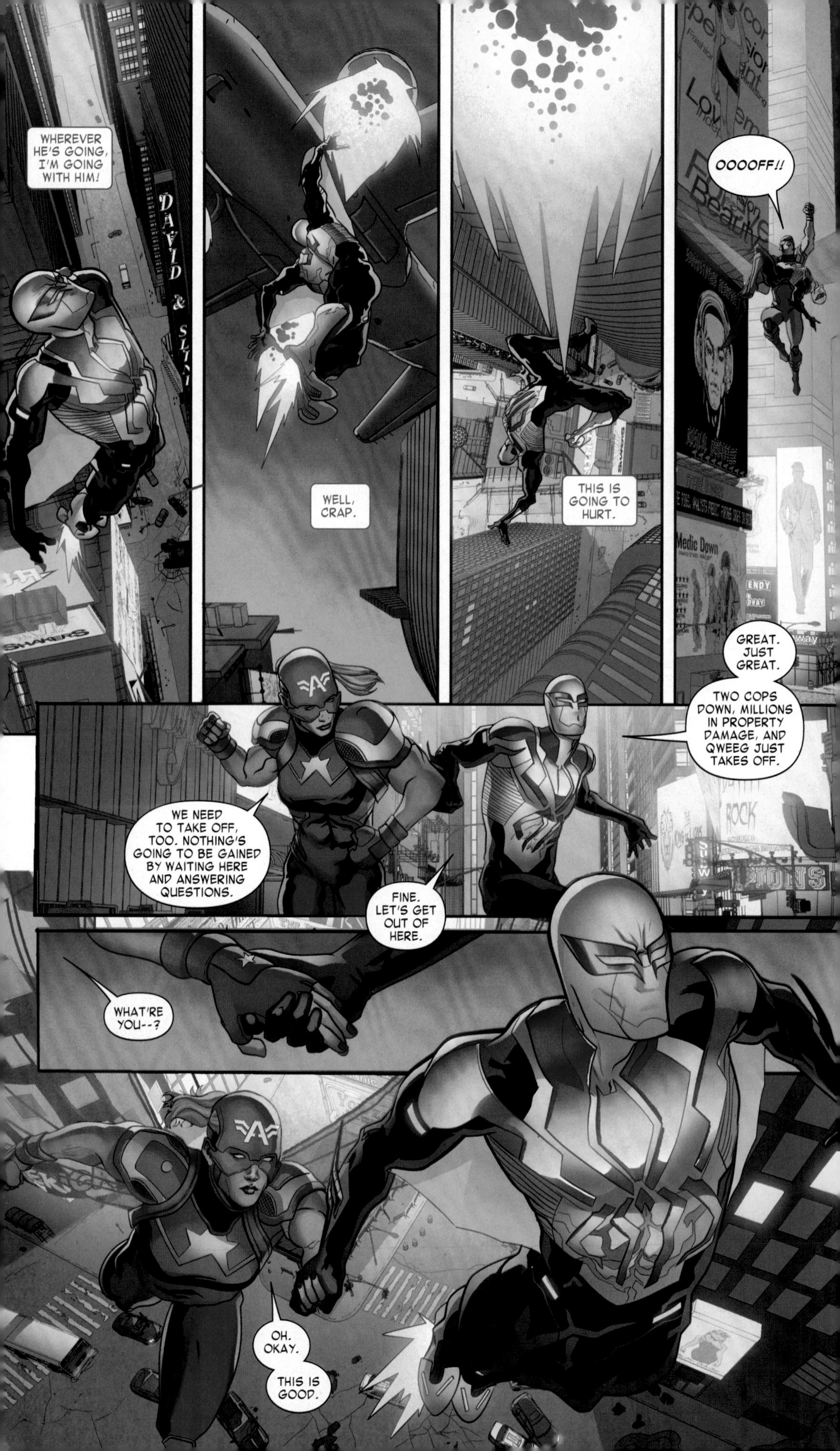
WHEREVER HE'S GOING, I'M GOING WITH HIM!
DAVID & SL
WELL, CRAP.
THIS IS GOING TO HURT.
OOOOFF!!
GREAT. JUST GREAT.
TWO COPS DOWN, MILLIONS IN PROPERTY DAMAGE, AND QWEEG JUST TAKES OFF.
WE NEED TO TAKE OFF, TOO. NOTHING'S GOING TO BE GAINED BY WAITING HERE AND ANSWERING QUESTIONS.
FINE. LET'S GET OUT OF HERE.
WHAT'RE YOU--?
OH. OKAY.
THIS IS GOOD.

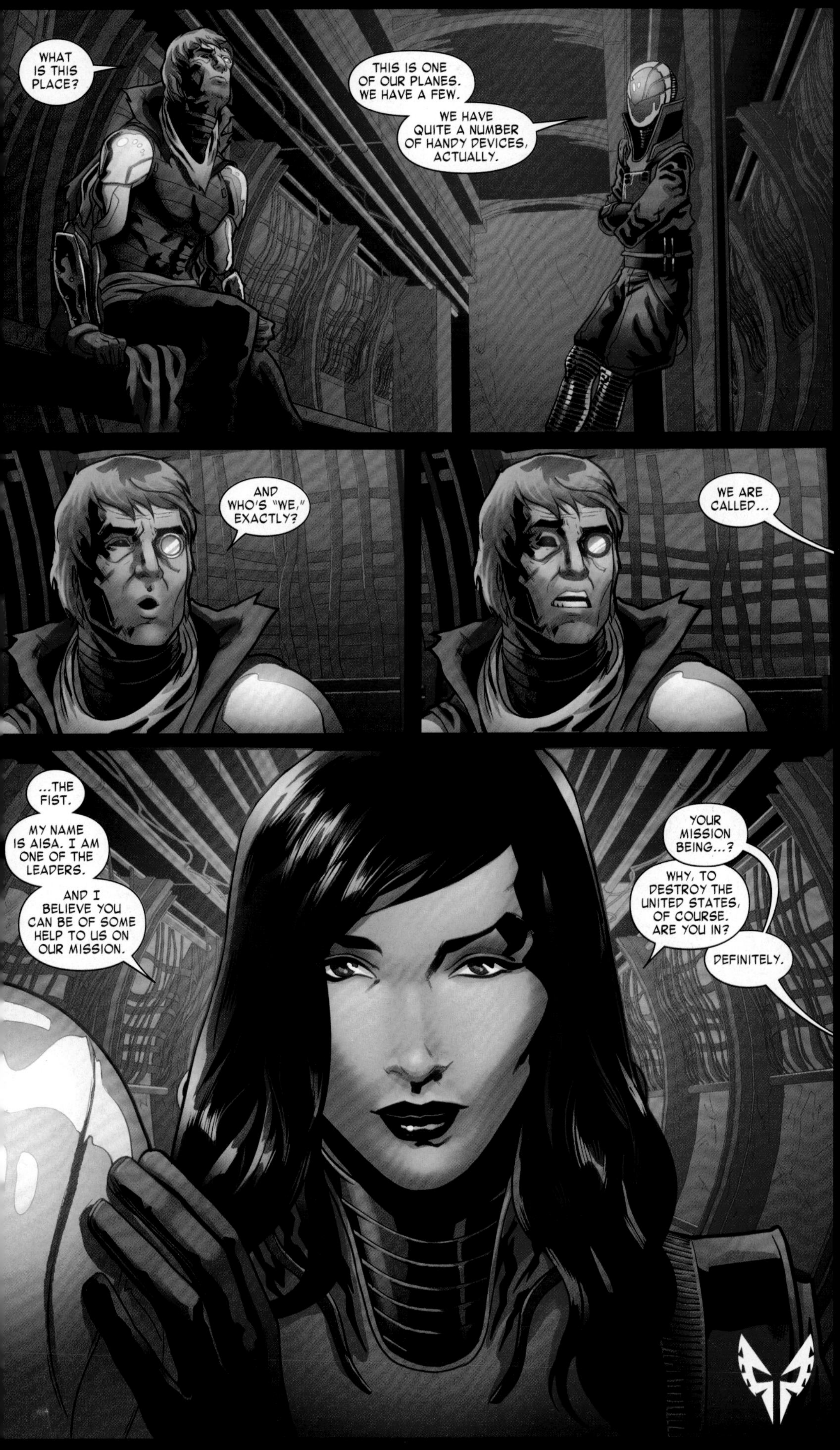
WHAT IS THIS PLACE?
THIS IS ONE OF OUR PLANES. WE HAVE A FEW.
WE HAVE QUITE A NUMBER OF HANDY DEVICES, ACTUALLY.
AND WHO'S "WE," EXACTLY?
WE ARE CALLED...
...THE FIST.
MY NAME IS AISA. I AM ONE OF THE LEADERS.
AND I BELIEVE YOU CAN BE OF SOME HELP TO US ON OUR MISSION.
YOUR MISSION BEING...?
WHY, TO DESTROY THE UNITED STATES, OF COURSE. ARE YOU IN?
DEFINITELY.

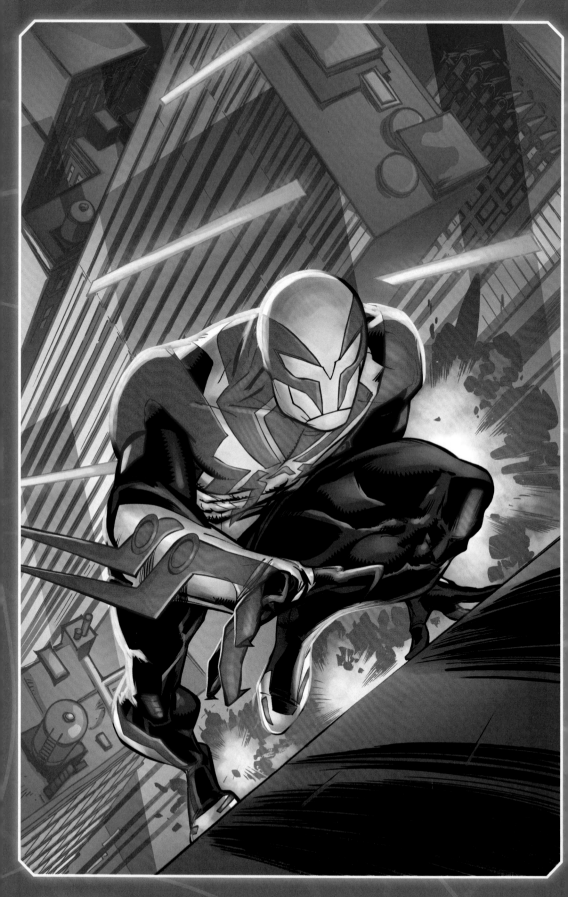

#1 variant by
RICK LEONARDI, DAN GREEN, & ANTONIO FABELA

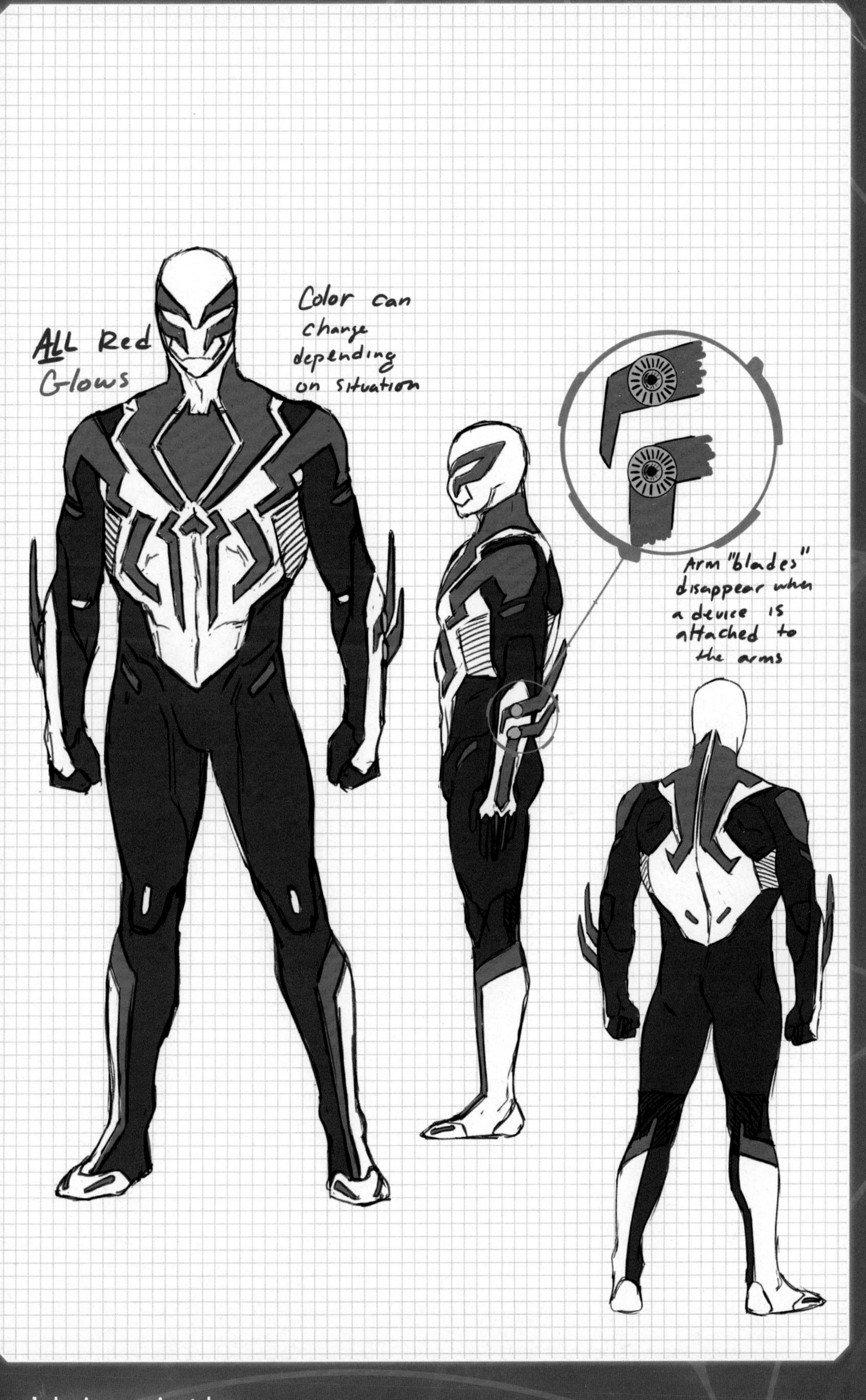

ALL Red Glows
Color can change depending on situation
Arm "blades" disappear when a device is attached to the arms

#1 design variant by
KRIS ANKA

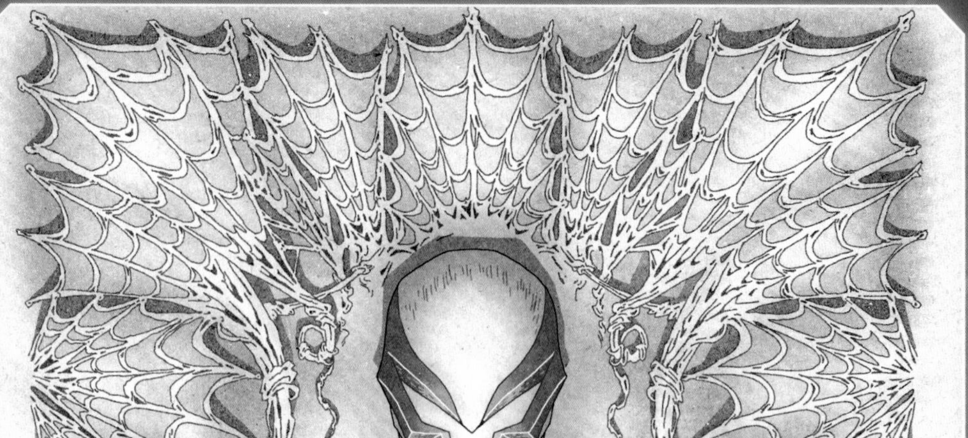

#1 hip-hop variant by **AFU CHAN**

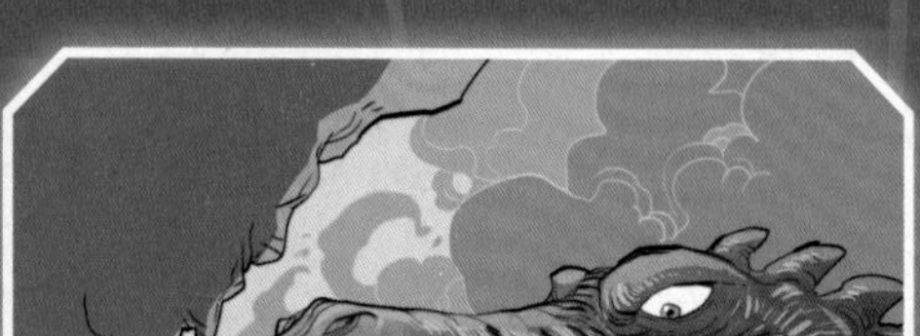

#2 Kirby monster variant by
MARGUERITE SAUVAGE

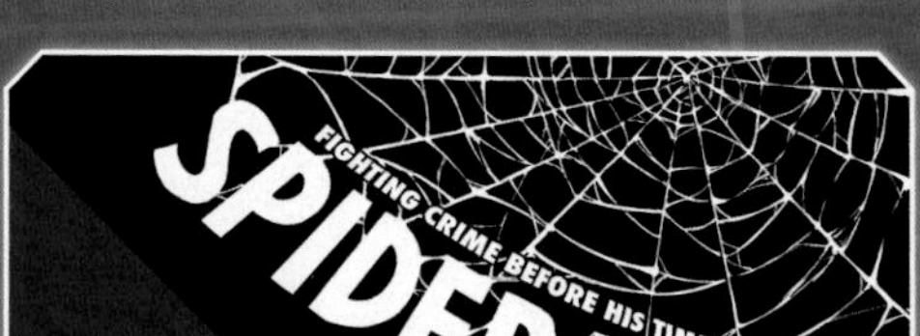
FIGHTING CRIME BEFORE HIS TIME!
SPIDER-MAN
2099

#2 variant by
DECLAN SHALVEY & JORDIE BELLAIRE

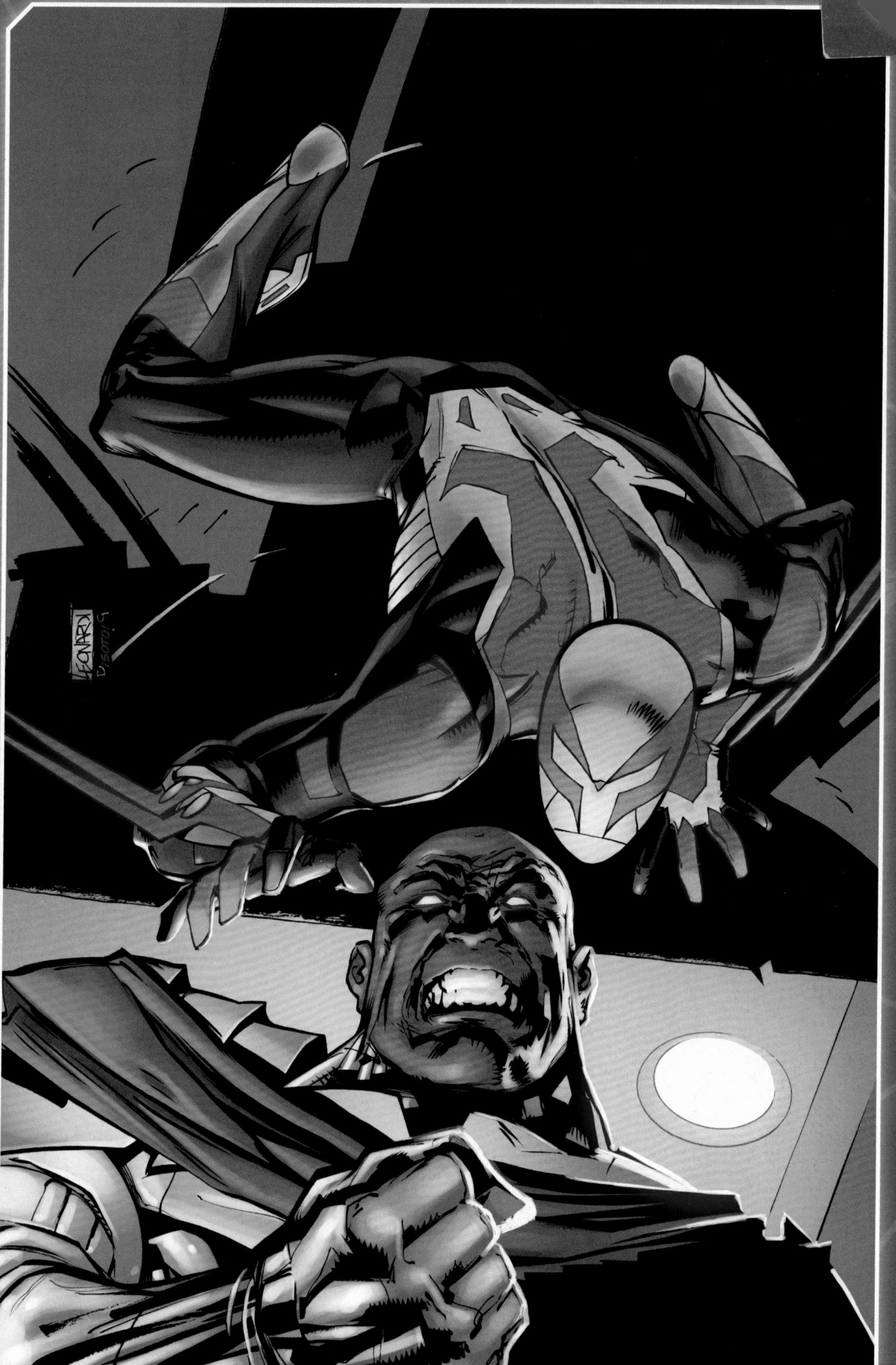

#3 variant by
RICK LEONARDI, DAN GREEN, & CHRIS SOTOMAYOR

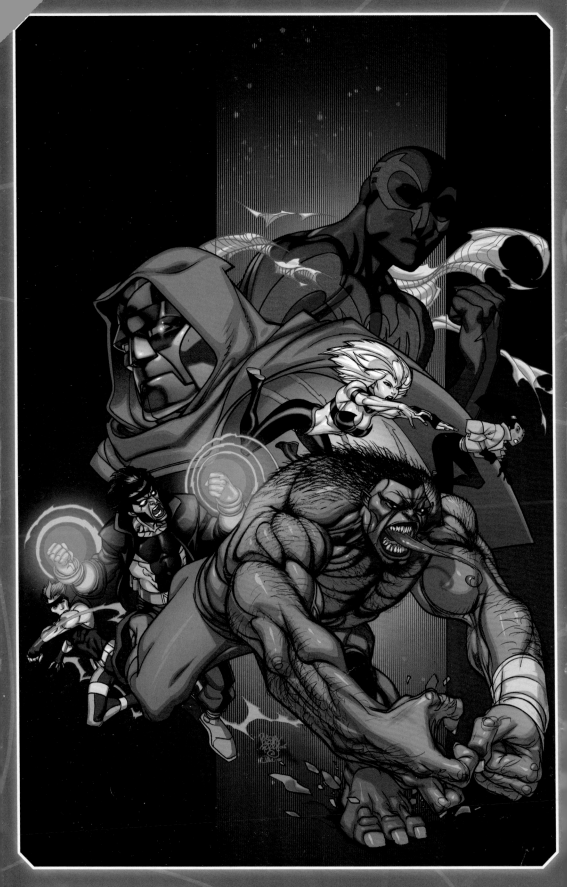

#4 Marvel '92 variant by
PASQUAL FERRY & DAVE MCCAIG